Willard Gayheart,
Appalachian Artist

Contributions to Southern Appalachian Studies

1. *Memoirs of Grassy Creek: Growing Up in the Mountains on the Virginia–North Carolina Line.* Zetta Barker Hamby. 1997

2. *The Pond Mountain Chronicle: Self-Portrait of a Southern Appalachian Community.* Leland R. Cooper and Mary Lee Cooper. 1997

3. *Traditional Musicians of the Central Blue Ridge: Old Time, Early Country, Folk and Bluegrass Label Recording Artists, with Discographies.* Marty McGee. 2000

4. *W.R. Trivett, Appalachian Pictureman: Photographs of a Bygone Time.* Ralph E. Lentz. 2001

5. *The People of the New River: Oral Histories from the Ashe, Alleghany and Watauga Counties of North Carolina.* Leland R. Cooper and Mary Lee Cooper. 2001

6. *John Fox, Jr., Appalachian Author.* Bill York. 2003

7. *The Thistle and the Brier: Historical Links and Cultural Parallels Between Scotland and Appalachia.* Richard Blaustein. 2003

8. *Tales from Sacred Wind: Coming of Age in Appalachia. The Cratis Williams Chronicles.* Cratis D. Williams. 2003

9. *Willard Gayheart, Appalachian Artist.* Willard Gayheart and Donia S. Eley. 2003

10. *The Forest City Lynching of 1900: Populism, Racism, and White Supremacy in Rutherford County, North Carolina.* J. Timothy Cole. 2003

Willard Gayheart, Appalachian Artist

by Willard Gayheart
and Donia S. Eley

Contributions to Southern Appalachian Studies, 9

Best wishes
Willard Gayheart
9/23/08

McFarland & Company, Inc., Publishers
Jefferson, North Carolina, and London

Library of Congress Cataloguing-in-Publication Data

Gayheart, Willard
Willard Gayheart, Appalachian artist /
by Willard Gayheart and Donia S. Eley.
p. cm.—(Contributions to southern Appalachian studies ; 9)
Includes bibliographical references and index.

ISBN 0-7864-1661-0 (softcover : 70# alkaline paper) ∞

1. Gayheart, Willard. 2. Artists—Appalachian Region—Biography.
3. Appalachian Region—In art. I. Eley, Donia S. II. Title. III. Series.
NC139.G225[...] 2003
741.973—dc21 2003014382

British Library cataloguing data are available

Cover illustration: Willard Gayheart, *Still in the Hollow,* pencil on paper, 1985

Manufactured in the United States of America

McFarland & Company, Inc., Publishers
Box 611, Jefferson, North Carolina 28640
www.mcfarlandpub.com

We dedicate this book to one
who is an inspiration to many people,
and who was the inspiration for this book.
We thank you for seeing potential we didn't see,
and for your unfailing support and encouragement
throughout our efforts:

To Dr. Grace Toney Edwards,
Director of the Appalachian Regional Studies Center,
Radford University

ACKNOWLEDGMENTS

At the risk of leaving out many, I owe a debt of gratitude to those who have encouraged my art and music over the years. They include Ms. Alice Sloan, Elmer Ray Combs, Becky Hancock, Etoile Berry, Brian Spencer, Bob McAllister, Joe Shannon, Crawford Maxson, Doug Hutchins, Tanya Rees, Ginger Correll, Jack Tottle, Helen and Leroy Martin, my supportive family, and Dr. Mitchell Wicker.

Willard Gayheart

Projects such as this one are not accomplished without help from many people giving of themselves over time in ways even they might not realize. Among those who have contributed in many ways to the successful completion of this endeavor is my husband, Randy. After educating two sons, he not only financed my late-in-life return to college, but has been a tremendous support to me as I pursued my curiosity about the Appalachian region, its history, culture, music, and people. He has enjoyed my journey perhaps as much as I. Hunter and Brook, our two sons, have been and remain my greatest supporters that keep cheering me on.

Dr. Ann Alexander, professor of history at Mary Baldwin College, taught my first class in Appalachian history and later, as my advisor at Mary Baldwin, helped me devise a plan of independent study towards earning a degree in Appalachian Studies. With her guidance my plan was accepted at Mary Baldwin and I earned my degree in May of 2002.

Another guiding force was Ricky Cox of Radford University, where I took Appalachian-related classes and shared in his wealth of information on folklore, music, history, and traditions. Dr. Dixon and Julie Williams of Pulaski, Virginia, spent many hours helping me with digital photography and computer technology, for which I am very grateful.

I am indebted to many others, including my mother, extended family, and my community of friends.

Donia Eley

TABLE OF CONTENTS

PREFACE

Willard Gayheart, a pencil artist from southwestern Virginia, represents Appalachia in a manner that is parallel to the kindness of his nature. Originally from eastern Kentucky, Willard lives now in the tiny community of Woodlawn, Virginia, between Hillsville and Galax, near the border of Virginia and North Carolina off Interstate 77.

A family business, The Front Porch Gallery, is located in Woodlawn. To reach the gallery, take the Hillsville/Galax exit off Interstate 77 and drive in the direction of Galax on Route 58. Turn right on Coalson Church Road in Woodlawn. The second building on the left is the Heritage Shoppe, and tucked away in the rear of that shop is Willard's gallery. Rocking chairs welcome visitors on the outside.

Once inside, guests are greeted by a chirping pet parakeet, art by Gayheart and others, and his son Michael and daughter Jill, who can usually be found doing framing work for customers. Sometimes Willard himself will be at his easel putting graphite to work creating memorable images of a region and its people. Willard's wife of 44 years, Pat, recently retired, and son Steve works in Mount Airy, North Carolina.

Willard's presentations of the region's history, people, occupations, pleasures, religion, and celebrations are drawn from his own experiences as a native Appalachian. His art has roots in his childhood, when he often drew unsuspecting classmates. He also draws upon his memories of that time to help provide images for his drawings.

Willard believes his life has bridged the transition from the old

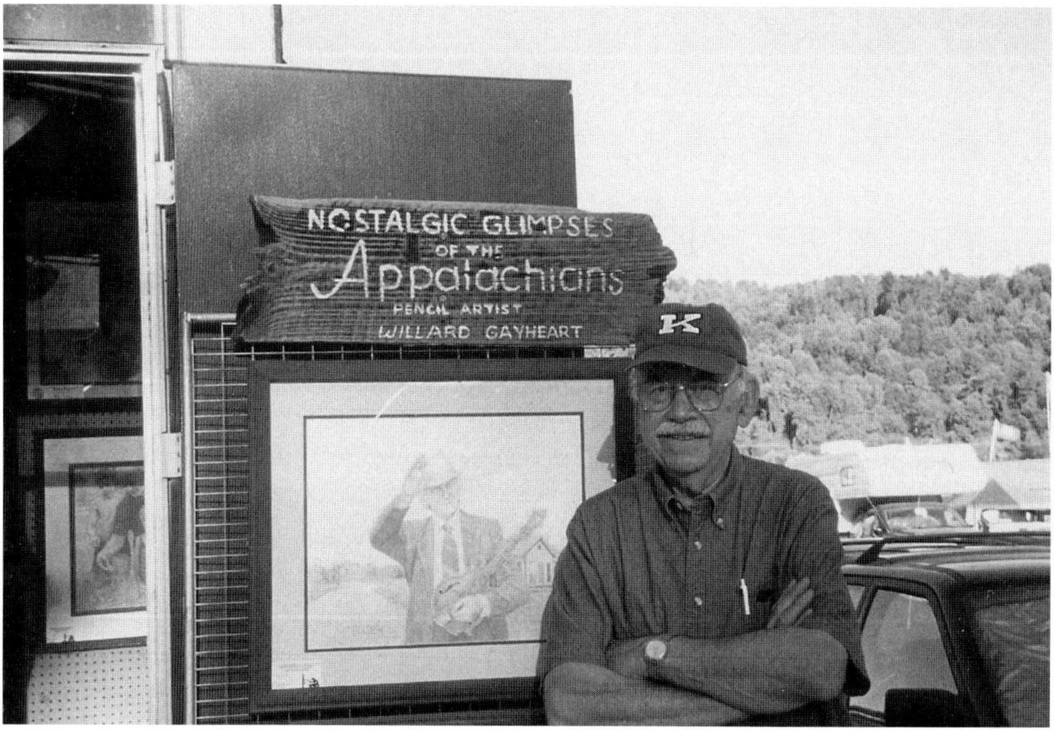

Willard Gayheart travels with his pencil drawings to numerous music events and arts festivals. His display here features a drawing of Bill Monroe, considered the father of bluegrass music.

Appalachia of small farms and coal mining to a time of widespread diversity in occupations and lifestyles.

His art is not an attempt to analyze a culture, nor is it an attempt to romanticize a region. Willard is a talented artist with broad experience in the folklife of the mountains. Famous and less famous people are equal in their importance to Willard as he portrays them in his depiction of life in the mountains, long ago and today. His art is not about change, but about preservation.

Throughout Willard's art, one sees self-reliant people living out their lives through their handicrafts, music, family rituals, work, and religion. Landscapes are important additions to many of his works, but the people and the presentation of the work of their hands and spirits are the artist's main purpose.

Willard often changes an actual scene to evoke an Appalachia typical of an earlier time, adding old-fashioned elements like the cabin drawn into the background of *Perfect Harmony*. Weathered and worn textures—the old cabin, the handle of the blacksmith's hammer—are significant visual elements of Willard's work. (See *Blue Ridge Blacksmith* and *Virgil*.)

The works of Willard Gayheart are positive images of the Appalachian culture, presenting the region as a place alive with interesting personalities.

INTRODUCTION

Early Life and Family

Willard Gayheart was born to Caney and Dora Gayheart in "a humble little house" on June 5, 1932, not far from Hazard, Kentucky, in the small community of Bulan. The house was located at the mouth of Sioux Branch, neither an address nor a town, but a little hollow that ran near the mouth of a creek. He lived there until about the age of four and was the oldest of four boys. A younger brother died at birth.

When he was four Willard's family moved to another house "up the road" and a year later moved yet again to a house in a nearby hollow called Clear Fork. He recalls that by the age of five or six he had lived in a couple of houses, the last one for two or three years.

During Willard's childhood, his father, Caney, went from one job to another. The first job Willard remembers his father having was driving a logging truck for one dollar a day, which Willard says "doesn't sound like much, but in those days of the Depression era any money was better than none." His family had few material possessions. Indeed, there was not even the assurance of shoes for school after a summer of running barefoot.

If money was available, then Willard and his brothers enjoyed a new pair of shoes, but if not, they made do with used or handed-down shoes and other clothing. "This was just the way life was in the thirties and until the War," according to Willard.

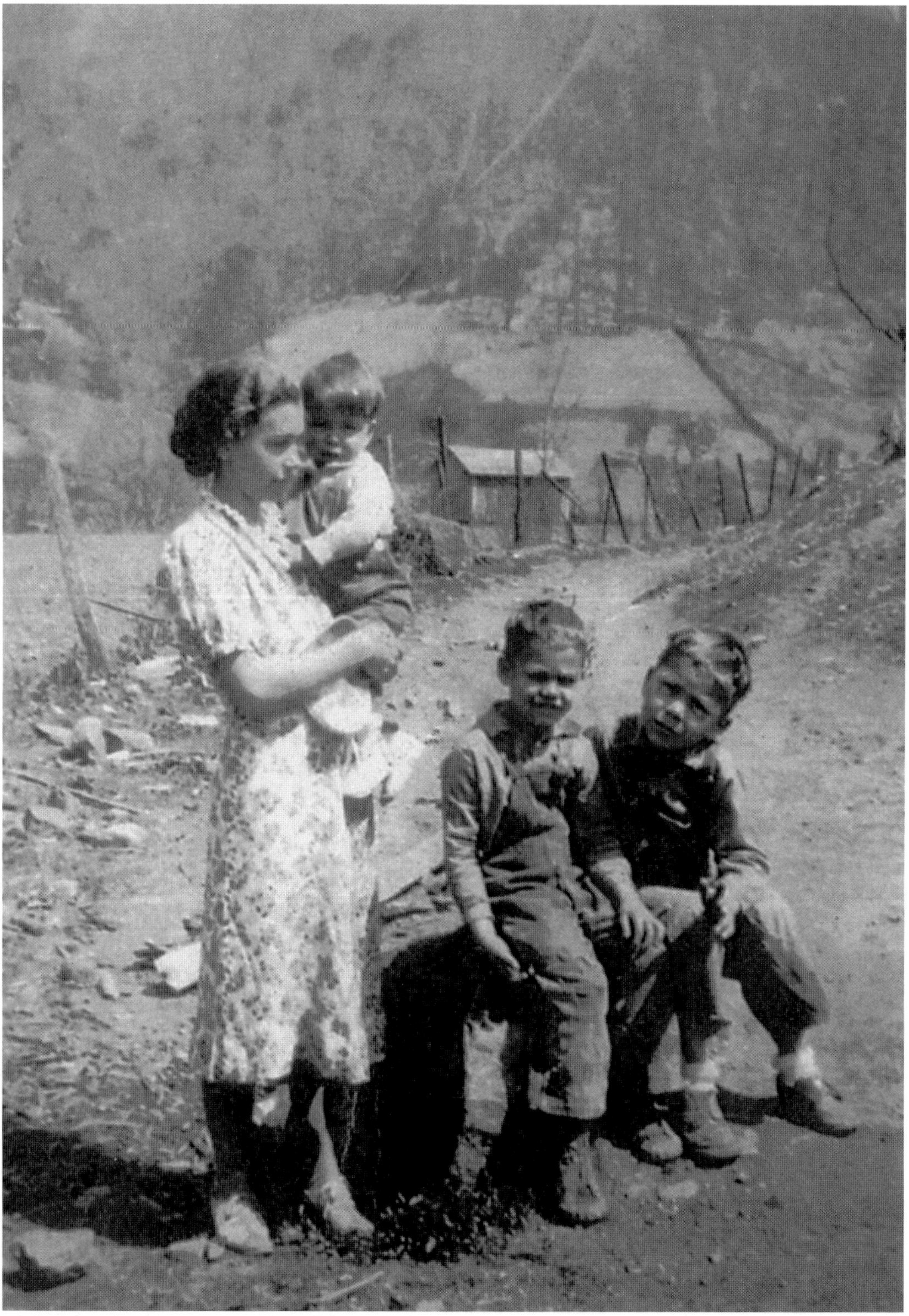

When Willard's father was thirty-five, he was drafted to serve in World War II, leaving the family to "make out the best we could," says Willard. The family had a small farm where they raised corn to feed the cow, horse, chickens, and hogs, and they were able to grow other food to eat along with the grain that fed the animals that provided meat for the winter months.

In 1946 Willard's father returned from the armed services. Willard recalls that 1946 was also the year the family got electricity in their small home. Until that time, the Gayhearts kept up with world events through a battery-operated radio purchased in 1939. Willard says, "That radio was quite a thing for us to have."

After returning from the war, Willard's father started in the carpentry trade. He had helped to build the house the family lived in, a small, two-room house for the family of six, but by the time Willard graduated from high school in 1949 his father was working more and more and had added rooms to the family home.

Life for the Gayhearts got a little better year after year. Willard says his father was quite a gifted carpenter, was good in math, and had a way with figures though he had only an eighth grade education. He "figured things out in his head." According to Willard, "he could contract a house and lay the block, the brick, do the plumbing, wiring, and build the cabinets." Willard says his father was unusual in that he worked by himself.

His father worked as a carpenter until the early sixties when he had an opportunity to teach young people in a government program for high school dropouts who did not have a trade. He taught young people through on-the-job training to work on and repair homes as well as build new houses throughout the mountains of Kentucky. These were government-sponsored projects for underprivileged people. Willard's father worked in this capacity until he was seventy years old.

Willard's father learned to do many things with his hands. He made furniture, had a small shop, and over the years acquired a great

***Opposite:* Dora Grigsby Gayheart, Willard's mother, holding Willard's younger brother Harold, who was born in 1939. Also pictured are John M. Gayheart, age five, and Willard (right), age seven.**

deal of equipment, which he used to indulge his hobby of woodcrafts in the evenings and on weekends. Unfortunately, soon after his retirement he became ill. He died at age eighty-three.

Willard feels he probably owes his father credit for some of his own artistic abilities. He says his creativity "came out in drawing pictures with a pencil" and his father enjoyed working with wood, but that all the creative and artistic desires in his family had to do with handwork.

Willard believes that people are happiest when being creative. He recalls his father "took a spell knitting" at one time. He learned to knit by helping Willard's mother learn the craft and eventually knitted many sweaters and hats for relatives and took great pride in his creations. Willard regrets his father became ill and was unable to enjoy his hobby in later years, but is grateful he did have a number of years doing the things he enjoyed. Willard is also grateful that his father left behind his legacy of the homes he built and the furnishings and cabinets he fashioned for them.

Dora Gayheart, Willard's mother, was a very strong woman, "only five feet tall if she stretched herself," says Willard. She turned ninety years old on December 2, 2001, still lives in the old family homeplace, and is now a mere 4' 10" tall. Willard describes her as always being a hard worker who remains active today and is still hard to keep up with, "though she has slowed a bit."

His mother encouraged his interest in art and music by providing him with paper and pencils for his drawings and by teaching him a few chords on an old guitar when he was a child. She perhaps set the stage for her son's lifetime of recording Appalachian history through his pencil art and developing his keen interest in music, which also remains a big part of Willard's life. She is a quilter who enjoys creating with her hands.

Willard believes his mother probably could have painted or drawn, but she was too busy with the care of the family to explore her own creativity outside the necessary sewing and quilting.

Times were hard, but Willard's mother saw to it that he and his brothers attended school regularly. Cordia School had four classrooms serving all twelve grades. Willard remembers that during his first year of school he was one of the few students who did go every day, even though he walked the two miles to and from the school. There were no buses to deliver students across winter snow, but he does not remember feeling any different from anyone else.

The difficult lifestyle was taken in stride as "just the way things had to be." Upon reflection, Willard says, "Those early struggles made me a stronger person and caused me to appreciate my life today."

The Cordia School building was heated in winter with pot-bellied stoves, and at the age of twelve Willard secured the job of starting fires in the stoves each morning. He lived close enough to the school that by the time other students arrived, the building was warm. Earning ten cents for each fire he built, at the end of the school year Willard "was paid three dollars, just enough money to buy an old guitar" he'd found for sale. The old guitar "didn't have but a few strings," but he eventually got the necessary strings and with help from his mother he began to play the old Appalachian music he continues to enjoy today.

Approximately forty students attended Cordia High School when Willard was there, and they used the two rooms on the second floor of the building while the younger grades were on the first floor.

Memories of his early life in the mountains of Kentucky include fishing, hunting, and playing high school basketball. Willard also spent a good bit of time in his teenage years trapping muskrats and minks to earn extra money. He says, "Today I wouldn't trap animals, but times have changed and back in that time trapping was a means of survival."

Once when Willard was checking his traps, which were up and down the creek behind the schoolhouse, he discovered one missing and the earth all around the area very disturbed and torn up. Fearing he had trapped someone's dog, he continued to search for the trap and finally found it halfway across the creek. Inside was the largest mink he'd ever seen. He was so afraid someone would steal the mink he hid it until lunch break when he could take it home to his father. The pelt was cured on a large board, and when he sent it off a month later he earned thirty dollars—"so much money I thought I was rich"—from a fur company in St. Louis.

Another way to earn money was collecting mayapple roots in spring and summer to send to the same fur company in St. Louis. A hempsack (made from burlap) would be filled with mayapple roots which were sent off to the company and made into a medicinal product. Each sack of roots earned Willard two or three dollars.

Because Willard advanced through the first and second grades of school in one year, and third and fourth grades the next year, he graduated at the young age of sixteen. He is quick to insist that his rapid advancement through the first four grades in just two years was not because he was smarter, but perhaps because he applied himself more than some students.

Willard believes the rapid advancement was actually more detrimental than helpful to his education. When he enrolled at Berea College in Kentucky, where he planned to study art, his youth and immaturity, coupled with his limited educational experience, made college hard for him. He was unhappy being away from home for the first time.

After struggling to succeed at Berea, Willard went into the Air Force in 1951 at age nineteen during the Korean War. He served as a cryptographer, working in code rooms sending and receiving classified messages, and he encoded and decoded messages until his release from the Air Force in 1955.

He then went back to Berea for a time, but left again to pursue a job opportunity with the Foreign Service as a cryptographer. Assured and encouraged by a friend that he would not have a problem getting a job, Willard left Berea College and went through all the necessary steps to secure a position with the Foreign Service. Much to his surprise and dismay, he failed the physical part of the exam, a possibility he had not considered. It was a great disappointment at the time, but today Willard feels blessed with the way his life has unfolded.

Willard put his college days behind him, took a job with a department store chain in Mullens, West Virginia, and wound up working thirty years in the store business. He says it was something he never really enjoyed, but it was a means to earn a living and support him and his wife, Pat Dooley, a native of Mullens whom he met and married while working in the town. In 1961 Willard and Pat moved with their oldest son, Steven, who was not a year old at the time, to Galax, Virginia, where Willard managed Ammars Department Store. Two more children, Jill and Michael, were born in Galax. The whole family still resides in the community of Woodlawn just outside Galax.

Steven married Kathy Robinson and has a daughter, Sarah, who is a frequent subject of Willard's drawings. Jill is married to Scott Freeman and is the mother of Dori, also a favorite subject. Scott is a musician and also writes bits of poetry for some pieces of Willard's art. Michael, the youngest son, is single.

Jill, Michael, and Willard own and operate the Front Porch Gallery in Woodlawn. "We try to make ends meet, but it's always a struggle," says Willard. "We're doing something we enjoy, though, and hopefully it will get better as time goes on."

Beginning a New Career

Though Willard has drawn all his life, he considered it an occasional hobby until his move to Galax, Virginia, in 1961. He noticed soon after arriving in the area that art was of interest to many in the community, and that several of his employees at Ammars Department Store painted. After granting permission for the employees to display and sell their art at the store, Willard started to draw more as well.

Around 1974 he gave a couple of his drawings to his church, Mount Olivet United Methodist, to sell at a community fundraiser called the Lord's Acre Sale, and he was surprised when the pieces were quickly purchased. When sketches began to catch the attention of shoppers at the department store, a new career began.

Willard feels "the drawings reminded people of their grandparents, their children, or brought back memories of childhood scenes or experiences." He sold his work "for a few dollars here and there." Then he did a more detailed depiction of a man with a fiddle and a boy (his own son Michael) with a guitar, and received one hundred dollars for the work. He called the drawing *Bridging the Gap*.

Following this drawing, he did a work entitled *Kilby Snow, Blue Ridge Balladeer* and eventually had limited edition prints done. By the mid–1980s, Willard realized he wanted to devote all his time to his art and left his job at Ammars Department Store.

Since about 1985 Willard has traveled extensively with his art and his music. His works have been displayed at the annual Old Fiddlers' Convention in Galax, where thousands of people converge from all over the world for one week each August. They come to compete, to camp, and to participate in or enjoy the many jam sessions during the week. Willard joins in with voice and guitar.

The very popular MerleFest in Wilkesboro, North Carolina, is held annually in April in memory of Merle Watson, the son of legendary Doc Watson; Merle was killed in a tractor accident in 1985. Willard's art is not only exhibited and sold there, but he has drawn the official poster for the festival for four years. This festival draws top name entertainment such as Dolly Parton, Alison Krauss, and many other acoustic and traditional musicians.

His work can also be found at music festivals and art events through South Carolina, Tennessee, West Virginia, New York, California, and Pennsylvania, as well as his website, Pencilart.com. Regional art centers, galleries, and businesses exhibit and sell Willard's art. Music CDs and cassettes of Willard and his band, Alternate Roots, are also for sale at these events and locations and on the website.

A story lies behind almost every piece of art Willard creates, and the faces often belong to people in his life, including his own children and grandchildren. Other faces belong to famous celebrities, but many are less well known or regionally known. Each one has played a part in some way in the history or culture of Appalachia.

Willard has received commissions for many works, among them drawings for the anniversary celebration of the original recording sessions of country music for the Bluegrass and Country Music Alliance Museum in Bristol, Virginia; official posters for the annual MerleFest; a fundraising drawing for a landmark building at Virginia Tech in Blacksburg, Virginia; local fundraising efforts for parks, humane societies, and civic clubs; and personal commissions from families wishing to celebrate a life or hobby or occupation. In the late 1980s Willard was commissioned to illustrate a book entitled *Mountain Summer* by William Mashburn of Blacksburg, Virginia, published by Pocahontas Press of Blacksburg.

His most recent commission and honor was for a drawing entitled *All in the Family*, initiated by Dr. Jack Tottle, director of the Bluegrass and Country Music program at East Tennessee State University in Johnson City, Tennessee, a part of the Center for Appalachian Studies at the university. The drawing depicts the contributions of African Americans to bluegrass and country music. Behind each famous musician in the drawing, including the Carter Family, Bill Monroe, Jimmie Rodgers, Earl Scruggs and others, Willard drew the face of the person who influenced each musician. All were African American except for one who was Hawaiian.

This work was chosen to be a mural on a wall in the lobby of the new Sherrod Library at East Tennessee State. Because Willard does not himself draw murals, he suggested a North Carolina muralist to interpret and complete the finished 7' by 10' project.

In February of 2002 a formal dedication honored Willard and muralist Marianne Mylet of Winston-Salem, North Carolina. Appropriately, a concert featuring bluegrass musicians from the university followed.

Getting to Know the Artist

Willard Gayheart is a gentle, modest, articulate and wonderfully talented man. Without knowing his 1932 birth date, it would be difficult to judge his age. His tall frame is agile and stout. He is also quick to smile and is a deeply kind and spiritual man.

With sincerity, Willard says that all the good things that have happened to him throughout his life have been because of the goodness of other people, and not a result of his own efforts. It is obvious he truly believes this.

He gives credit for his artistic and musical success to his mother and to Alice Sloan, his beloved teacher at Cordia School. Both women gave him tremendous support and encouragement. Willard credits Miss Sloan with the education of many mountain children who otherwise would not have had the opportunity. She is featured in his drawing *A Gift of Love*. Alice Sloan founded the Cordia School after being educated herself at Alice Lloyd College and then in Cleveland.

He names many others who have helped him, including his parents, Becky Hancock at Pulaski County High School, and Dr. Grace Toney Edwards of Radford University, whom he credits with encouragement and motivation. He includes the recent dedication of his work for East Tennessee State University and this writer's interest in developing a book about his life, art, and music among examples of how others have contributed to the goodness in his life.

Willard's responses to questions are honest and thoughtful. There is nothing superficial or false to be found in his personality. When he tells the story behind a piece of art, his voice takes on the sentiments expressed in the drawing.

One hears a smiling voice as he talks about *Dori* and *Her First Castle*, both of which feature his grandchildren. Or one might hear another emotion as he talks about his mother, Dora, the subject of a 1993 drawing entitled *A Lone Quilter*. He proudly says that through the sale of prints of that drawing, his mother is "living in people's homes all over the country."

Humor is evident in his voice as he describes *Still in the Hollow*, which depicts a moonshine still. His idea for this one was inspired by the still exhibit at the Folklife Center at the World's Fair in Knoxville, Tennessee, in 1982.

The Artist and His Music

Willard's first memory of music was at about age four, when his dad bought a windup phonograph and brought it home to the family with records featuring the Carter Family and Jimmie Rodgers. He remembers the excitement of hearing the old time music and knowing from that time on that he wanted to learn to play the guitar and sing.

When a visitor to the family home brought a guitar for his mother to tune, Willard was surprised to learn of his mother's talent, and he says that knowledge further excited him. He began to comb through catalogs looking at and being fascinated by the instruments. Then came the opportunity to build the coal fires to heat the Cordia School classrooms, for which he was paid three dollars at year's end. His first guitar, a small Montgomery Ward brand minus several strings, was purchased with the money. When money became available for strings, Willard's mother tuned the instrument and taught him the chords she knew. "I practiced all summer that year," says Willard.

By fall he was able to play well enough to accompany himself and sing. "I could always sing harmony, had an ear for it somehow or another." Willard and a friend, Elmer Ray Combs, performed duets for school programs. All these experiences served as motivation for continuing to practice and learn. The childhood fascination has never diminished, and rarely has Willard been without a guitar.

Until the Gayhearts moved to Galax, Willard had not played with an organized band. He says, "There was music everywhere here, traditional music, almost the center of what we know as bluegrass or old time traditional music, and it wasn't long before I had an opportunity to play in a band, and so I did."

Willard's first band was called the Mountain Ramblers, one of the oldest continuous local bands in the area. He recalls being very nervous the first time he performed in public with the group in competition at a fiddler's convention.

After a couple of years with the Ramblers, he became part of a group known as the Mountain County Boys. With this group he had his first chance to play on a recording.

The Mountain Ramblers became the Highlanders in 1970, and the group is still active today. The Highlanders have performed in New York, Kentucky, North Carolina, and the group performed at the World's Fair in Knoxville, Tennessee, in 1982. They recorded seven

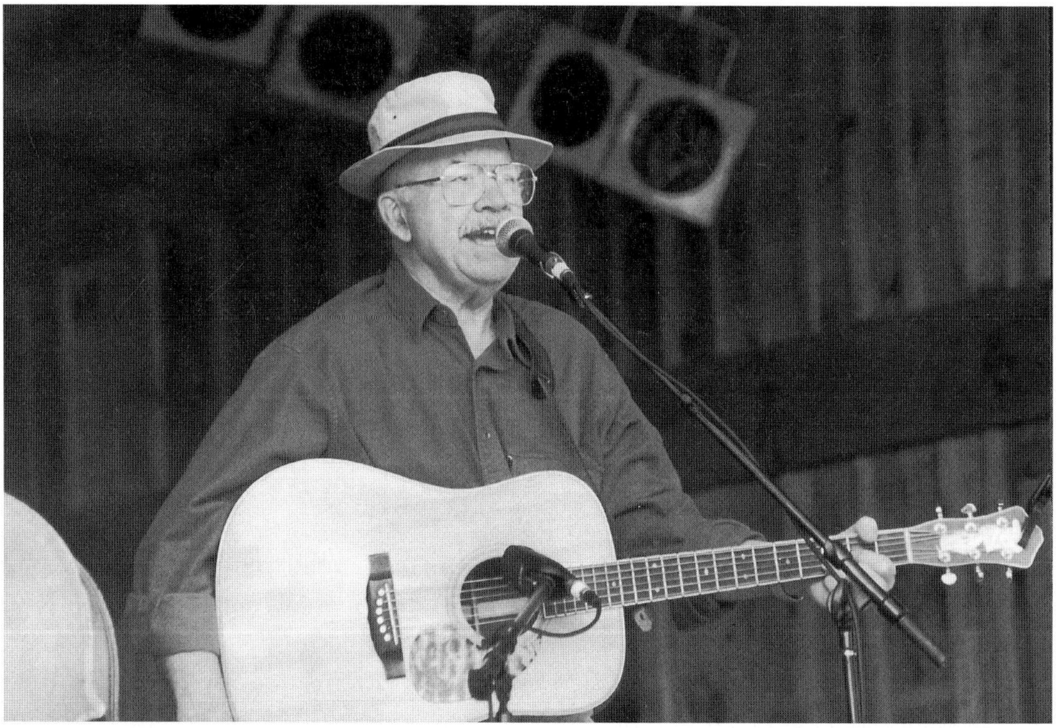

Willard Gayheart the singer, guitarist and songwriter has appeared at such prestigious venues as MerleFest in Wilkesboro, North Carolina, and the 1982 World's Fair in Knoxville, Tennessee.

albums. When Willard left the group several years ago to join his son-in-law's band, he was the last remaining original member.

Willard and his son-in-law Scott Freeman, along with Edwin Lacy and Sandy Grover, formed a band called Skeeter and the Skidmarks to play old time traditional music.

"It was quite a bit different," Willard explains. "I'd always played bluegrass and there's a distinct difference between old time and bluegrass, with bluegrass being identified with a three-finger style banjo playing and old time identified with a claw hammer style and nearly always a fiddle." This group didn't always have a fiddle, but Scott could play both the fiddle and mandolin and would alternate between the two instruments. The band cut an independent album and later cut two albums with a producer from Blacksburg, Virginia.

During the three or four years the band played together, they traveled extensively, performing twice in Grass Valley, California, several times in Maryland, and during one summer, weekly at North Carolina's Tweetsie Railroad near Blowing Rock. When Edwin Lacy decided to enter a Presbyterian seminary out of the area, the group of musicians disbanded.

Shortly afterwards, a new band called Alternate Roots emerged and eventually recorded two projects on its own label. The group enjoyed a highlight review in *Bluegrass Unlimited* and then was one of the featured bands at the International Bluegrass Association's annual meeting in Louisville, Kentucky, in 2000. Original band members included Katy Taylor on guitar, Randy Pasley on Dobro, Tony Testerman on bass, Scott Freeman on mandolin and fiddle, and Willard on guitar. Everybody took part in the singing.

Then, in 2001, a young man named Steve Lewis joined the group. He plays banjo, guitar, and sings, and is, Willard says, "an awesome musician." Steve's list of accomplishments is perhaps topped by winning the banjo contest at MerleFest. His prize was an Earl Scruggs model Gibson banjo. He also placed second in the guitar competition. At the Don Reno Festival in South Carolina earlier in the year, Steve won first place in banjo. In 2001 he won second place at the national championship contest in Winfield, Kansas, on both guitar and banjo.

A new CD by Alternate Roots entitled *Branching Out* was released in June 2002.

"Music, like art, has been a big part of my life," Willard says. "It's almost something you can't separate from what you do every day. It's as much a part of me as anything. Art and music seem to go together with me and always has. At my age a lot of people start slowing down and I feel like I'm just getting started."

Willard has also written a few songs, and one, "The Last Run," was recorded by a group called Richochet and was listed in the top 25 in *Bluegrass Unlimited* for several weeks.

He says he probably plays now more than ever before and it keeps him young. "It's hard to play music and not be uplifted and have fun. It's therapeutic and for that reason alone I think I'll continue to play and sing. I think talents are something we need to use or they'll be taken from us," Willard said.

Along with the traditional music Willard loves, he says he's learned to appreciate all kinds of music from classical to pop. His first exposure to classical music was at Berea College where he learned to enjoy some of the great symphonies the teachers used as background music in his drawing and painting classes, music he found, and continues to find, very soothing.

Techniques of the Artist

Drawing unsuspecting classmates at their desks or in the library and other places around school is the way Willard Gayheart remembers getting started in a hobby that has evolved into a full-time vocation—that is, when he's not on stage performing with his band, attending to one of the many tasks involved in owning and operating an art gallery and frame shop, traveling to a festival to exhibit and sell his art, or responding to one of the many civic, church, or family related opportunities that come his way. He was once described as "unflappable," and that is just how he handles the demands on his time and talents.

He says, "I've always drawn and sketched, and I've always enjoyed drawing people though I did a lot of still life drawings early in my childhood." Only when he went to Berea College for a time did he receive any formal instruction. While there, he took a beginning class in drawing and painting, and he had an opportunity to study the techniques of famous artists.

A time in the armed services, followed by beginning a career in retail management, marriage to Pat, and raising a family, took Willard in new directions for some years. "Then along in the early seventies I started experimenting in drawing with charcoal and pencils of various sizes as a hobby and to relax in the evenings, and I slowly started getting back into it," he said.

After working with charcoal for a time he found he could get better results and detail using pencils. He also discovered that by drawing from a photograph and taking the time he needed, which in some cases was as long as two weeks, he could accomplish the kind of detailed drawing he'd long envisioned.

The first completed work, which Willard feels was indicative of what was to come later, was *Bridging the Gap*. Because he was working from several photographs, he was able to take the necessary time to study all the details.

He describes his methods as follows:

"The trick is the shading, especially in portraits and faces. It's so important to get the shading right. That's what creates the realism in pencil drawings, filling in all the details. So it's a very meticulous thing. First, I generally rough sketch the picture and then I start filling in all of the details. Working from the photographs I have in front of me on the drawing table, I can come and go whenever I have time to work on it.

"I also discovered there were some tools I could use that would be an asset, and one was a magnifying glass with a fluorescent light mounted on the drawing table so I could see the details. It's a matter of sketching the drawing and filling in all the details, paying attention to the shadows. It's hard to explain, but it's all tedious and about observation and knowing when I get the likeness. It's hard to know in some cases when I'm finished, but I have to stop someplace and when I get to the point I think it's about as good as I can do, I just stop.

"Over the years I've learned many things about what tools to use. In the beginning I used whatever pencil and paper I could come up with, but I discovered that if I bought and used good quality paper and art pencils, I could take advantage of the different grades of lead, which are indicated by the hardness of the leads. I use anything from 2H lead to a 2 to 3B, 2 and 3B being the softest and the darkest, and 2H harder which makes softer marks. I control the light to dark by using the different hardnesses of leads. I keep several pencils handy and I use a kneaded eraser, which I can shape any way I want, something else I discovered. There's a whole lot you can do to lift out highlights.

"The tools I use are paper, pencils, eraser, magnifier, a light, and a slanted table like a drafting table or drawing table.

"The plus side of this medium is there aren't too many tools to work with and no mess to clean up as with paint. I work until I'm finished and come back to it like I leave it, so I don't have a lot of preparation. Every day that I draw I'm learning. There's something to learn all the time. I never quite get to where I want to be and everything's a challenge. I guess that's what makes it exciting. I've never been satisfied, and there's always that goal to strive for, that picture that someday I'll do that I'm satisfied with, totally satisfied. It'll never happen, but I keep striving for that."

Willard has even started to tint some of his drawings with colored pencils. He does this upon request, and sometimes will randomly select a piece to color. He says he's discovered which pieces are most popular in color. *Her First Castle* and *Mary Faith* are two that are popular. He claims the technique is simple—he goes over the drawing with a colored pencil, which automatically picks up the same shadows and lines as the original pencil drawing.

Drawing on the Appalachian Experience

Willard says he is a product of the Appalachian Mountains. He has lived in the region all his life, and he feels his life has bridged the transition from the old to the new Appalachia. He talks of his love for the mountains, the people and the culture, and how his art is caught up in the nostalgia of this lifestyle. He feels the pencil medium is especially suited to portray the rustic lifestyle that existed in the Appalachian Mountains, a lifestyle fast fading into memory.

Long before settlement by immigrants, Indian tribes lived in these mountains, but by 1800 few were left. Immigrants from England, Scotland, Ireland, Germany and Italy found their way to the foothills, mountains, and valleys of the Appalachian chain and settled there. Even today their names and folkways can be found in the region. Willard's name comes from the German name Gearhardt, which was changed at some point after the arrival of his ancestors to what is now Kentucky.

Some of the immigrants came as indentured servants and moved on to this area because land was available, but probably were thought of as poor, ignorant or less educated than some of the landed gentry to the south or east. Even today the stereotype of the mountain immigrant is a "hillbilly," an ignorant individual as portrayed in film, cartoons, and fiction. These immigrants, however, had to have resourcefulness and fortitude just to eke out an existence in the rugged mountains. They had to make their own tools, grow their own crops, and provide on their own just about everything else they needed.

The attributes of Appalachian people can be traced back to the times when the settlers first experienced how harsh their new free life could be. It was imperative that they show solidarity and neighborliness with a measure of self-reliance, and they had senses of humor, beauty, individualism, and pride in their heritage.

Today these values and characteristics are still very much evident. Writers like James Still, Loyal Jones, Jim Wayne Miller, Wilma Dykeman, and so many others carry on the traditions through their wonderful poetry, fiction, and nonfiction, just as Gayheart does with his artistic renderings of life in the Appalachians and the music of his guitar.

Traditional culture of the region is found in the hollows and valleys and coves. It has been preserved by people like Ray Hicks, a subject of Willard's art who told stories using words, phrases and dialect from hundreds of years ago. (Hicks died in 2003.) The people sing the same ballads and play the same instruments their ancestors brought with them to this country. The fiddle was the instrument most immigrants carried with them because of its small size and light weight. The banjo has African roots.

This brief discussion of the region would not be complete without some mention of coal, the fuel that helped supply the nation with the energy it needed. Coal still today comes out of West Virginia, Virginia, and Kentucky in large quantities. Outside interests controlled the buying and selling, and the Appalachian people suffered from the abuse of companies that bought mineral rights to land for much less than the real worth.

As the economy changed for better or worse, so did the lifestyle of mountaineers who became laborers in the mines. Whole communities sprang up when coal was king and just as quickly died when coal ceased to be king.

Out-migration began to occur in the mountains as people who had no diversity in their economic opportunities fled in search of jobs in the North. At least three million people left the region between 1940 and 1970.

Today the people of the Appalachians are a diverse population who live in rural areas, small communities, and cities; work in businesses; enjoy educational opportunities; and raise families in beautiful settings surrounded by people who care about one another and enjoy a culture many envy.

Appalachian Values

Willard's description of his life in the mountains of Kentucky and Virginia brings to mind the work of another mountain native, who wrote about "Appalachian Values," the typical qualities of Appalachian people. Loyal Jones, originally from North Carolina, lives in Kentucky and is retired from the Appalachian Center at Berea College, the school Willard attended. According to Jones, the values are individualism, self-reliance and pride; neighborliness and hospitality; familism; personalism; love of place; modesty; sense of beauty; and sense of pride.

Gayheart's drawings bring to mind many of the values and explain the Appalachian experience from the perspective of an artist.

Religion, through fundamentals of faith, is not necessarily the organized weekly church attendances, but more locally autonomous individualistic church gatherings. Willard's drawing entitled *Blue Ridge Baptism* is a good example of the importance placed on religion in the region.

Individualism, Self-Reliance and Pride are probably the most obvious characteristics of mountain people, Jones says. Early Appalachians were individualistic from the beginning or they would not have risked so much to find their way here to the mountains. Appalachians don't want to be beholden to anyone and take great pride in being able to make and build the things they need such as clothing, furniture, houses, musical instruments, or other such items. Willard's drawings of Kilby Snow in *Blue Ridge Balladeer* and Sherman Wooten in *The Chair Maker* are good examples of these values.

Neighborliness and Hospitality started long ago on the frontier when migrating Appalachians helped each other build homes and barns and took each other into their homes as they traveled. The term, according to Jones, used to describe hospitable people was "clever" and no greater compliment could be paid to a mountain family. The drawing depicting this trait is Willard's *Stir-off at the Crib.*

Familism is the deep loyalty between family members. In James Still's book *River of Earth,* the father takes in extra relatives even though there isn't enough food in the home to feed his wife and children. *Christmas on the Mountain* and *The Sweetest Gift* are only two of many of Gayheart's works that show love of family.

Personalism involves Appalachians being respectful of others with quiet tolerance of people's differences, not crusading their prejudices, but accepting or at least tolerating others, and having little interest in credentials.

Love of Place is a unifying value of mountain people, an attachment to one's physical location.

Modesty is a character of many talented Appalachian people: no airs, no boasting or "getting above their raising." Loyal Jones feels Appalachians have a pretty good view of themselves and don't take themselves too seriously.

A Sense of Beauty comes in many forms and often is tied to functional necessity. Good craftsmanship in such things as handmade chairs, rifles, stitchery, quilts, musical instruments, and beautiful music are all a part of this Appalachian value. Many of Willard's drawings exhibit these four characteristics.

A Sense of Humor is probably best portrayed in Willard's *Study of a Storyteller,* his drawing of Ray Hicks, the famous storyteller from

Beech Mountain, North Carolina. This teller of Jack Tales is the perfect illustration of humor in man and the human condition.

Patriotism has driven Appalachian people to turn out for all national wars, and draft quotas in Appalachia have often been filled with volunteers.

Willard Gayheart embodies each of Jones' "Appalachian Values." He is a religious man, as evidenced by his local church involvement, where he contributes his time and musical talents. His faith is also frequently evident in conversations with him.

He is an individual who is self-reliant and has a lot of pride, particularly where his family is concerned. Self-reliance is seen in his ongoing effort to accurately and lovingly portray mountain people through his strokes with graphite, and to earn a living for himself and his family from his gallery and frame shop. He has a very modest pride in his work.

He is definitely hospitable or "clever." One only has to open the door to his business or telephone or write to him to see this quality in his enthusiastic responses.

It is hard to imagine one more proud of and dedicated to his family than Willard Gayheart, as evidenced by his closeness to his wife, their children and grandchildren, and to his mother Dora.

Personalism, or interaction with other people, is another value seen in Willard. Never a seeker of the limelight, he quietly treats everyone he meets as though they are the most special things to him at the moment.

His love of place is evident in conversations with him, his music, and in his work. A sense of beauty shows through in all his drawings, whether of a dirty coal miner or a child planting a garden.

Quick to laugh, Willard has a wonderful sense of humor and often makes self-deprecating remarks.

A huge American flag hangs in a prominent spot on the front porch of Willard's gallery, an unspoken tribute to his country. Clearly he has strong patriotic values.

As written in *Appalachia Inside Out*, edited by Robert J. Higgs, Ambrose N. Manning and Jim Wayne Miller, "We cannot define precisely where Appalachia begins and ends geographically, and neither can we say exactly where the culture and customs of the region begin and end." Willard Gayheart's art is of and about the region, yet it transcends boundaries in many ways.

The people in his art might be the people of other regions as well as Appalachia. The music and instruments he draws and sings about have certainly transcended boundaries. What he has tried to keep alive through his artistic drawings and his music is being sought today by Americans everywhere, as illustrated by an August 2001 article in the *Washington Post* titled, "America Is Heading for the Hills," following the release of the popular movie *O Brother, Where Art Thou*, which featured mountain music. There is a resurgence of interest in the music, history, and all things Appalachian.

The book entitled *Appalachia Inside Out* also questions whether Appalachia will become indistinguishable from American culture in other parts of the country. It concludes that even if Appalachia were lost, "there still would be a need for knowledge of the history of Appalachia."

Willard Gayheart has done his part to insure that the history and culture will remain alive through his art and music. He has fulfilled the "Appalachian Values," and he has not migrated, but stayed in and celebrated this place.

THE ART OF WILLARD GAYHEART

Text in italics, as well as other quoted text, comes from interviews with Willard Gayheart.

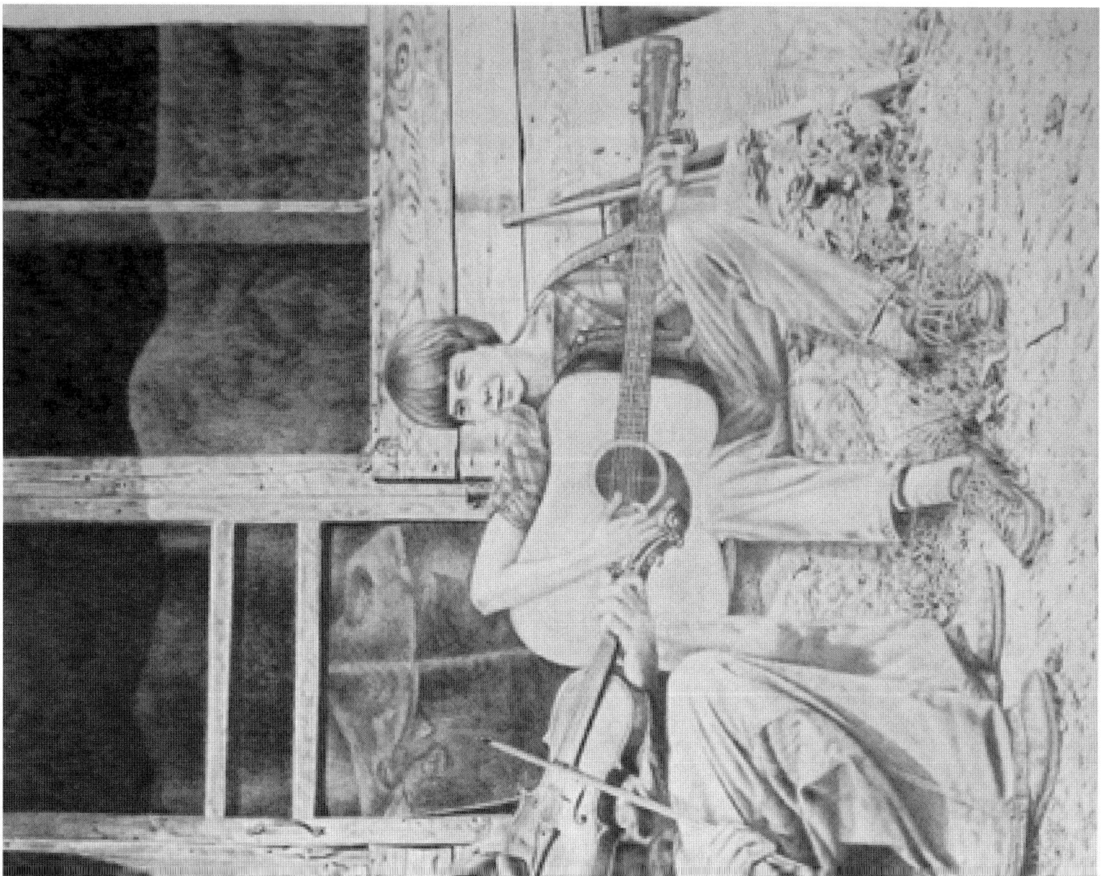

Bridging the Gap
1979

In an effort to represent how traditional music bridges the generation gap, this drawing with Michael Gayheart as the young model was the first the artist recalls including such background details as the wood grain in the building, and shading and detail of the screened porch. The older man was taken from an old photograph belonging to Willard.

> *This is typical of what you see a lot at fiddlers' conventions and other places where you find traditional music, especially in jam sessions. You'll find the old and the young playing together. And that's one of the particular styles of music I think works really well to bridge the generation gap.*

Kilby Snow
Blue Ridge Balladeer
1983

Kilby Snow was an autoharp player from Fries, a small town in Grayson County, Virginia. When Willard knew him he lived near Galax, Virginia, home to the annual Old Fiddlers' Convention, which celebrated its 67th year in 2002.

A carpenter by trade and an instrument maker who probably made some of the autoharps he played, Kilby was a great autoharp player. He was innovative in that he was left-handed and played on the wrong side of the bars. This method gave his playing a different sound, and he could play anything he ever heard. Willard recalls one tune in particular called "Yakkety Sax" which Kilby had heard on the radio by Boots Randolph, a Nashville saxophonist who played with Chet Atkins and other Nashville musicians.

Willard drew Kilby in his overalls in front of an old house to symbolize cabins of the Blue Ridge Mountains and titled it *Blue Ridge Balladeer* because he wanted to say something about past Blue Ridge culture and thought Kilby a good model for this kind of project. Only later did he learn Kilby was known all over the country as one of the great autoharp players and that Mike Seeger, a traditional folk musician from Rockbridge County, Virginia, had discovered him years before and had taken him to festivals where he became known for his music and eventually did some recording.

Another note of interest about this drawing is that the original was sold to a former employer of Willard's in Galax and at his death the family asked Willard to sell the piece. He sold it at the Black Gold Festival in Hazard, Kentucky, an annual event to honor coal, one of Kentucky's major resources, that features parades, crafts, and entertainment. At the time a movie called *Fire Down Under* starring Steven Seagal was being filmed in the area and Willard said, "there was lots of excitement." He sold the art to Mike Brian, a young stunt man with the movie, and "off to Hollywood it went."

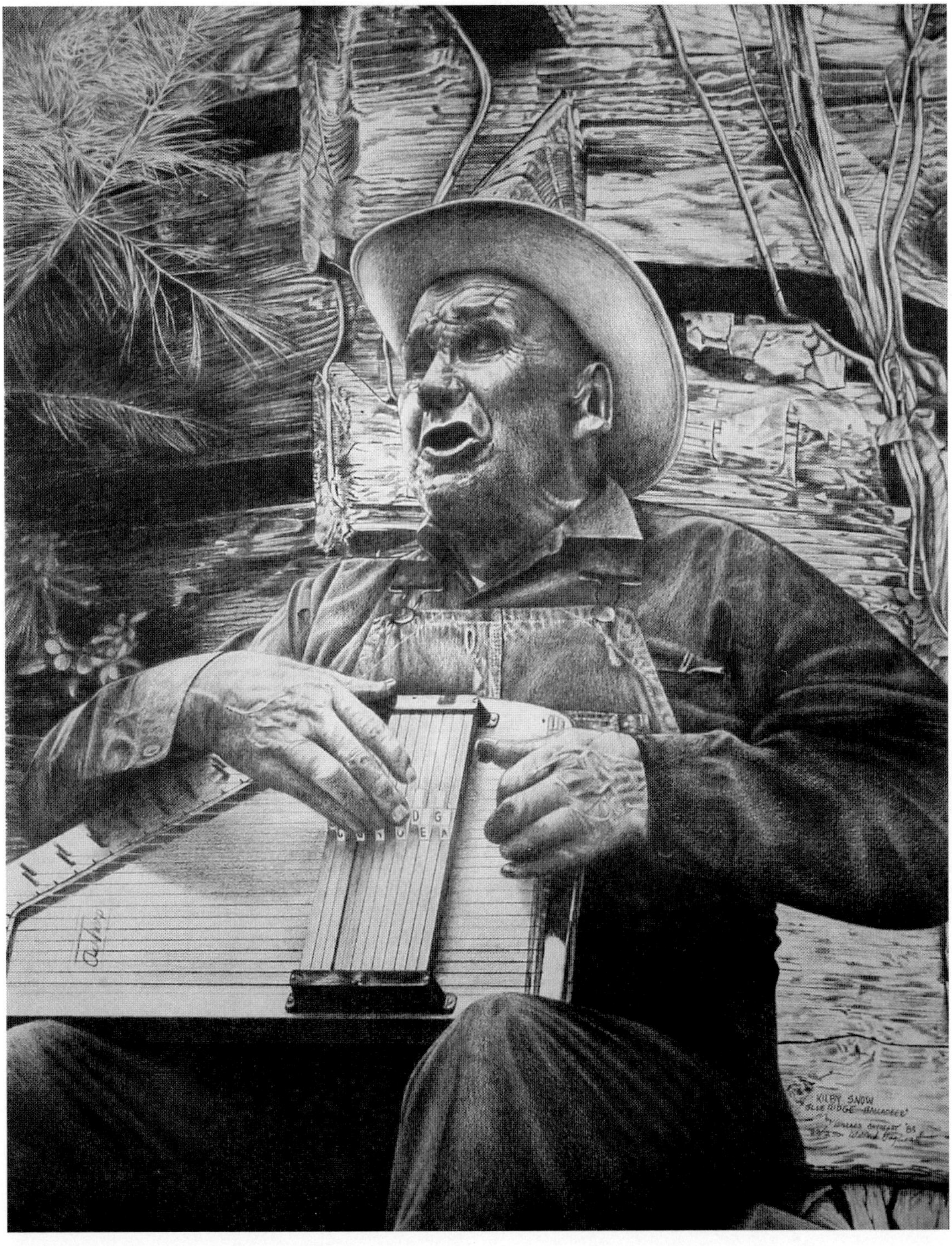
KILBY SNOW

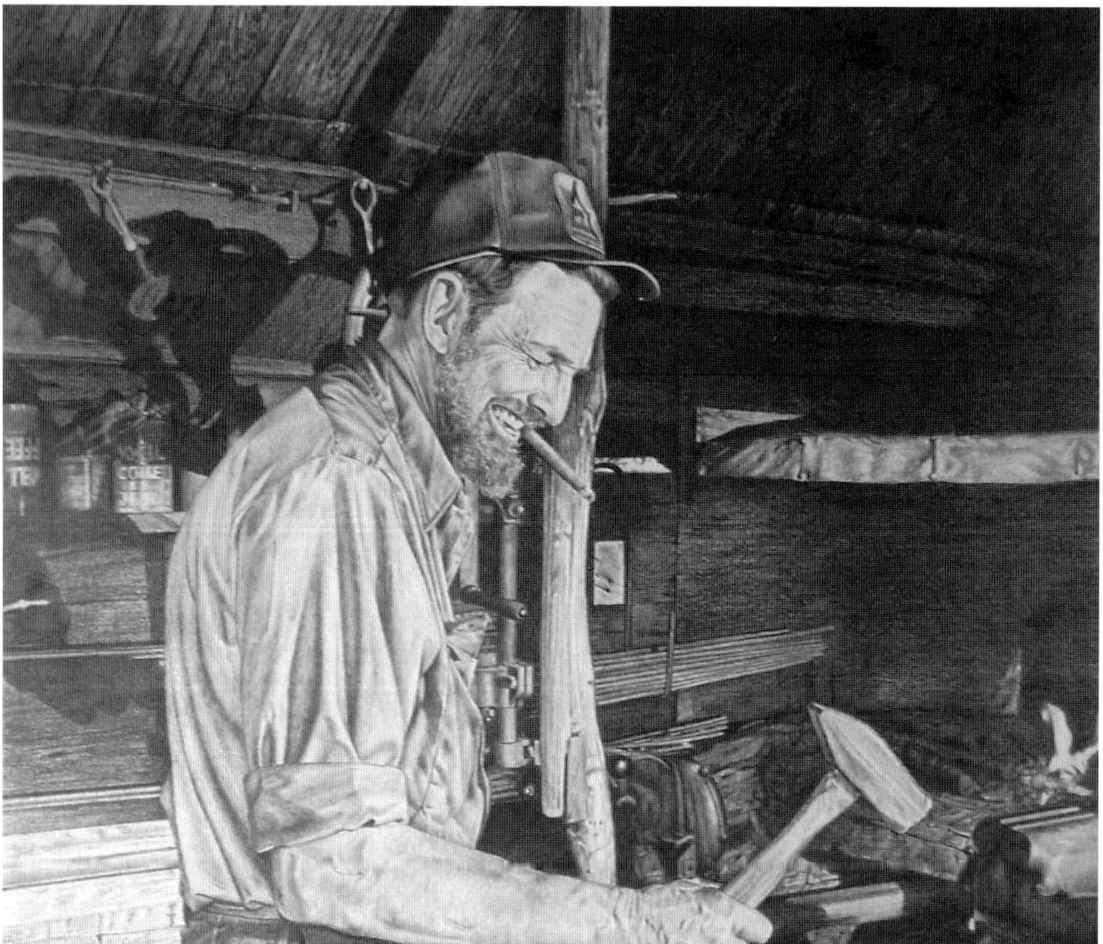

Phipps Bourne
Blue Ridge Blacksmith
(Early 1980s)

Phipps Bourne is shown in his blacksmith shop at Mabry Mill, a scenic location at milepost 176 on the Blue Ridge Parkway near Floyd, Virginia. A very creative person, Phipps was known around Mabry Mill as "Festus," a name perhaps taken from the character in the television show *Gunsmoke* or from Hephaestus, the Greek god of fire, frequently depicted as a blacksmith. Or the nickname might have come about because of his strong mountain dialect, "the way he pronounced his words, the way he talked."

For many years Phipps worked in the blacksmith shop for the National Park Service to demonstrate the art of blacksmithing. Willard is unsure whether any of his creations were sold at the Mabry Mill gift shop, but he recalls that Phipps had a shop at home and sold fireplace tools, shovels, and pokers that he made. Willard says Phipps must be called an artist for his creativity in blacksmithing, wood carving, drawing, and painting.

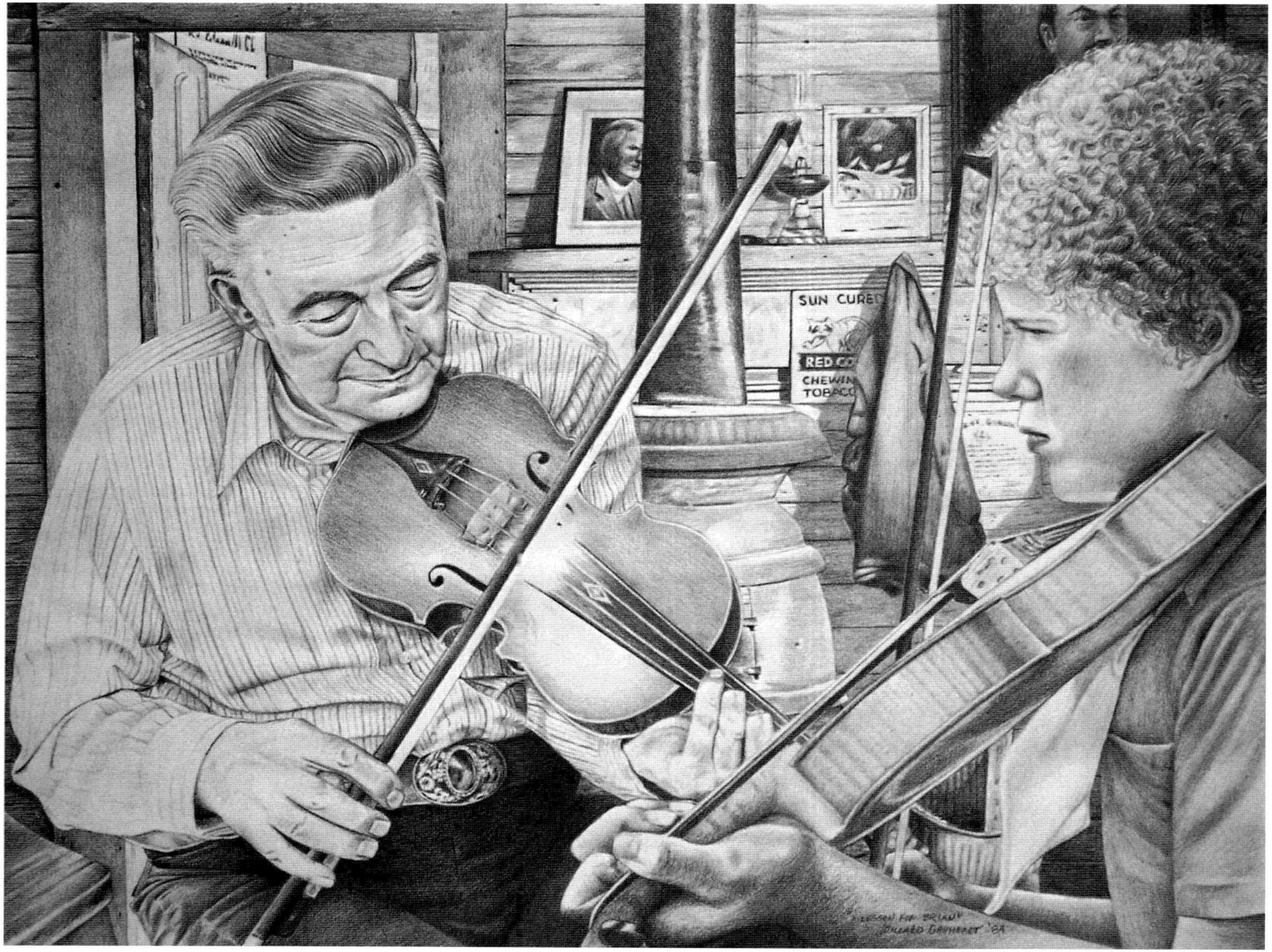
SUN CURED
CHEWIN
TOBACC

Lesson for Brian
(1984)

Albert Hash, an award-winning musician at many fiddlers' conventions, lived near White Top Mountain, in Grayson County, in the national forest recreation area of Mount Rogers, the highest peak in Virginia. He was an innovative and inventive machinist who designed and made most of the tools he used as a gifted instrument maker.

Albert crafted beautiful fiddles, dulcimers, and guitars, but was mostly known for his fiddles. Owners of a fiddle crafted by Albert Hash now own a collector's item.

At Mount Rogers High School, where the enrollment wasn't large enough to have a marching band, Albert helped to organize a string band for a community with great interest in traditional music.

The kids learned how to play the fiddles and guitars and banjos and to dance, and they played all over the place and still do today.

After many requests for a drawing, Willard decided to feature Albert teaching Brian Grimm a lesson in playing the fiddle. Brian is now an adult with his own band, the Konnarock Kritters.

Albert's daughter, Audrey Hash Hamm, carries on a family and cultural tradition by making fiddles and lap dulcimers. Dulcimers are stringed wooden instruments commonly found in Appalachia and can be played by plucking or strumming the strings. Audrey sells her instruments at the annual Blue Ridge Folklife Festival held on the campus of Ferrum College near Rocky Mount, Virginia, each October.

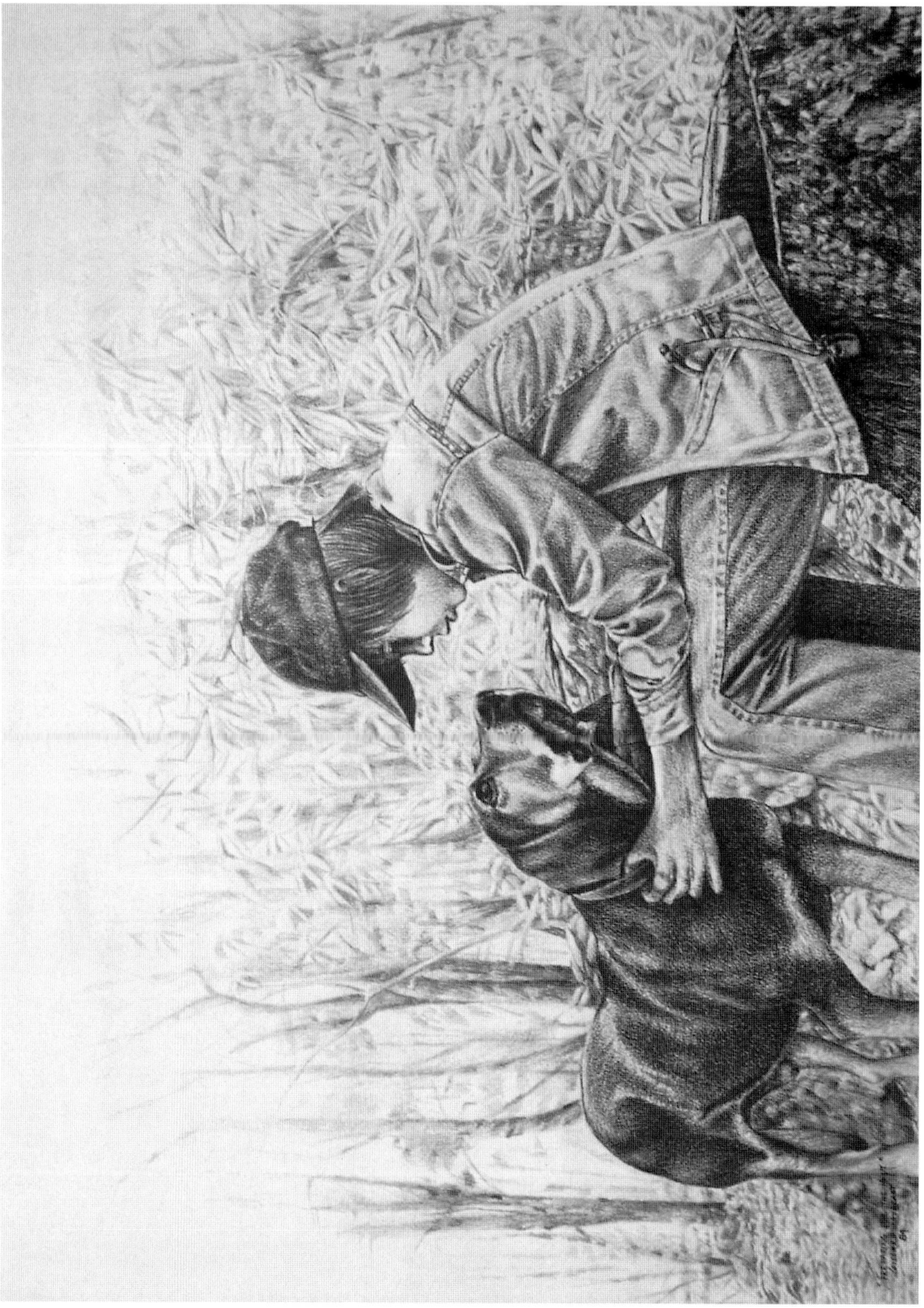

Preparing for the Hunt (1984)

This drawing developed from photos Willard took of a friendly black and tan coonhound called Old Drum, a dog featured in several of his scenes. His son Michael is the model for the young hunter. As Michael holds Old Drum "kindly by the neck and stares into his eyes, he's making plans for some kind of big game hunt or whatever he can bring down with his slingshot," says Willard.

> *This represents what I thought was kindly typical of the Appalachian Mountains and a boy growing up in the country with his dog and things they would do in times past.*

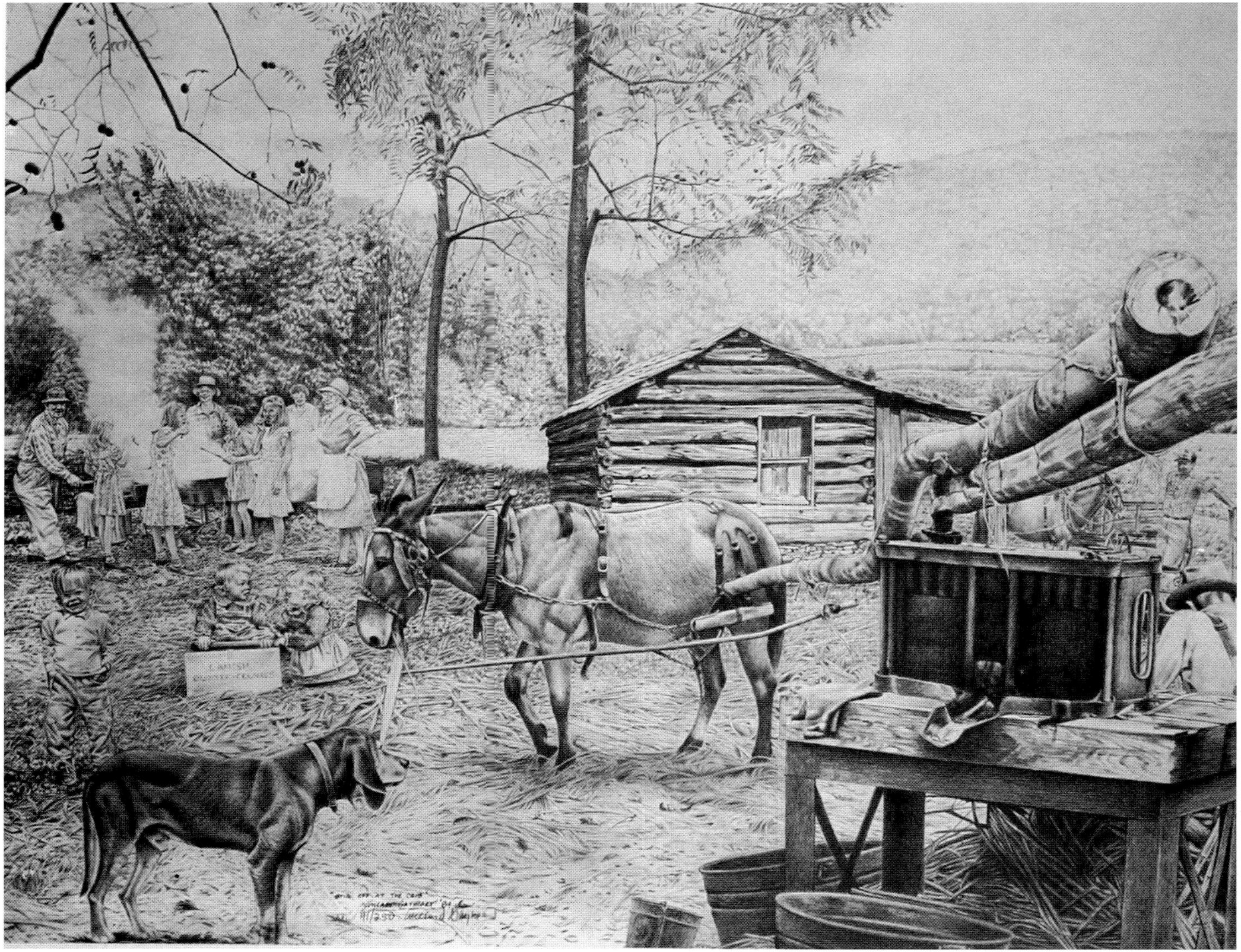

Stir-off at the Crib (1984)

Making molasses in the fall was a yearly tradition for Willard Gayheart.

> *The intent here was to depict family unity or community, a large family or small community, however you want to see it.*

He has drawn the old mule and gin as they grind the cane to squeeze juice for the molasses.

> *They'd stir those all day, and just at the right time they'd bring them off and put them in containers and put them away for winter.*

A favorite subject of the artist is the dog Old Drum, who is frequently found in Willard's art.

> *I thought surely in a scene like this you'd probably find an old hound dog like you would find in the Appalachian Mountains. There's also a cabin there, probably a corncrib or blacksmith shop, and children playing; typical of what might have been fifty or sixty years ago.*

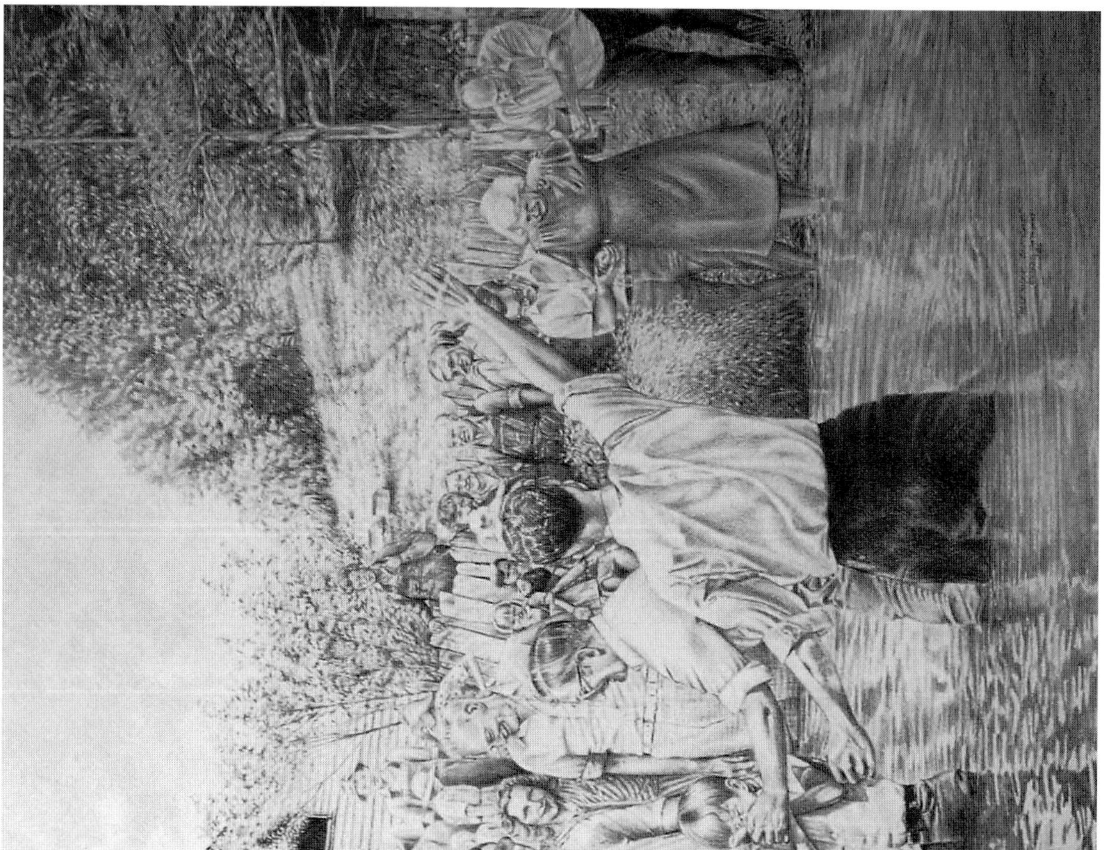

Blue Ridge Baptism
(1984)

This drawing focuses on a father and son ministry team. The grandfather, Bob Adams, and his son, Gary, are baptizing grandson Mathew Adams. From a collection of photographs of baptisms, Willard created what he thought was a good representation of a typical baptism in a mountain stream with people lined up waiting their turn and bystanders or a congregation as witnesses.

The original drawing was sold to an acquaintance of the artist, and at his request it was personalized by using the faces of family members.

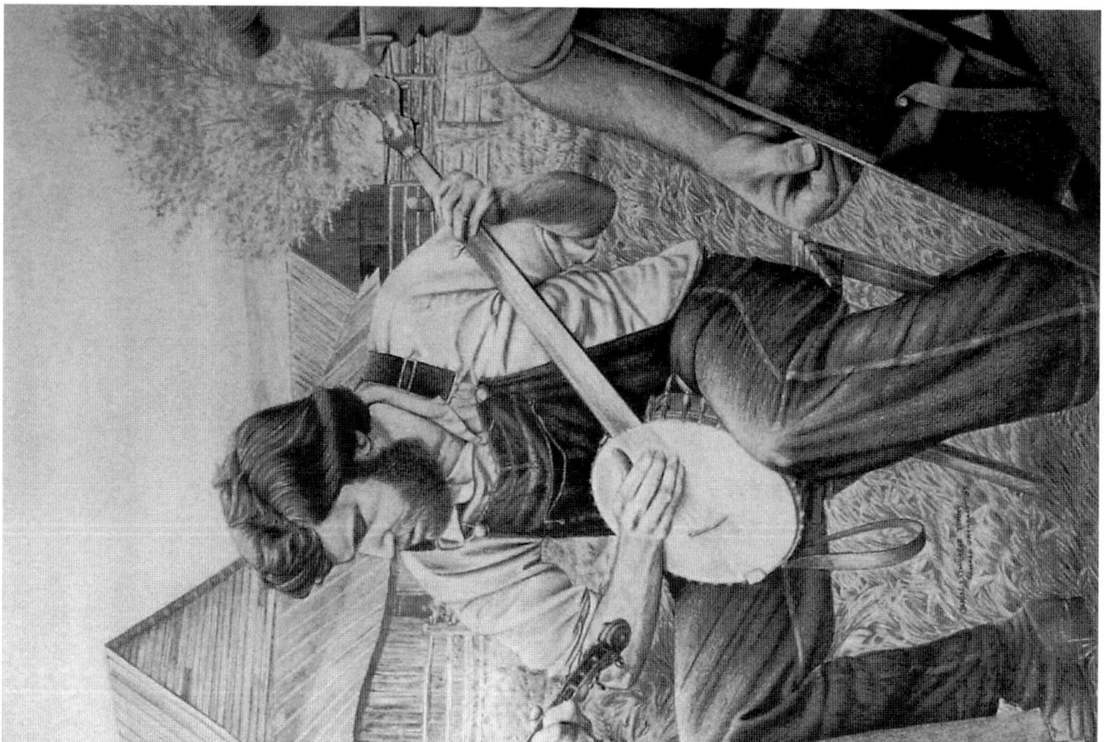

Jammin' with Uncle Tommy (1984)

"Known by people the world over" is the way Willard described Tommy Jarrell, the fiddler from Mount Airy, North Carolina, who is featured at the left in this drawing. In 1982 Tommy was a winner of the National Heritage Fellowship award from the National Endowment for the Arts.

This drawing resulted from a summer afternoon picnic hosted by Alice Gerrard, another well known old time musician who lived at the time near Galax, Virginia, where several fiddlers came together for an afternoon to play, some meeting for the first time. Other musicians attending the picnic included John Rector and John Patterson.

Featured in this drawing with Tommy is Andy Cahan from New York City, one of many who came to live with and learn from Tommy Jarrell.

Young people from all over the world came to learn from Tommy and he let 'em stay as long as they wanted to.

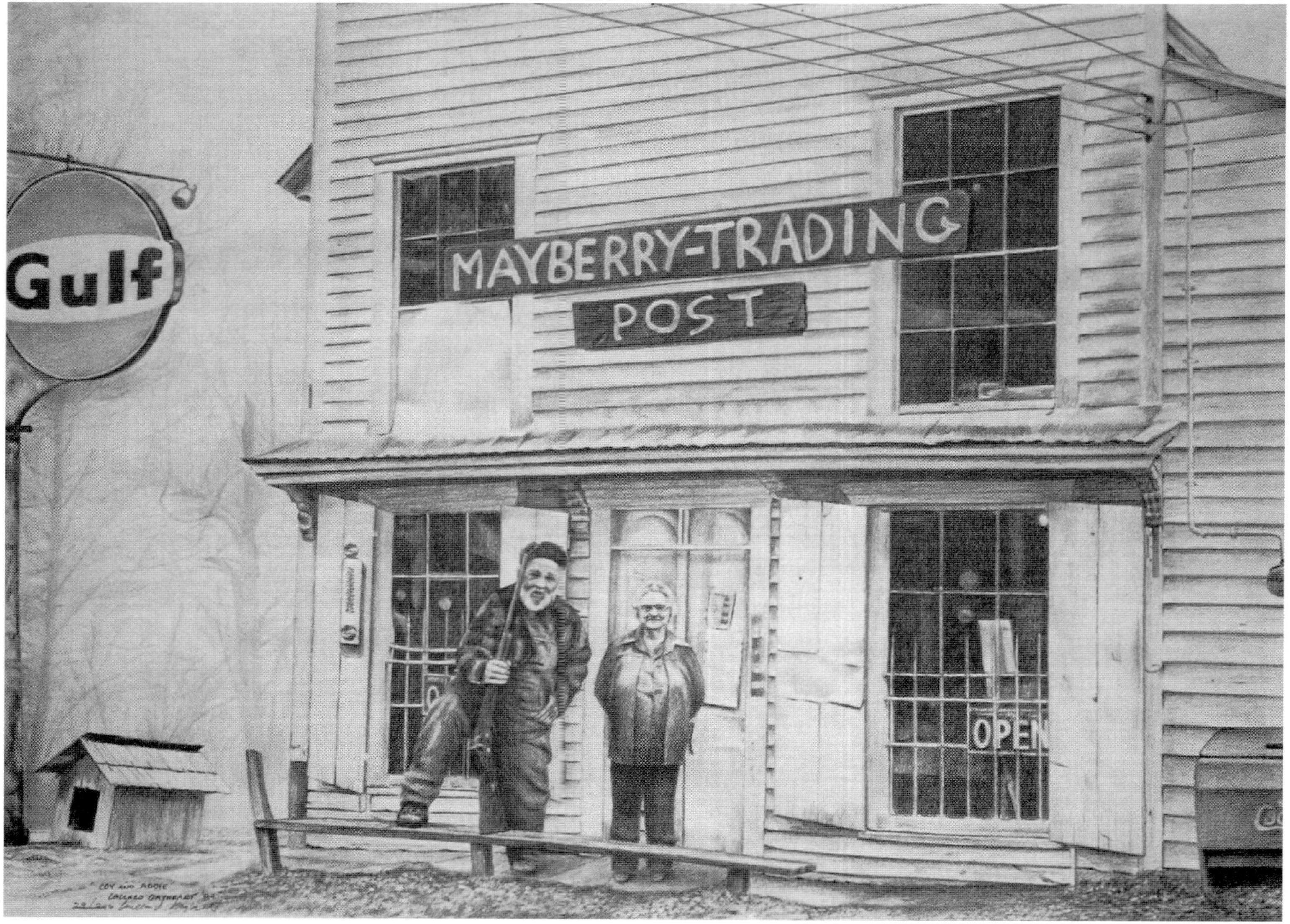
Gulf
MAYBERRY-TRADING
POST
OPEN

Coy & Addie
1984

Coy Yates owned the store in this drawing, which is probably still in operation today on the Blue Ridge Parkway at Meadows of Dan, Virginia, in Floyd County.

Everybody loved Addie Wood. She was a storehouse of stories and loved to tell her memories to people who stopped by the store.

Because of the proximity of the store to the Parkway, people were always stopping by to visit or to buy handmade products and homemade items such as apple butter.

All prints from this drawing have sold.

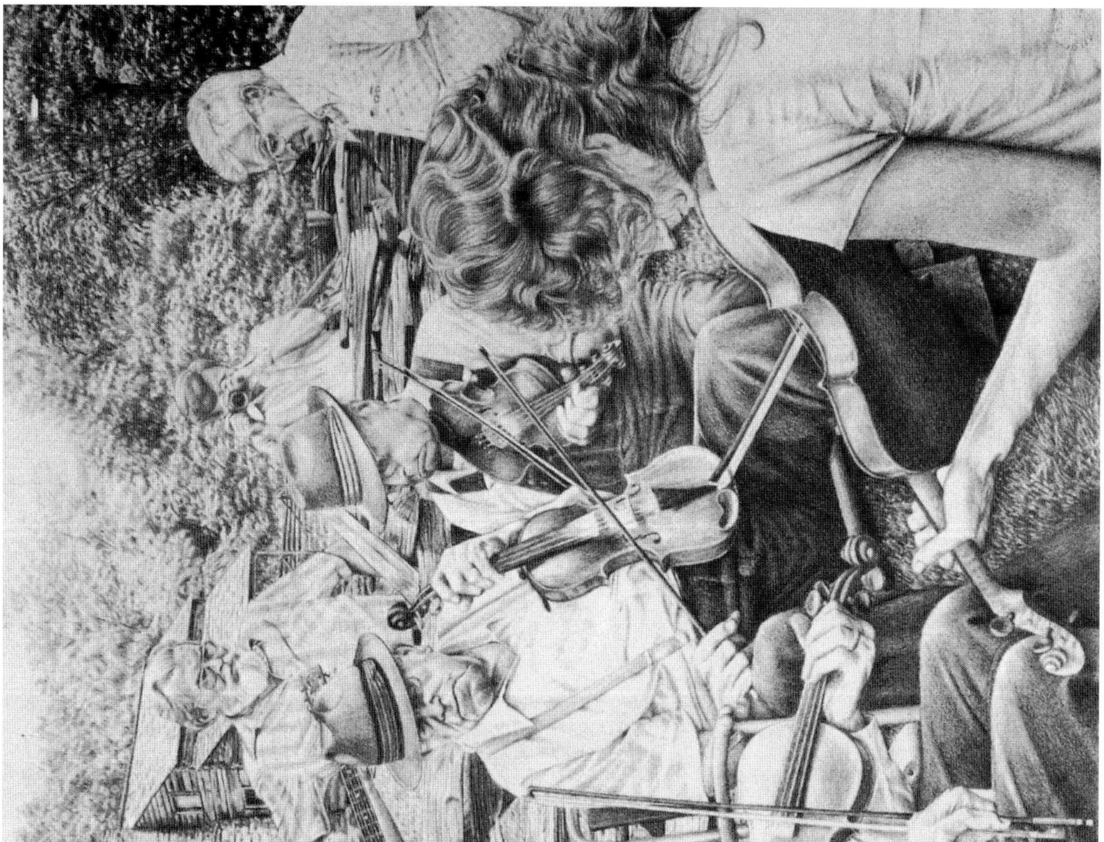

Fiddle Workshop
1984

On a Sunday afternoon in 1983, many notable musicians in and around the southwestern Virginia community of Galax gathered for a picnic and afternoon jam session. This drawing was a result of that afternoon, which included local notables such as Tommy Jarrell, John Patterson, Ernest East, John Rector, and Alice Gerrard, also publisher of *The Old Time Herald* magazine.

> *Alice was very interested in older old-time musicians and one summer Sunday afternoon in the early eighties a lot of us went and had a big old time jamming and visiting. I took some pictures of the older musicians there. Many are now gone. I called this Fiddle Workshop because so many played fiddles and they were comparing notes and swapping licks or teaching each other moves on the fiddle.*

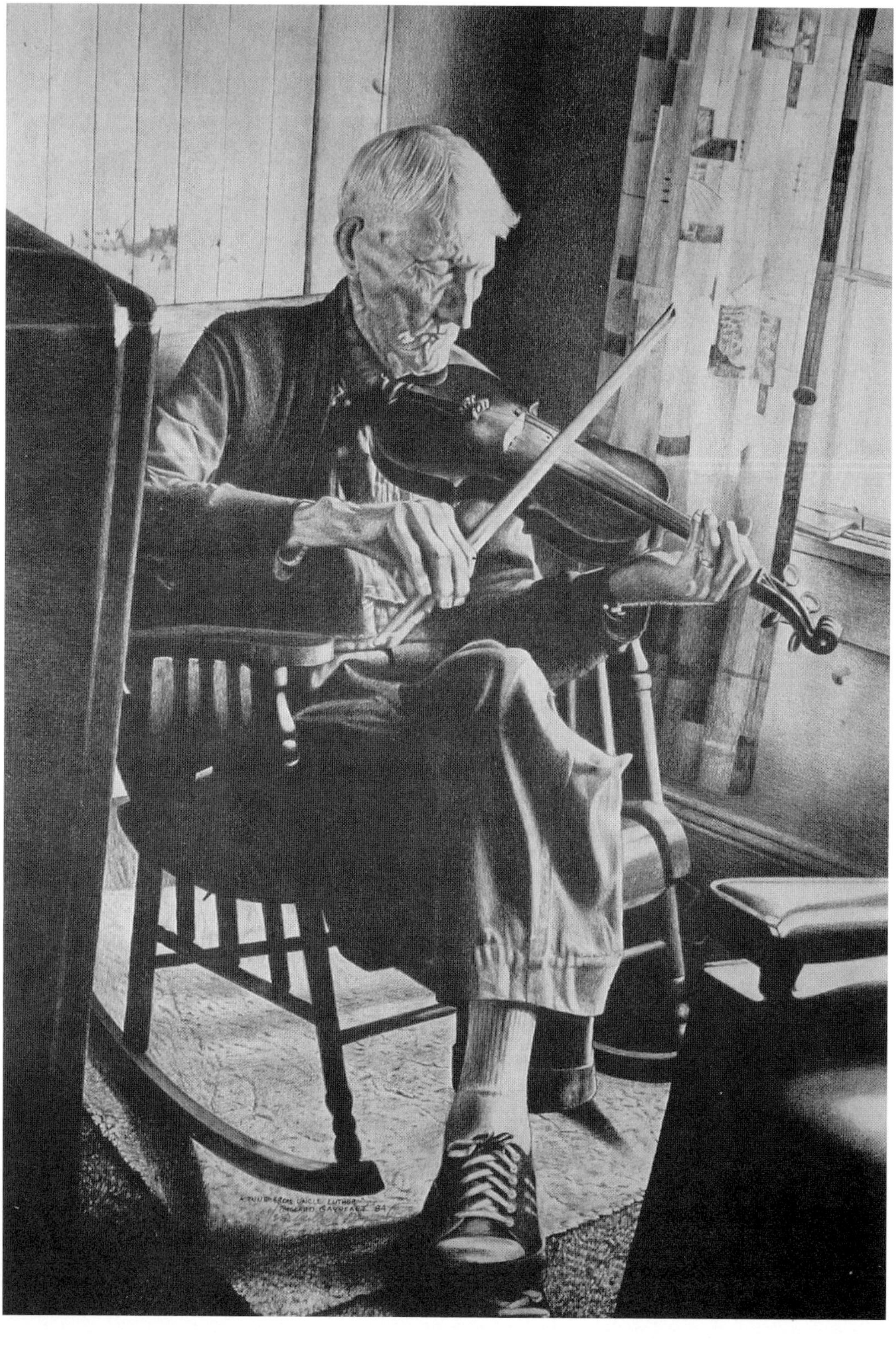
A TUNE FROM UNCLE LUTHER

A Tune from Uncle Luther
1984

Luther Davis was a humorous, witty, magnetic kind of fellow. People liked him, especially young people. He was a local personality who was a good fiddle player and worked at a stockyard as an auctioneer.

Willard recalls that this man was "kindly discovered in his eighties" by young people who were amazed at his great memory of the past and his "storehouse of old fiddle tunes."

Luther lived to be 99 years old, and his family has said the spark brought to him by young people added years to his life. His family physician has told of his humor on his 99th birthday, as he was hooked up to all sorts of equipment and joked about his situation not being the way one should spend a 99th birthday.

A recording of Luther Davis playing his fiddle is owned by Bobby Patterson of the Heritage Shoppe located in Woodlawn, next to Willard's Front Porch Gallery.

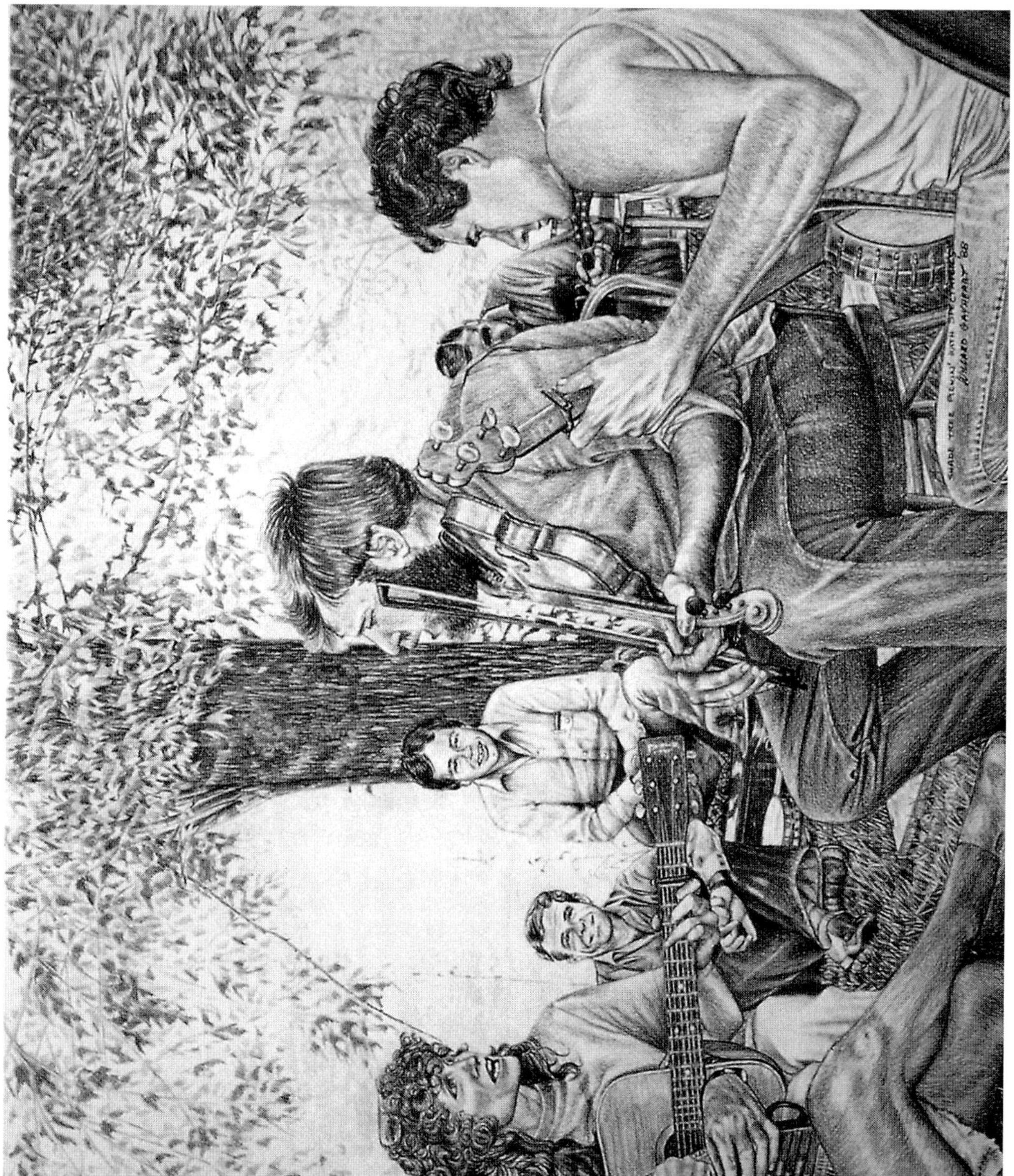
Shade Tree Pickin' with
Willard Gayheart '88

Shade Tree Pickin'
1985

This drawing resulted from a jam session out in the country near Galax back in the summer of 1981-82. Alice Gerrard, recording artist and publisher, had a picnic one Sunday afternoon and invited a lot of old time musicians. Willard said, "We had a big jam session." He did several drawings from that afternoon. The people in the drawing are Andy Cahan playing the banjo, Drew Smith from New Jersey playing the autoharp, and the man sitting in front of the tree enjoying the music is Bill McFarland. This drawing was actually McFarland's wedding present from Willard. McFarland graduated from Galax High School and went on to a school of music in Boston and worked for National Public Radio in Minnesota. Then, he became the director for a national jazz educators' association and booked shows across the country featuring jazz musicians. "We're real proud of him, a local boy," states Willard.

Alice Gerrard's magazine devoted to old time musicians is called *The Old-Time Herald.*

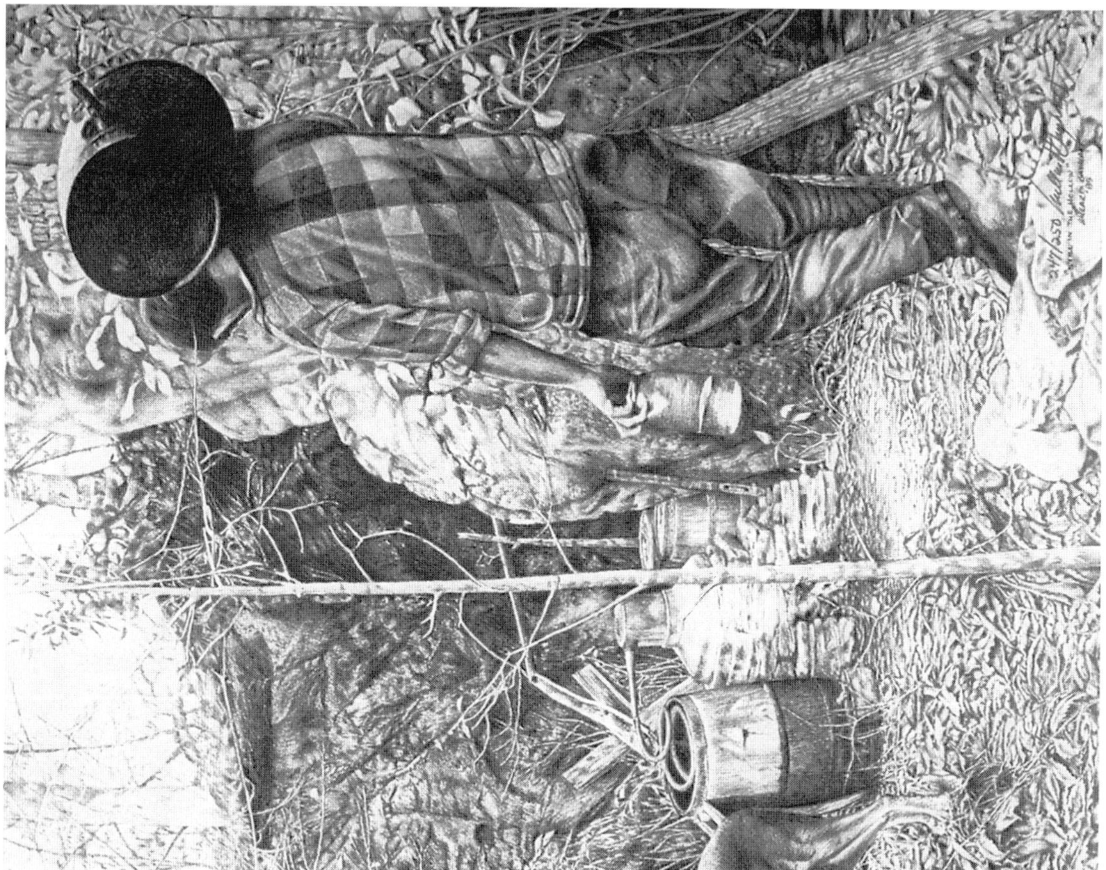

Still in the Hollow
1985

In 1982 our band called the Highlanders played at the World's Fair in Knoxville, Tennessee, and I met down there a moonshiner from east Tennessee, a Tennessee mountain moonshiner, bona fide. They'd hired him to do that every day at the Fair so people from all over the world could see how Tennessee moonshine was made and every day he'd make a run of moonshine and at day's end destroy the makings.

A year or so later Willard was exhibiting at a festival and had a request for a drawing of a still from a former ABC officer who had been involved in locating and destroying illegal distilleries in the mountains. Working with photos from the World's Fair and other pictures of old stills, plus photographs of the model still at Mabry Mill on the Blue Ridge Parkway in Floyd County, Virginia, Willard once again added Old Drum, a hound dog found in several of his drawings. The result was *Still in the Hollow.*

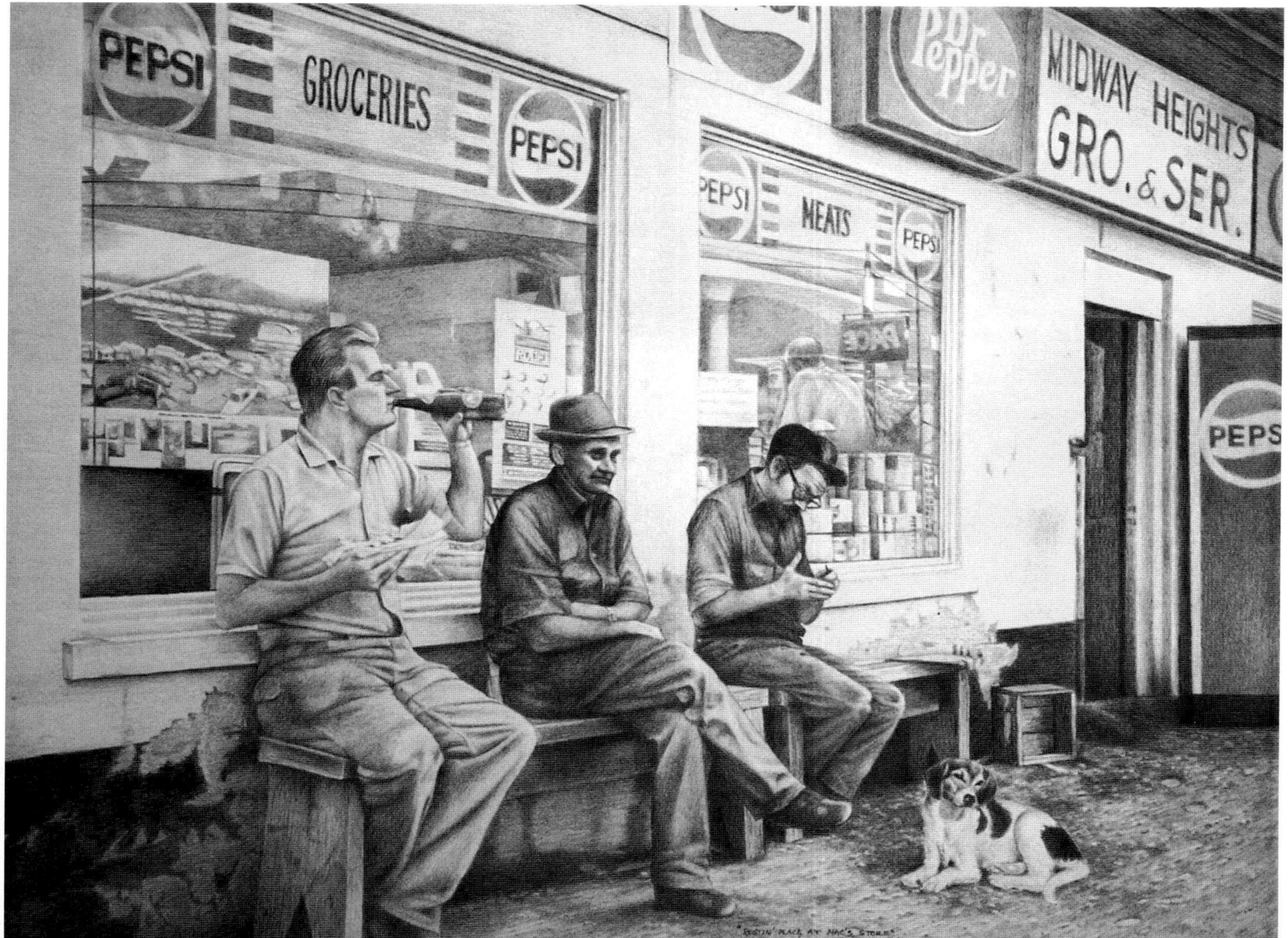
PEPSI
GROCERIES
PEPSI
Dr Pepper
MIDWAY HEIGHTS
GRO. & SER.
PEPSI
MEATS
PEPSI
PEPS

Resting Place at Mac's Store
1986

This is a result of stopping at a little store one evening to get gas, milk, and bread. There was a bench in front of the store and it was almost twilight and there were three fellows sitting there. One of them was picking splinters out of his hand where he'd been working, one was just staring off into the distance, and the other was eating a sandwich and drinking a Dr Pepper. I thought, boy, what a scene to draw. I got my camera and told 'em, 'Boys, don't pose, just do what you've been doing.' I did two or three photographs and a few weeks later did the drawing and added a dog.

Mac's Store was a neighborhood store on Route 58 between Hillsville and Galax, but is no longer in existence. On the left is Bruce Higgins, Cecil Horton is in the middle, and B. B. Delp is getting splinters out of his hand.

Canning Peaches
1986

"Canning peaches, apples, beans, and tomatoes was the old way of preserving food for the winter," explained Willard. In this commissioned drawing of a couple from Southwest Virginia, a big square wash tub is being used.

> *People would heat water outdoors and after cold packing the peaches in glass jars, they would place the jars in the hot water and cook the peaches all day. In the evening they would take the peaches out of the water, tighten the lids to vacuum pack them, and store [them] in a cellar or some other cool place for winter use.*

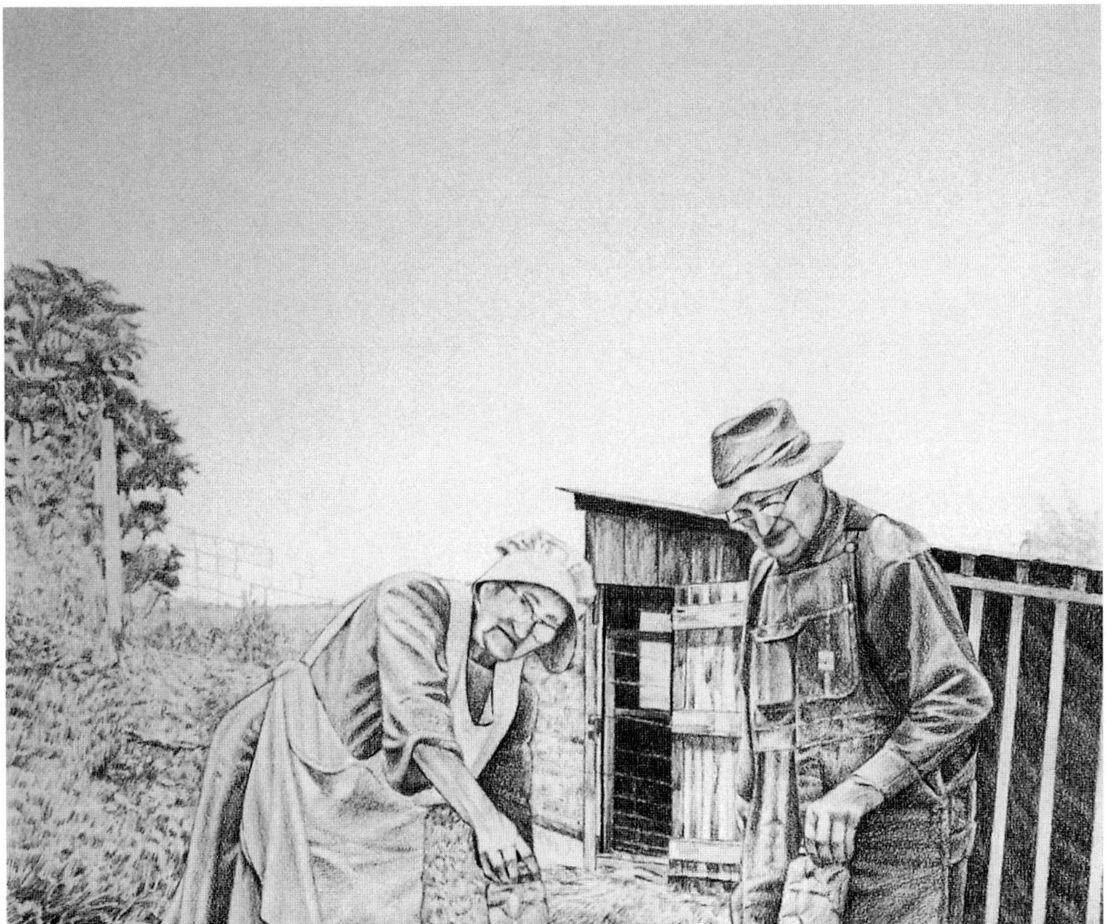

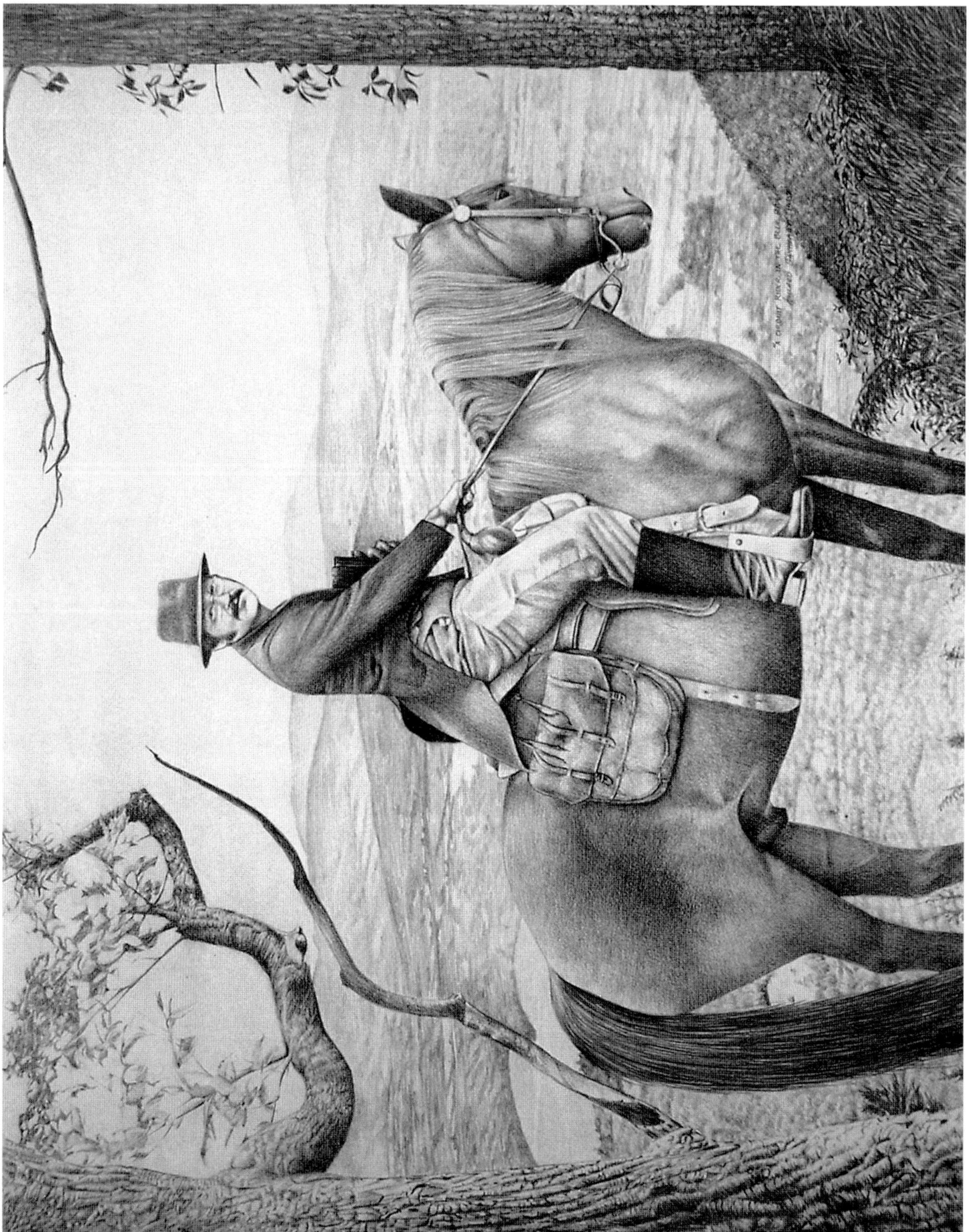

The Circuit Rider
1987

Using a former church pastor, Joe Marine, as the model, Willard did this drawing as a gift for him, but changed the background to a view from the Blue Ridge Parkway in Virginia.

The drawing was done from a photo taken of Joe on Heritage Day at Mount Olivet United Methodist Church in Galax, Virginia. Joe was wearing authentic 19th century clothing borrowed from a church member.

Portrait of a Coal Miner
1987

Willard grew up in eastern Kentucky where coalfields were common. Although there were no coal mines in the community where he grew up, he could cross the mountains in any direction and go into a coal camp with mining facilities, the tipple, and trains that came and went to haul the coal away.

This commission work portrays a typical miner in front of the tipple as he might have come from work with his dinner bucket, his light for the dark mines on top of his cap, and garb he might have worn to work back in the 1930s and '40s. This would have been a familiar scene in Kentucky, as well as in West Virginia and southwestern Virginia.

The drawing was done from a small photograph brought to Willard by a lady from eastern Kentucky some years back. The photograph showed the barely visible and coal-blackened face of her father, who had been a miner in Pike County, Kentucky. Willard stated he could not get the exact likeness of the man's face because his features were so covered with dust.

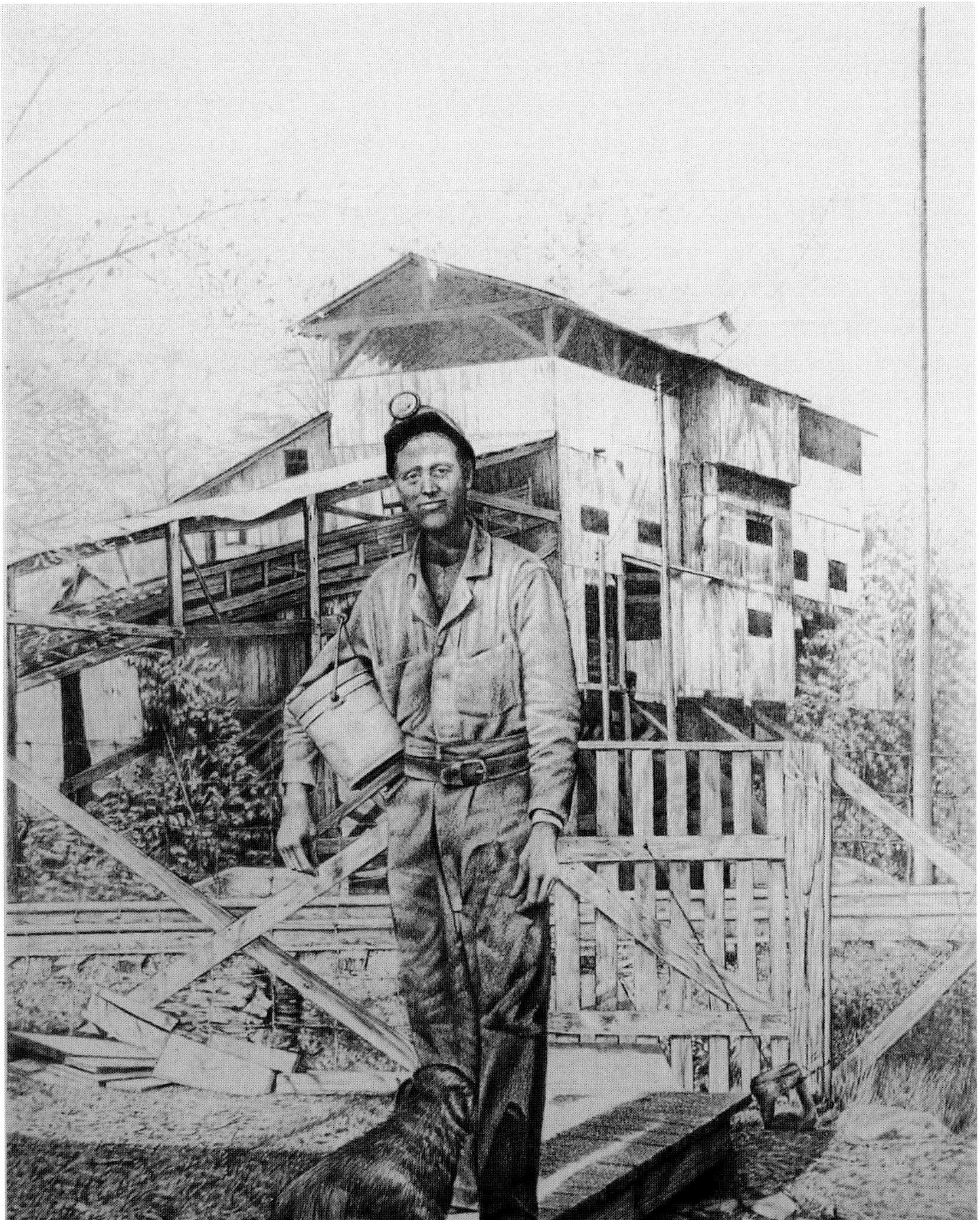

Josh
1988

We were at a family reunion in West Virginia and Josh, my wife's nephew, was digging and playing in the dirt with a spoon and cup from one of the tables. He was so caught up in what he was doing. I did what I often do with drawings of children and don't show much of their faces. Consequently, Josh could be many little boys at that age.

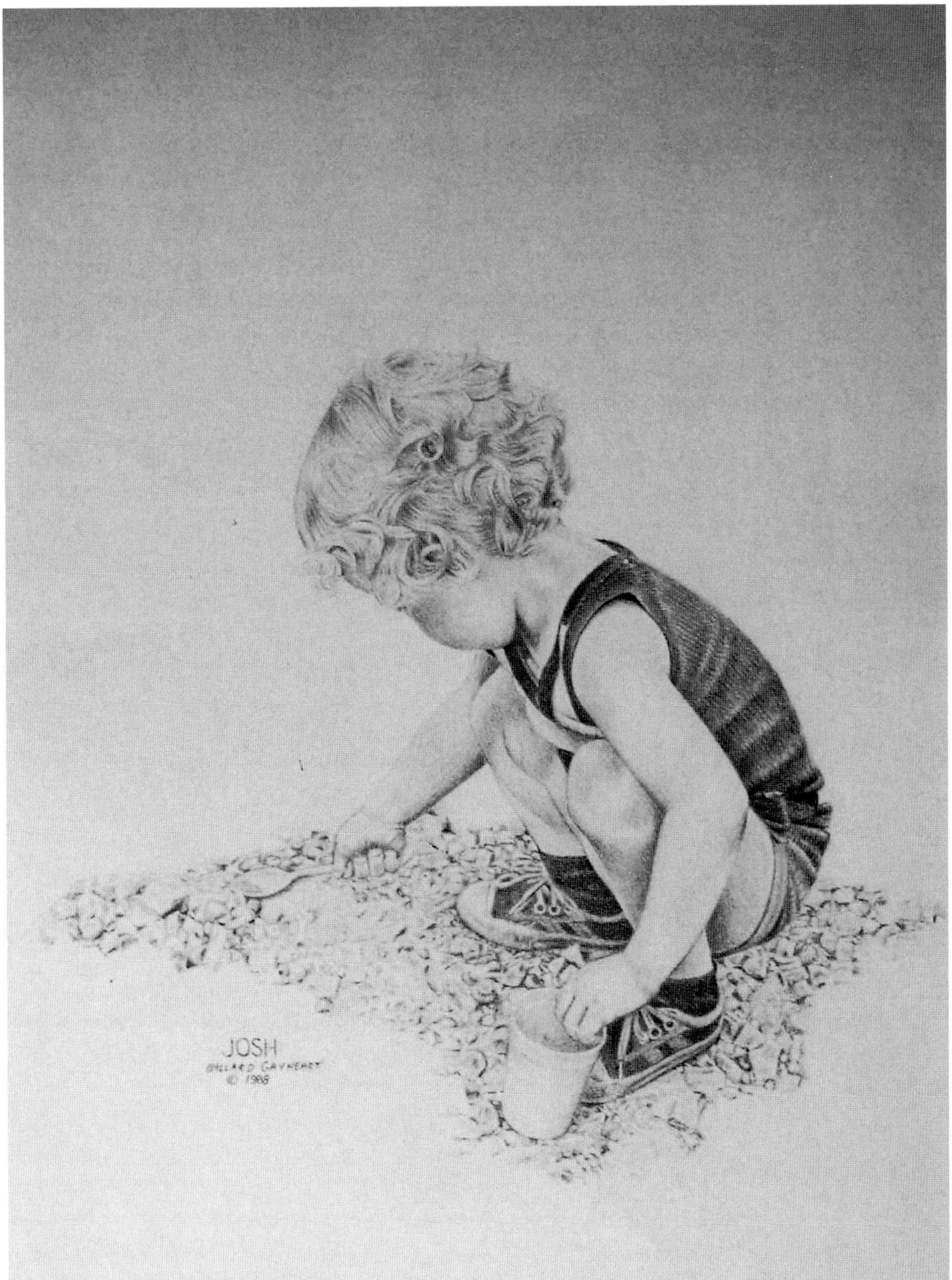
JOSH

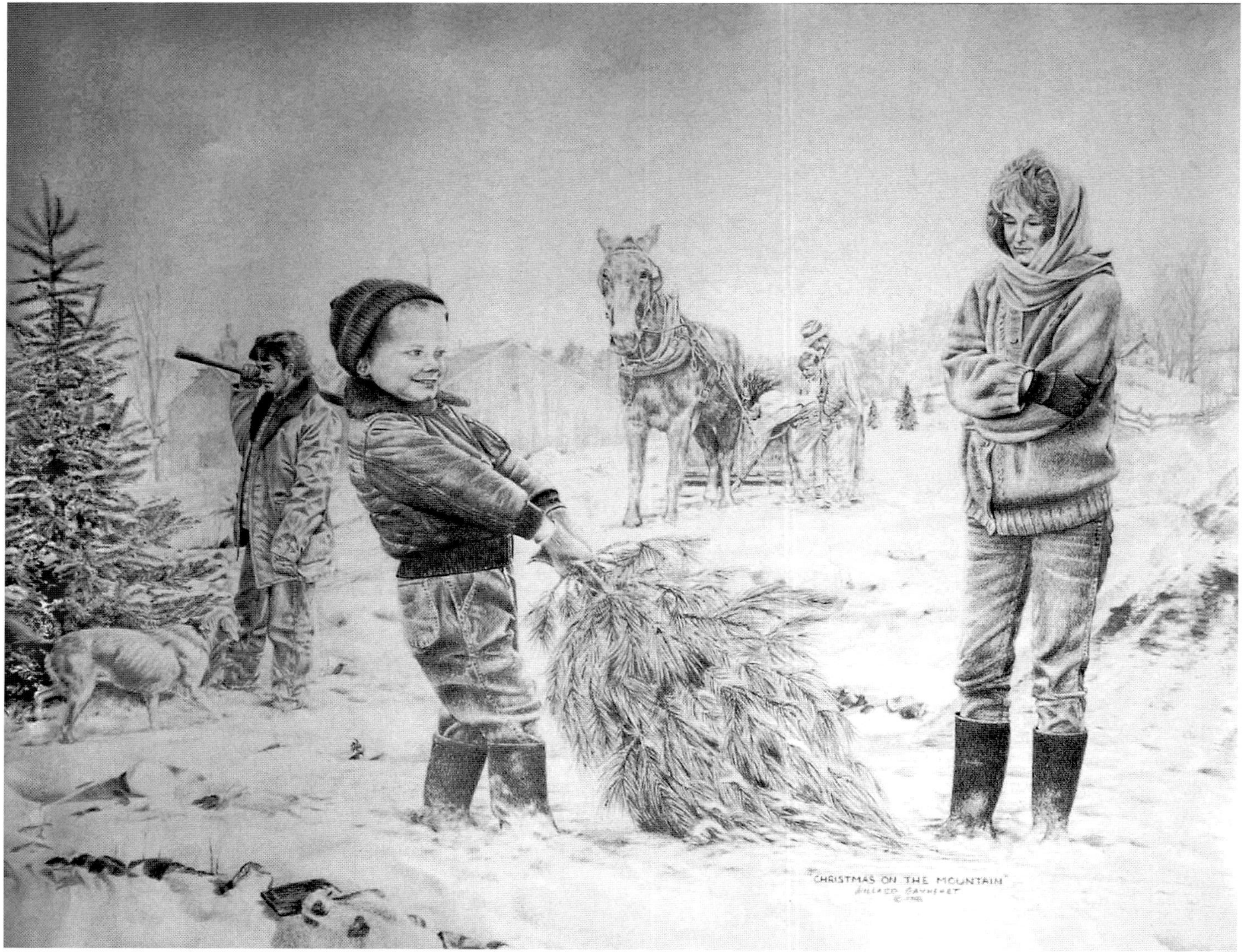
"CHRISTMAS ON THE MOUNTAIN"

Christmas on the Mountain 1988

In 1988 a young man newly hired by the Downtown Merchants Association asked Willard to create a drawing to sell as a fundraiser for the association, a group suffering after the influx of shopping centers to the area. Calling the idea a "most brilliant plan," Willard did the commissioned drawing of a Christmas activity featuring friends of his daughter. The scene of the family getting their Christmas tree in the woods in the snow with the grandfather and mule and sled was eventually recreated on a Christmas Parade float. Willard Gayheart was the grand marshal for that parade. The original of the drawing hangs in the Galax City Hall. Christmas notecards were also available for sale at that time.

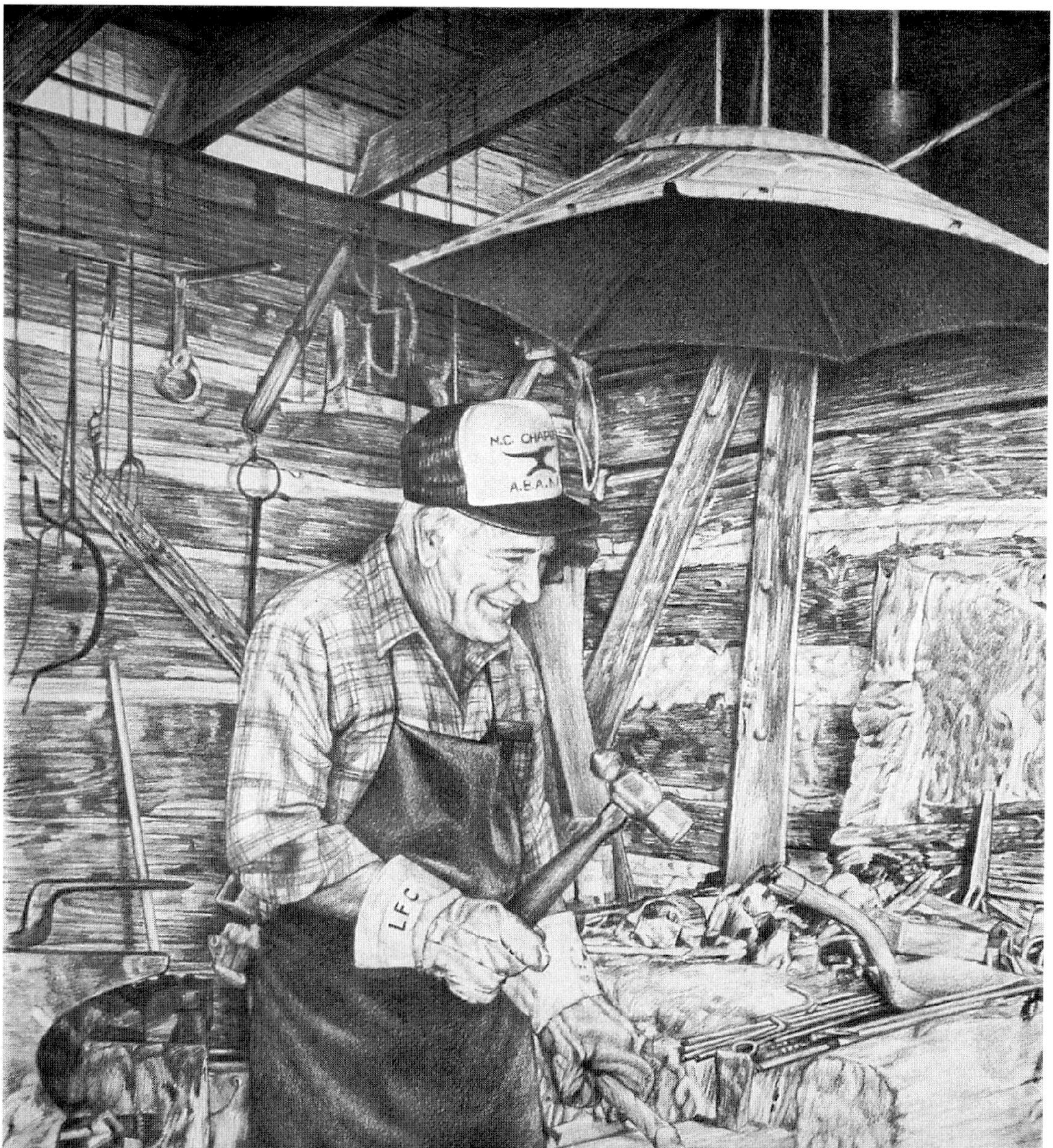
LFC
"VIRGIL"

Virgil
1988

Virgil Lily was a blacksmith with a shop near Christiansburg, Virginia, and this was a commission piece.

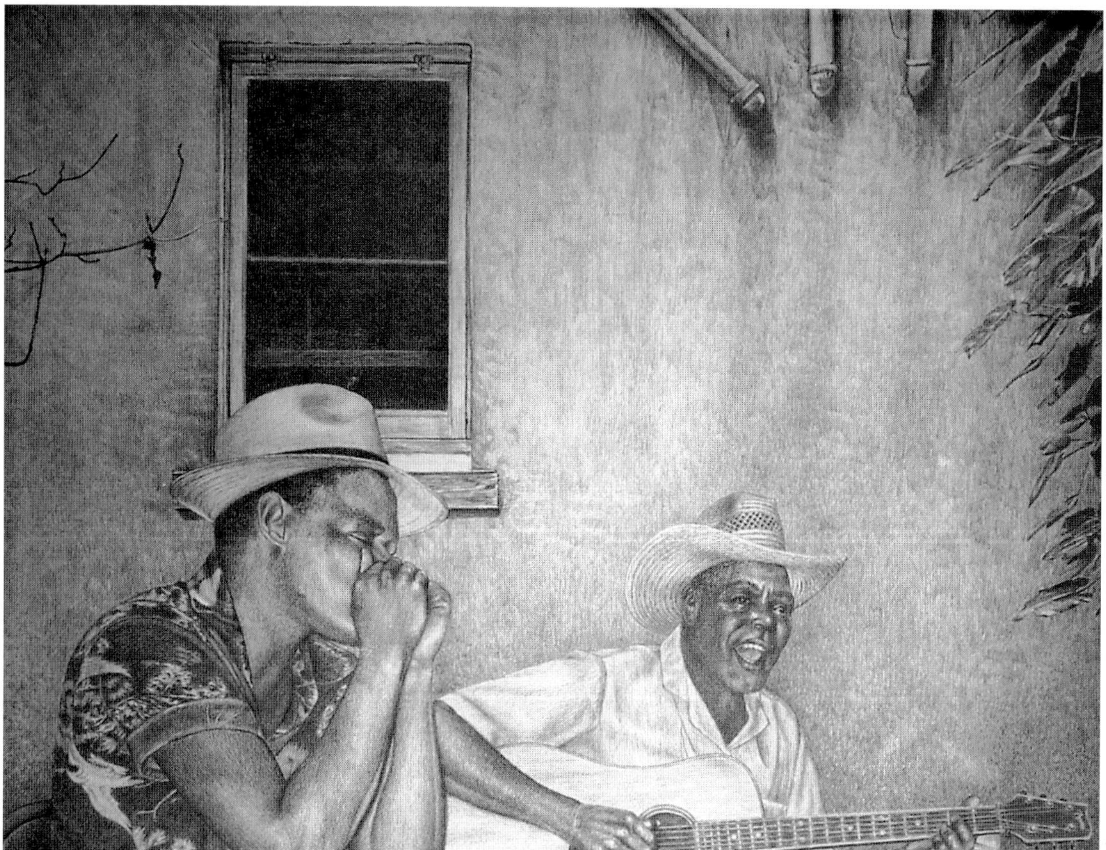
IN TOUCH WITH THE BLUES
WILLARD GAYHEART

In Touch with the Blues
1989

After performing with the Highlanders at a dance in a renovated barn that dated back to the late 1700s in Middletown, New York, a duo unfamiliar to Willard followed the Highlanders' performance. Their names were John Cephas and Phil Wiggins.

I noticed everybody seemed to know them up there, and there were a lot of young people there and they all gathered around them and sat down on the floor cross-legged to listen, and I understood why when they started to play because they were awesome. I grabbed my camera and took some photos of them. Later when I did the drawing, I changed the setting, didn't use the barn. I simulated them being on a street someplace.

They are probably two of the best there is in that kind of music. I know Phil Wiggins is probably the best harmonica player I've ever heard. John Cephas is no slouch either and plays guitar and sings.

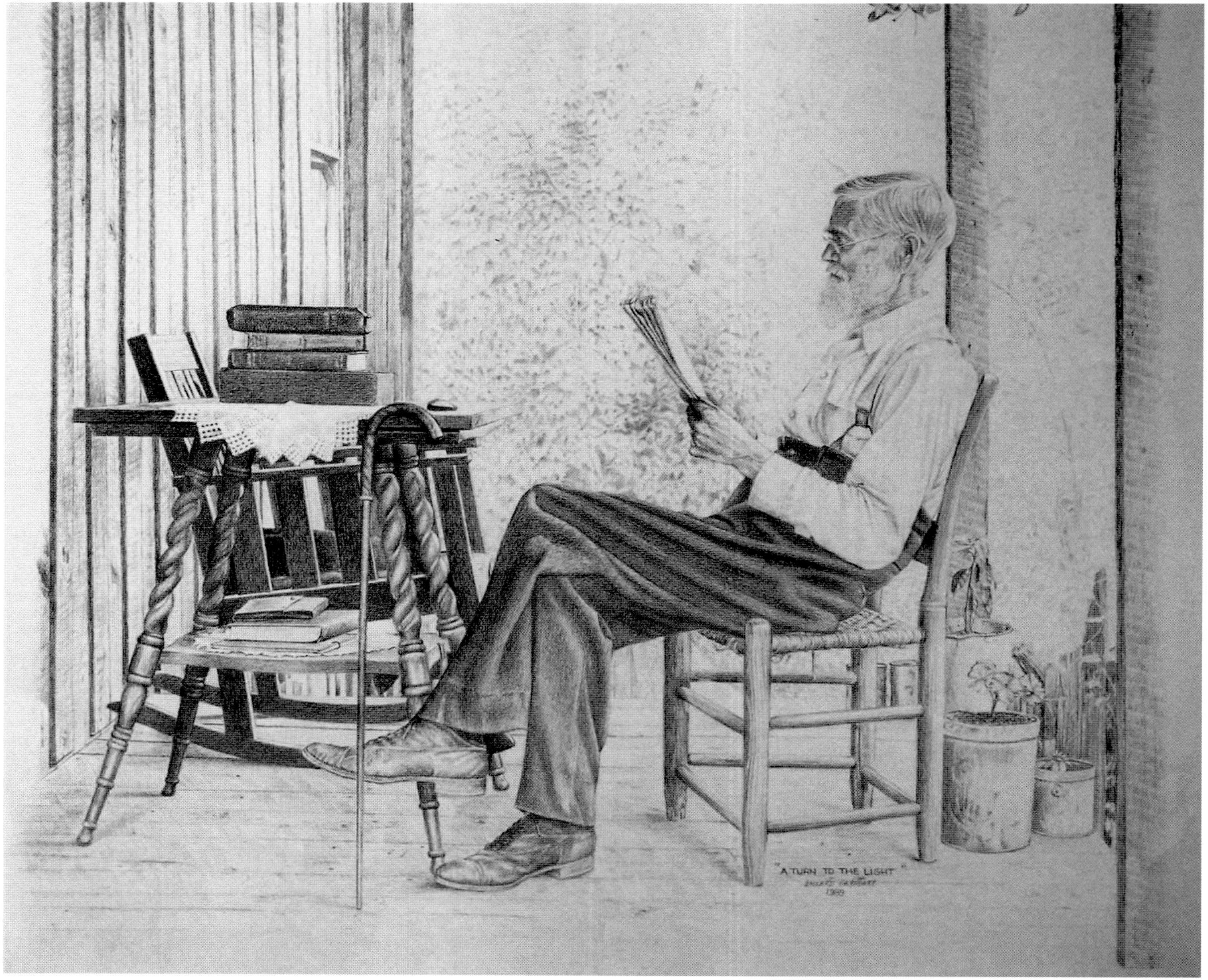
"A TURN TO THE LIGHT"

A Turn to the Light
1989

Manton Cornett, a cousin's grandfather, has his back to the light, perhaps sunlight or twilight, in this drawing taken from an early 1920s small photograph. The table was a popular style from that era.

Willard remarked that the subject had turned to catch the light on his paper, "but there were other points of light on the books and I thought this a fitting title with more than one meaning." This drawing has been very popular with teachers and librarians.

> *Mr. Cornett was a self-taught man, an unusual man, a school teacher, blacksmith, carpenter, and loved to read. There's a Bible on the table as well.*

Roy Vass
The Carroll County Playboys
1989

Roy Vass was a local musician who played several instruments, including the banjo, guitar, autoharp, and fiddle. He was one of the finest men I ever knew, and I was a real fan. His daughter commissioned me to do this in his memory after he died at a fairly young age, and I have him in the background with his band in the foreground.

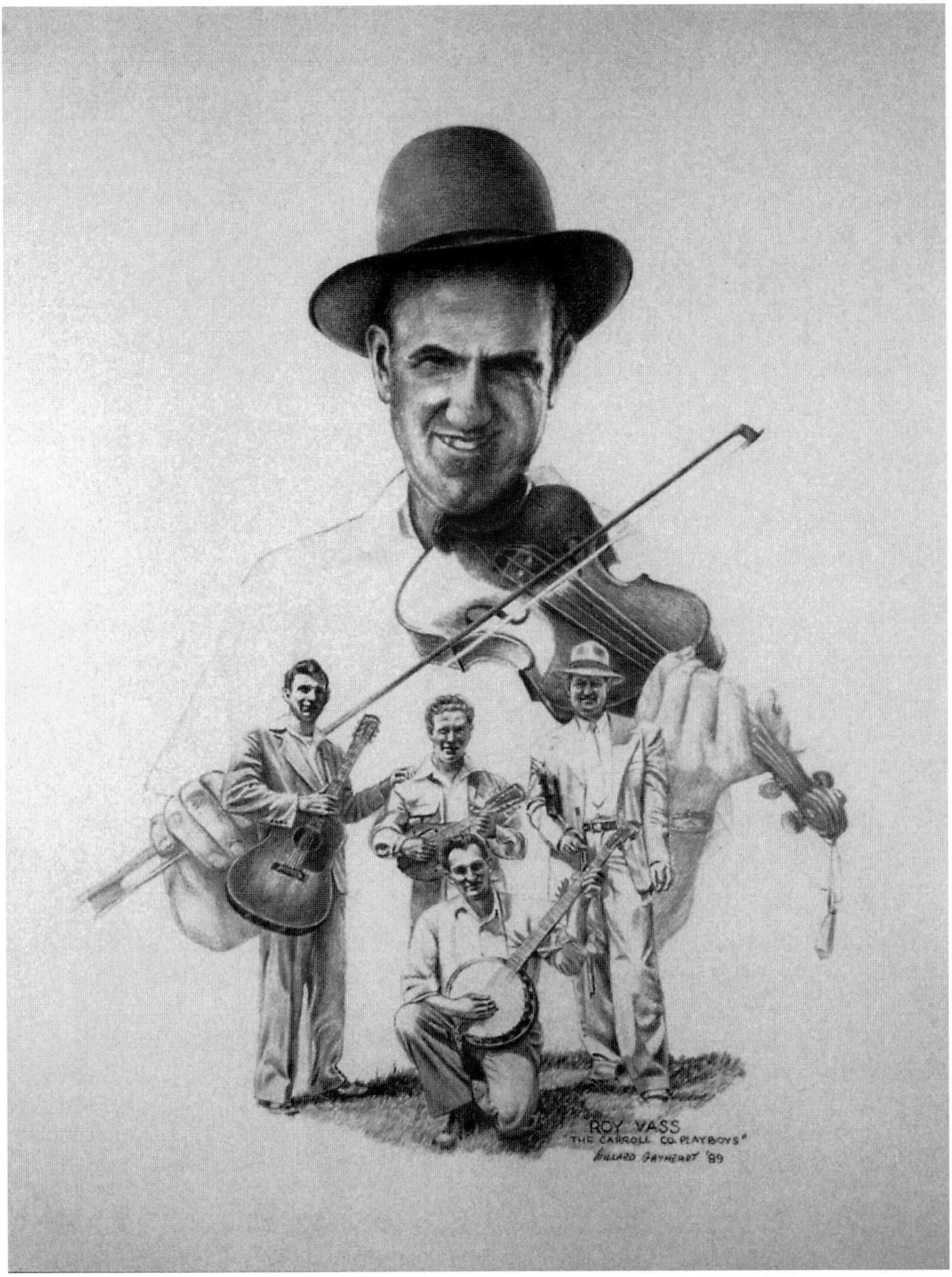
ROY VASS
"THE CARROLL CO. PLAYBOYS"
WILLARD GAYHEART '89

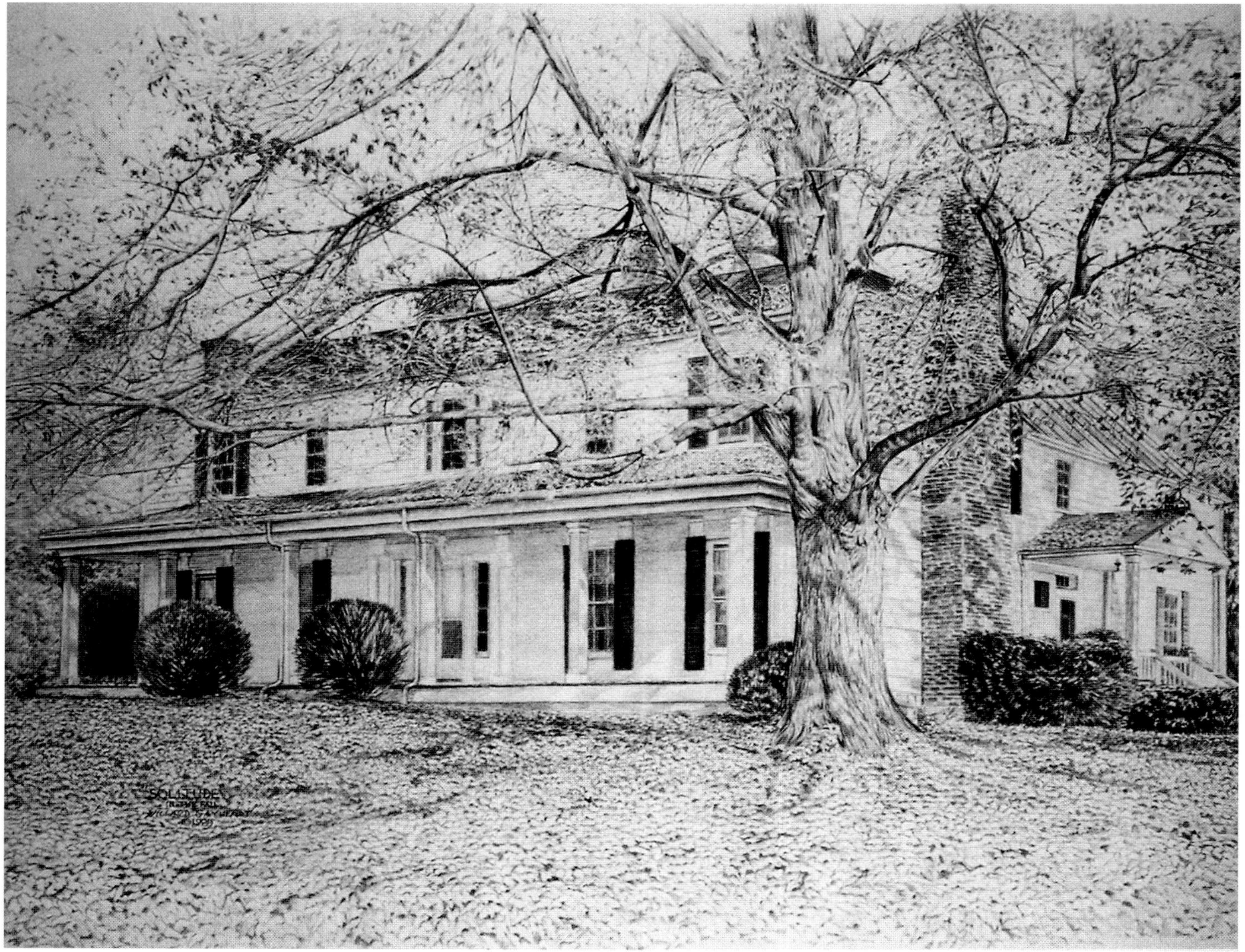
SOLITUDE

Solitude
1989

Solitude is one of the oldest buildings on the campus of Virginia Tech, in Blacksburg, and is located near the Duck Pond. This was a commissioned work at the request of Dr. Jean Haskell, who was head of the Appalachian Studies Department there at that time, to raise money to renovate the building.

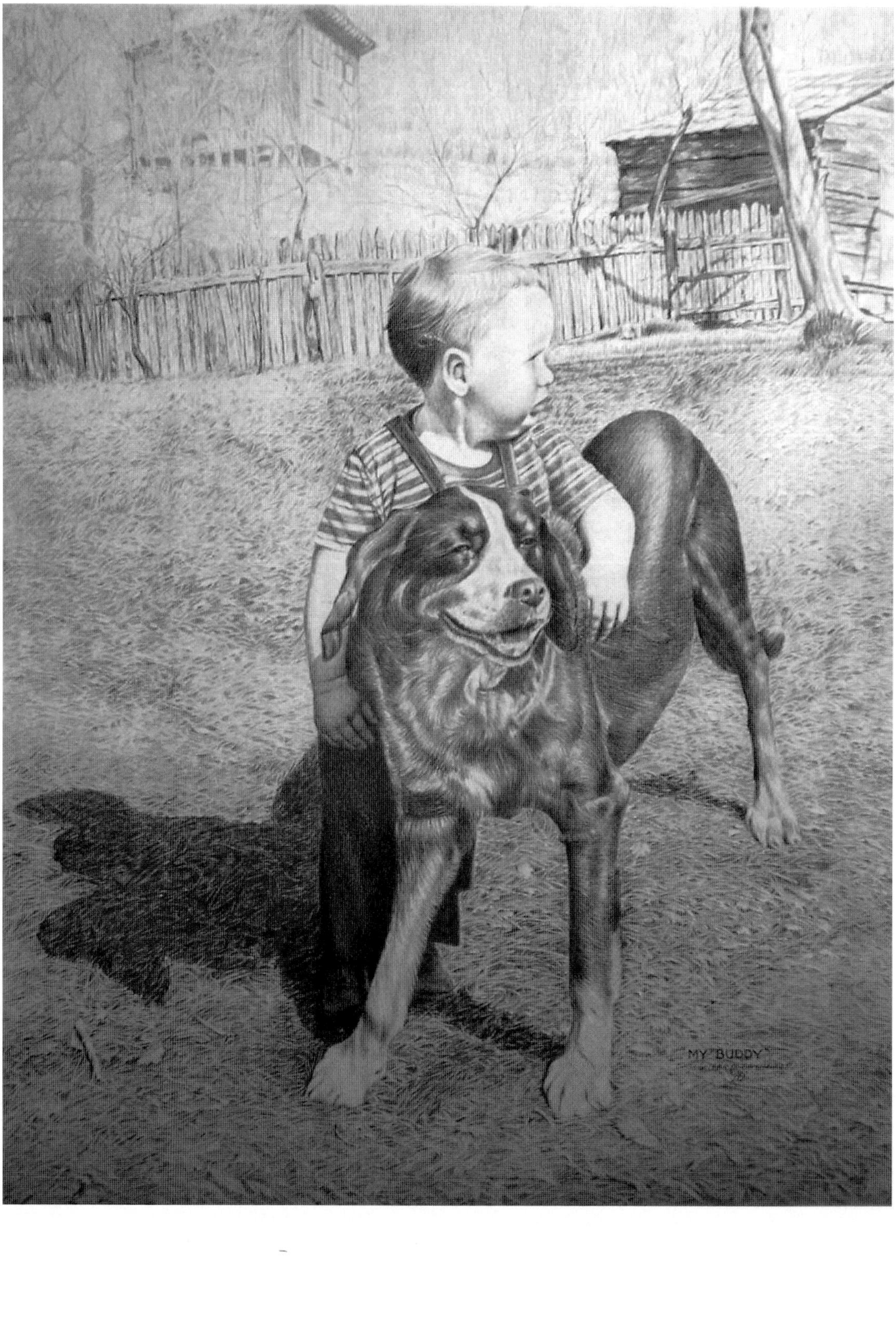
MY "BUDDY"

My Buddy
1989

A popular piece, this drawing was commissioned as a fundraiser for the Humane Society of Pulaski County, Virginia.

Using old photographs given to him by a relative, Willard drew a scene from the mid-forties featuring a family member with his dog. Willard recalls that the family of this boy lived near his home in eastern Kentucky in a little community called Big Fork. He told me that back in the days he grew up most rural addresses for the small communities had names ending in Fork or Creek.

Willard describes this particular family as a model for the families of the area at that time. Like many other families they were hard working people seeking to better themselves, they believed in the pursuit of education for their children, and sacrificed so they could be educated. Doing what was necessary to learn, the children often walked as much as two miles each way to attend school from first grade through high school. "We did what we had to do," stated Willard.

A Visit to Wayne's Shop
1990

National Heritage Award winner Wayne Henderson is an acoustic and traditional musician from Rugby, a southwestern Virginia community in Grayson County. He is also a maker of fine guitars.

> *Wayne is a big talent in this area. I did about five views of him making guitars and one of him playing a guitar. Wayne is quite a picker. Doc Watson, a frequent visitor to the shop, is in the drawing along with Wayne and Gerald Anderson, a great instrument maker in his own right. He assists Wayne and also makes mandolins. The reason for this drawing is I'd been wanting a Wayne Henderson guitar and couldn't quite afford to buy one. So I devised a way of doing a drawing and swapping it for a guitar, and it was a piece of my artwork for a piece of his; and now I actually have a beautiful guitar that I play all the time. It's one I use to do all of my playing and recording with, and Wayne has the original of this drawing hanging in his living room, which I'm quite proud of.*

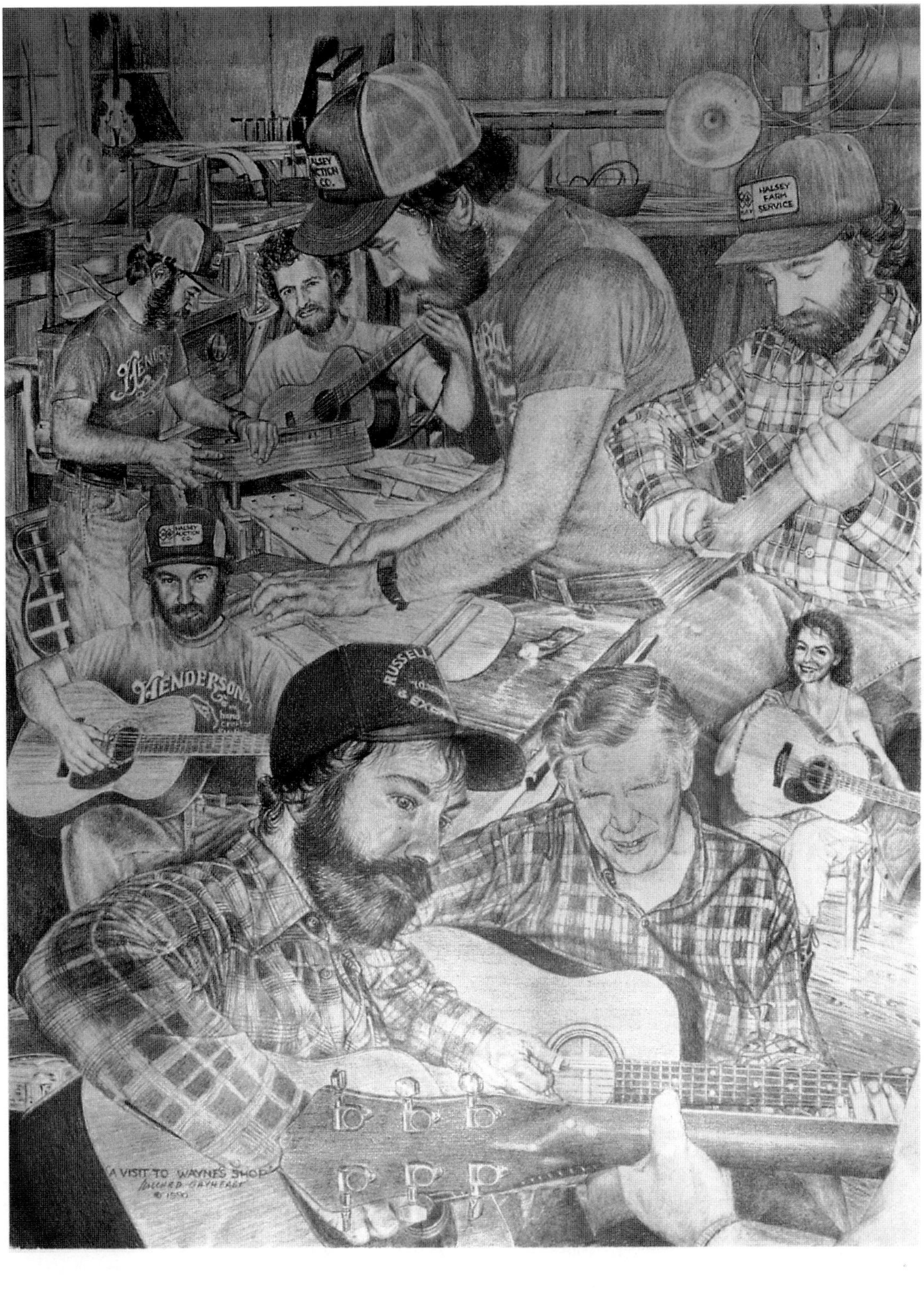
HALSEY
FARM
SERVICE
HENDERSON
A VISIT TO WAYNES SHOP

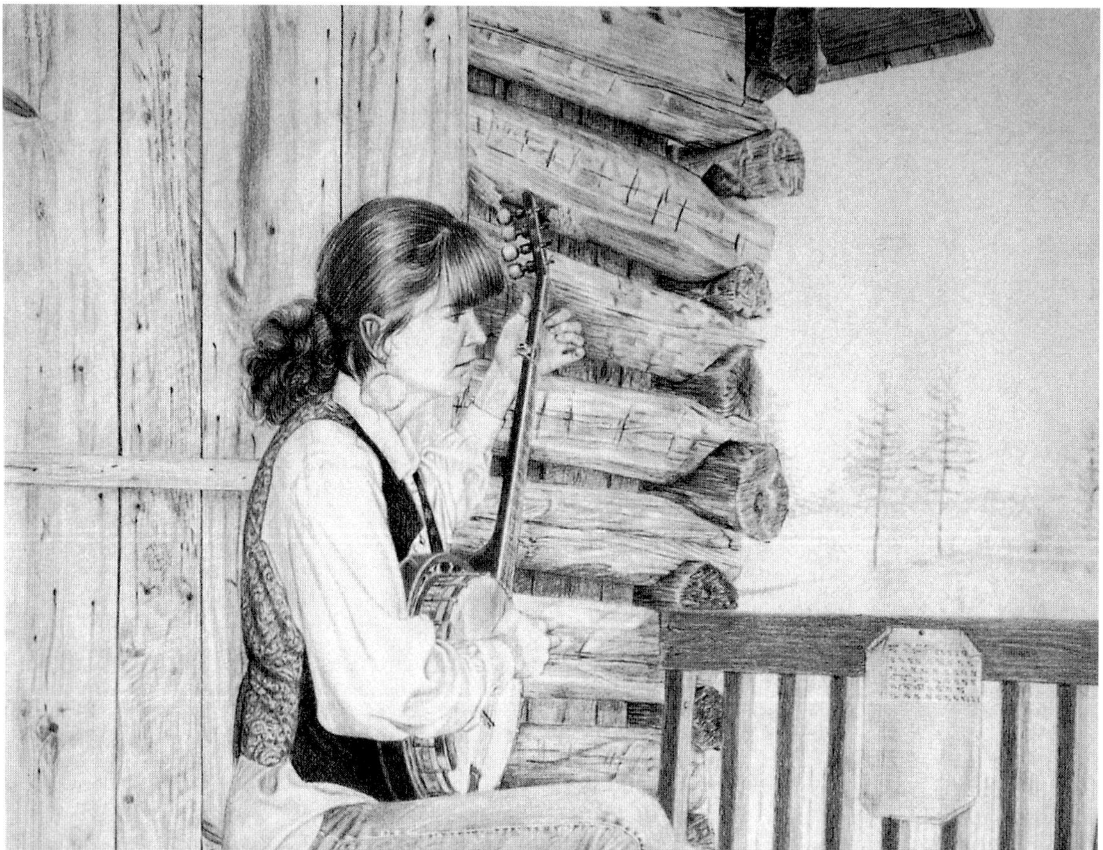

A Pickin' Place
1990

My daughter Jill was taking banjo lessons and I put her in a setting on a quiet porch of a log cabin sitting on an old stool made by a friend of mine with a hickory bark bottom and walnut legs.

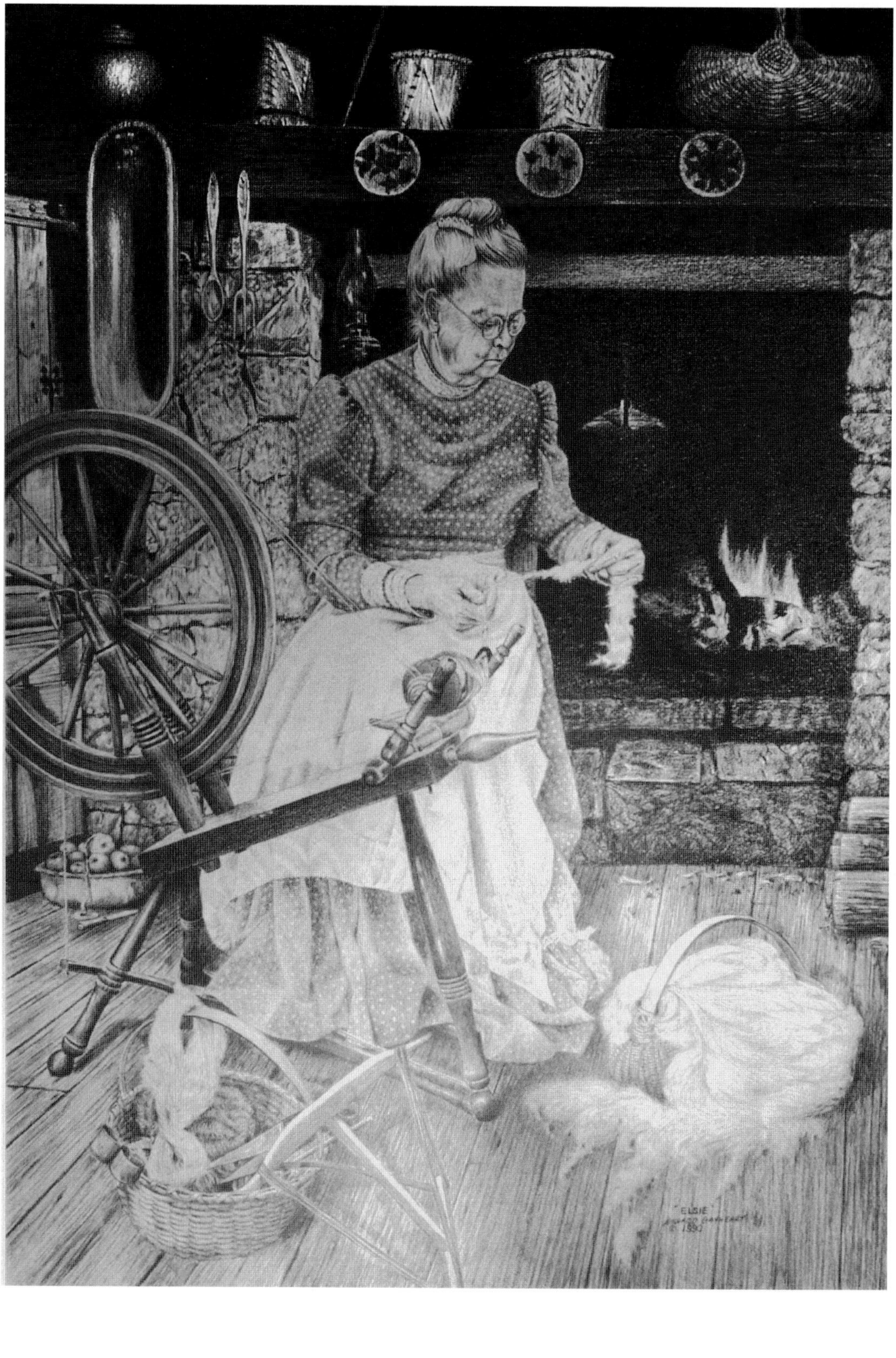
"ELSIE"

Elsie
1990

Elsie Trivett was from Zionville, North Carolina, a little community near Boone, in Watauga County. She died at age 89. Willard met Elsie about fifteen years ago at a festival in Damascus, Virginia, called Appalachian Trail Days. She was demonstrating spinning on an "old-timey" spinning wheel and Willard took pictures of her from which he later did the drawing. He sent Elsie and each one of her daughters prints of the piece, and in return she sent him a chair cushion she had made "kindly like you make a hook rug. It was a beautiful little thing with a bird on it," says Willard.

Following the start of their friendship, Willard saw Elsie at Merle-Fest and other places the two of them would be doing shows, such as the Storytelling Festival at Beech Mountain, North Carolina. He says they became "buddies," and she was a wonderful lady who could do so many things she'd learned as a young girl. He was asked to be a pallbearer at her funeral, but could not because of the illness of his own mother.

Elsie probably learned the creative crafts of tatting, spinning and weaving out of necessity growing up, and later turned her art into a way of earning extra money.

A few years ago actor Kurt Russell was in North Carolina to make a movie, and his wife, Goldie Hawn, there with him, took an interest in spinning. In a craft shop in Mountain City, Tennessee, a small town close to Boone, they bought a spinning wheel. When they asked for someone to teach them how to use it, they were referred to Elsie. They called Elsie and she agreed to teach them, though Elsie didn't know who they were because she'd never seen a Goldie Hawn or Kurt Russell movie. Willard says, "They got acquainted and they took to Elsie." They made many photographs, which Elsie kept as souvenirs.

Elsie Trivett left a legacy of teaching and example to follow her, and her daughters continue her work. She won a governor's award in North Carolina for the contribution to the culture of her crafts and was featured at the North Carolina State Fair for many years. She was a wonderful lady, a special one-of-a-kind person.

Perfect Harmony
1990

This drawing depicting family is of Dick Culbertson of Blacksburg, Virginia, and his grandson, Luke. One of the most popular drawings Willard has done, the original is owned by a man from Florida, and the 300 limited edition prints sold out long ago.

Dick Culbertson also has a home in Grayson County near Independence, Virginia, which is in the southwestern part of the state. He is featured here playing the harmonica with young Luke, who is by now grown up. In the drawing the child is holding the harmonica backwards.

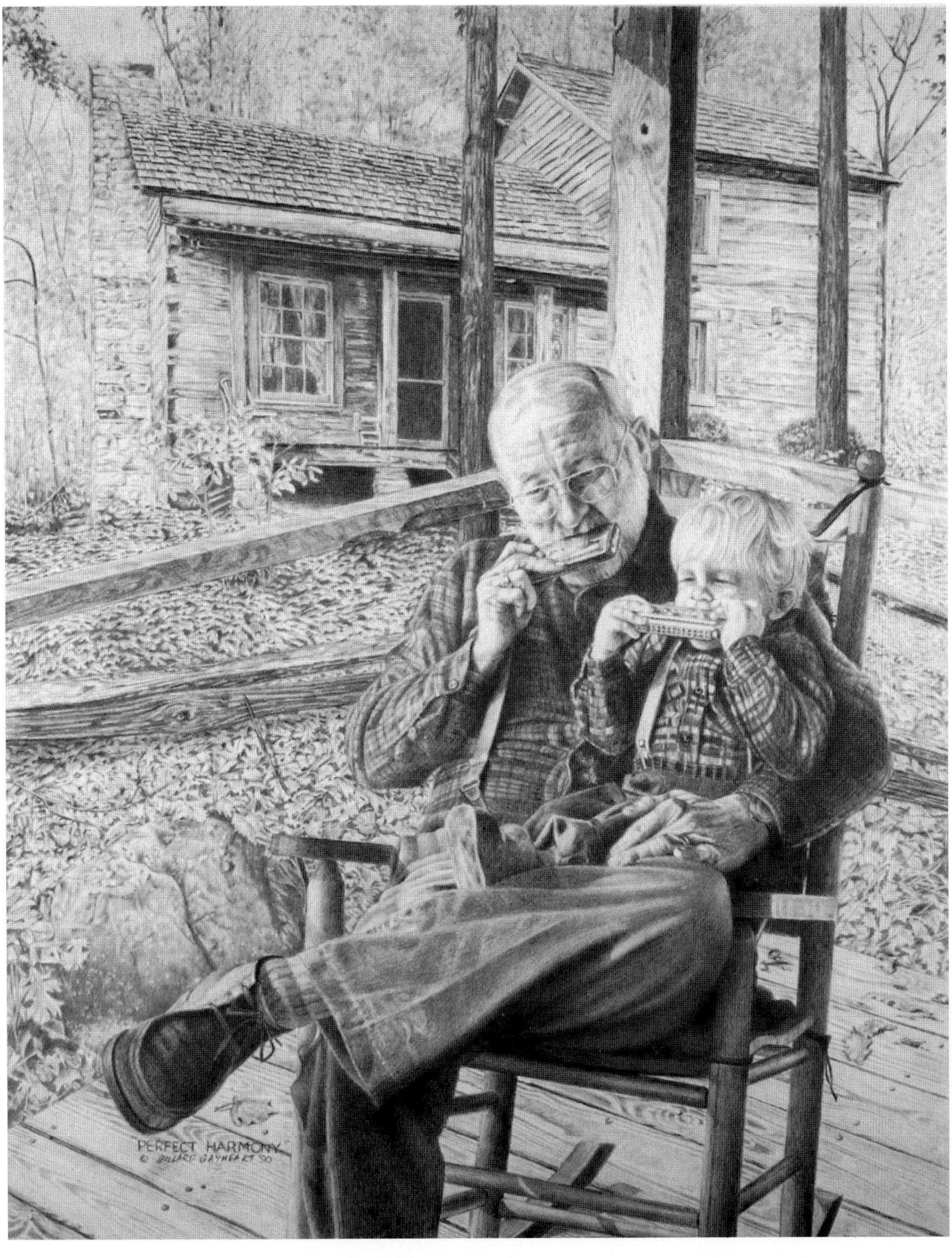
PERFECT HARMONY

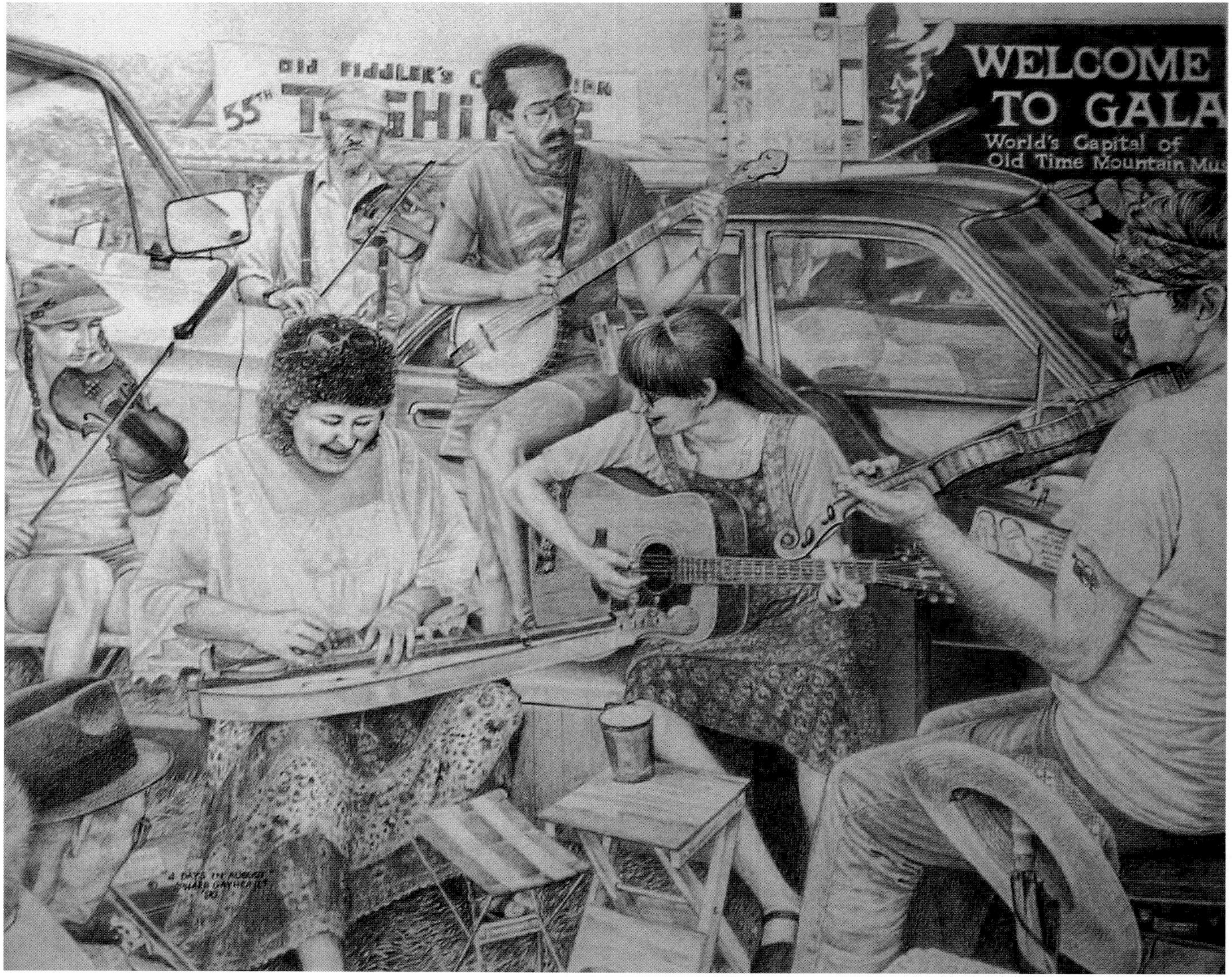

WELCOME
TO GALA
World's Capital of
Old Time Mountain Mus
OLD FIDDLER'S
55TH

Four Days in August
1990

In the early days of the Old Fiddlers' Convention held annually in August in Galax, Virginia, the convention lasted only four days. Now the convention goes on for one week each year. This drawing, done as a fundraiser for the Rotary Club in Galax, was a successful piece featuring Lois Hornbostel.

Lois Hornbostel is one of the country's leading dulcimer players who also teaches and instructs in different places and has written instructional books on how to play the instrument.

Study of a Banjo Picker
1990

This is Roger Sprung from Connecticut. Roger has been coming to the Galax Fiddlers' Convention for probably 35 years. He's one of the most consistently attending contestants that we have at the convention. He hasn't missed a year since he started and he's one of our really good progressive banjo players and has cut several albums. He cut one with Doc Watson several years ago that I remember really well because it was some of the first really innovative progressive banjo picking that I'd heard and he was playing some of the old popular songs on the bluegrass banjo, he and Doc Watson. Roger is unique in that he makes his living with the music, he teaches the music, and he also sells instruments. He's been a figure in bluegrass music for many years.

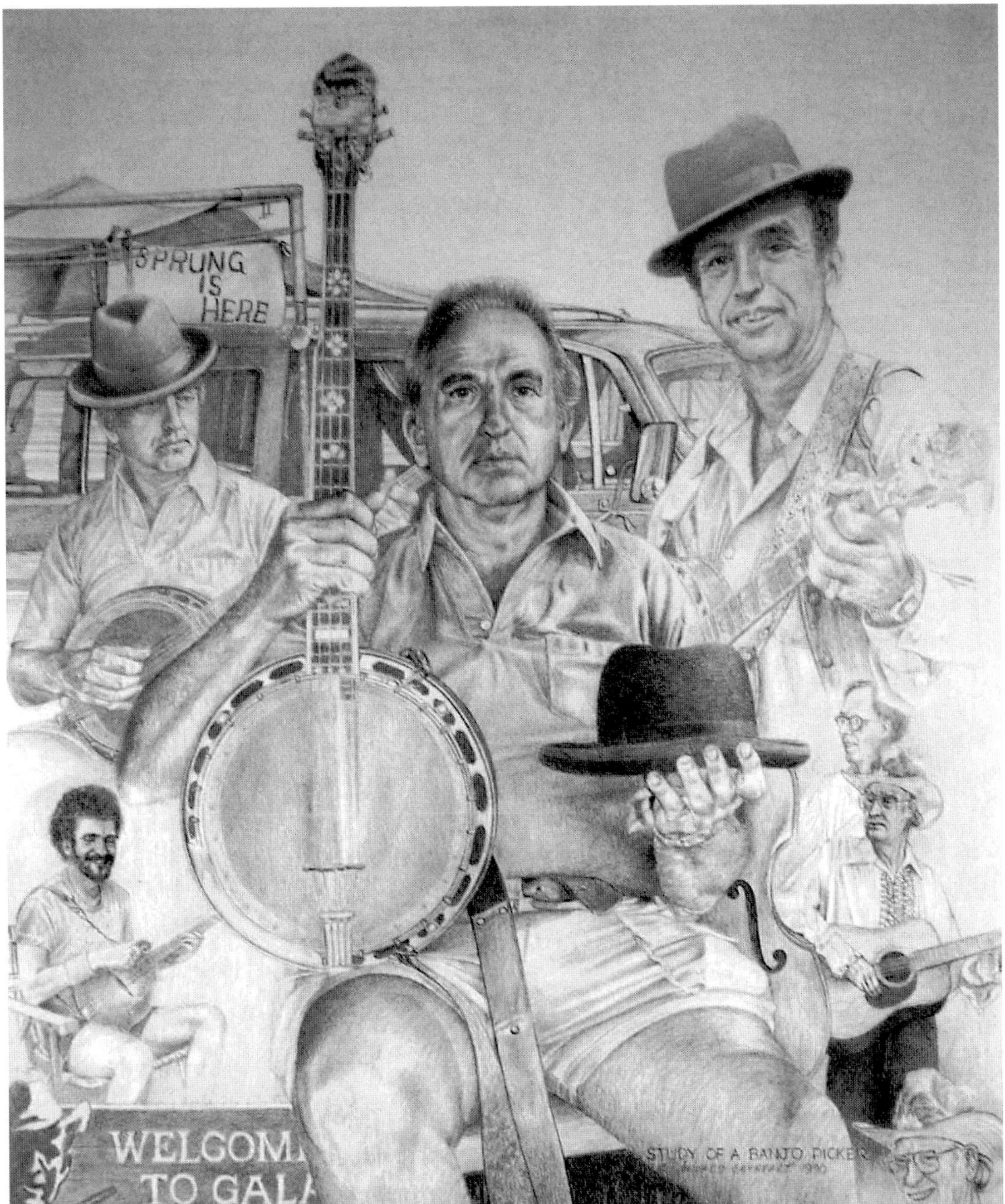
SPRUNG IS HERE
STUDY OF A BANJO PICKER

A Tune for Granny
1991

A state grant provided a teacher at West Salem Elementary School in Salem, Virginia, with the opportunity to have an artist-in-residence at the school for two weeks. Upon accepting the invitation, Willard's responsibility was to start and complete a drawing in the two-week period, and the drawing would then belong to the school. He recalls this experience with fondness.

> *I had a big time, a memorable time with the children. I played music with them, sang songs, and the children were all so responsive and motivated me so, both the children and the teachers. It played a big role I think in my motivation to continue and to be excited about doing these drawings. I did this drawing from a photograph I had, and I did it mostly because of the little boy being about the same age as some of the kids at the school.*

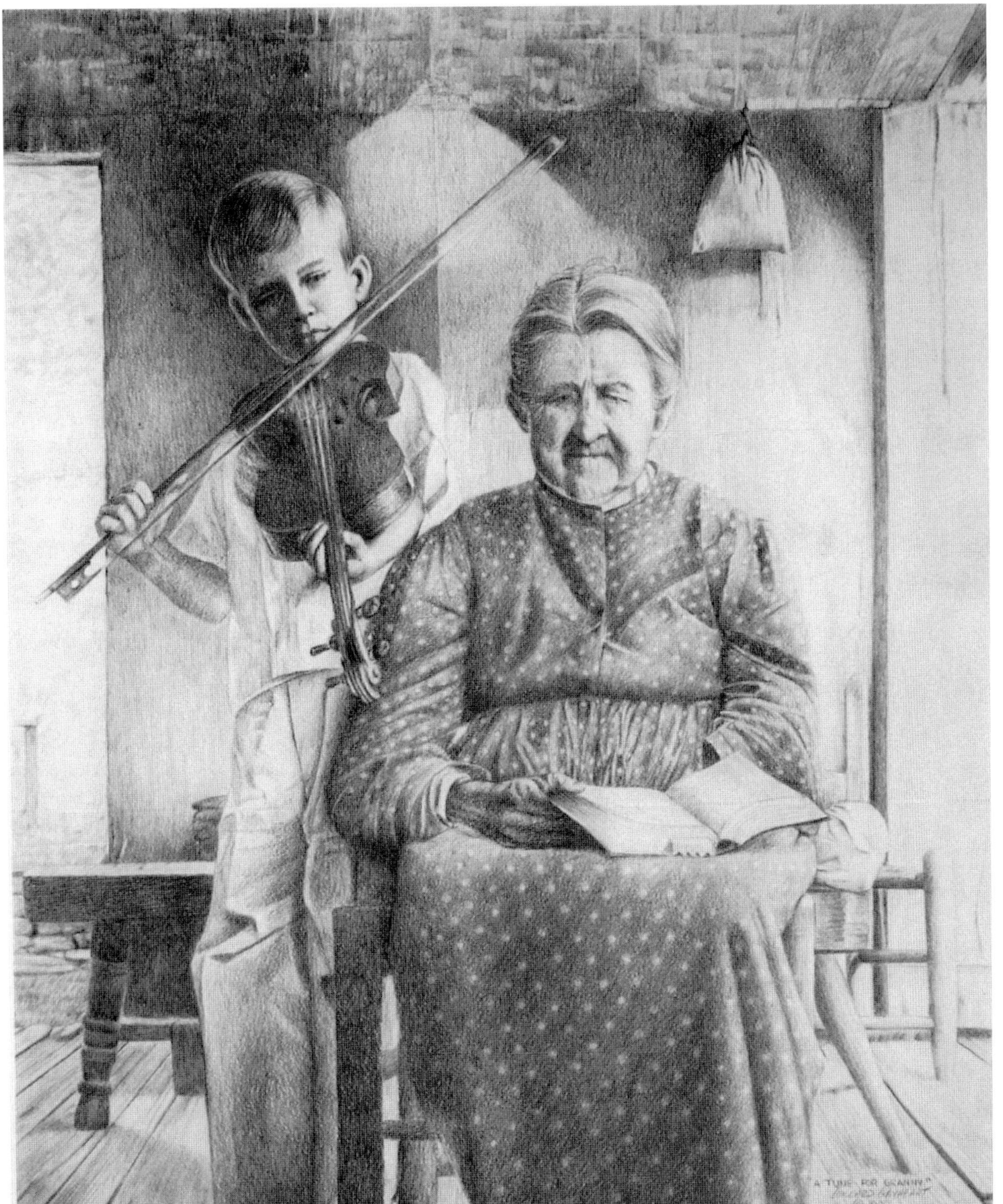
"A TUNE FOR GRANNY"

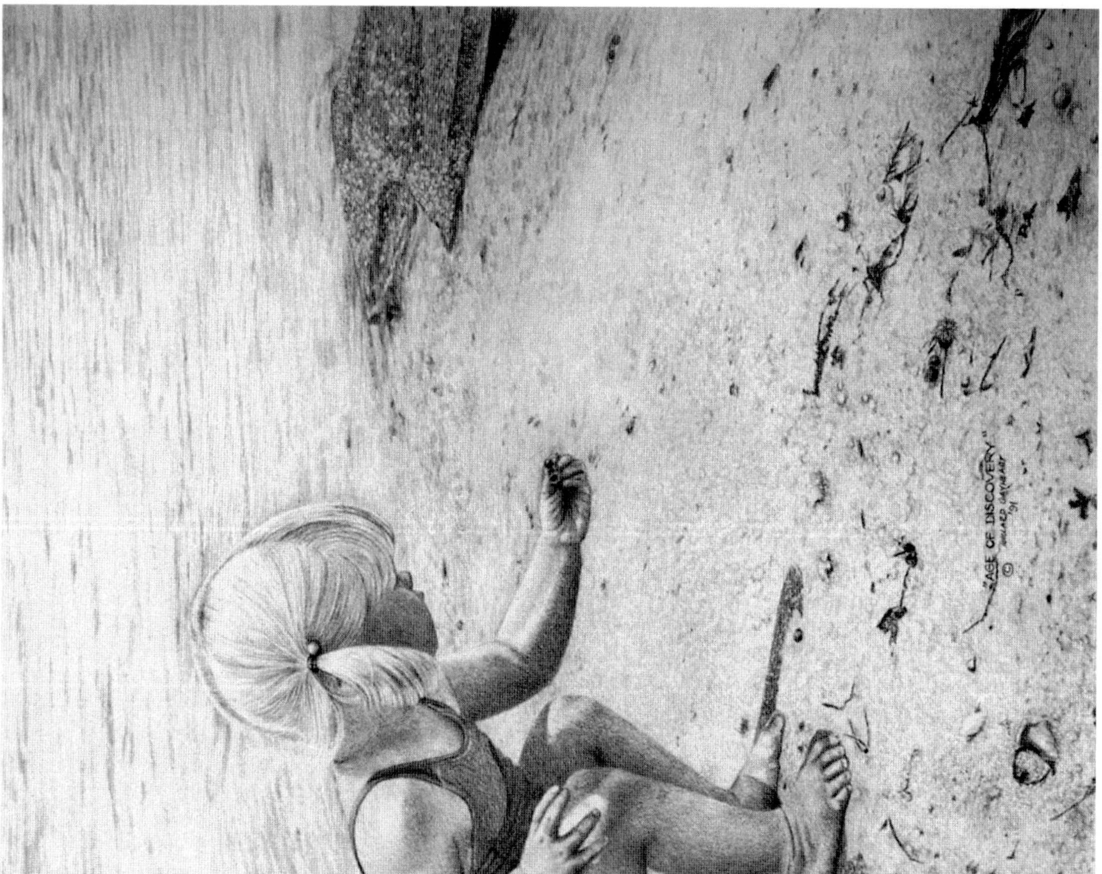
"AGE OF DISCOVERY"

Age of Discovery
1991

For several years Willard participated in a show sponsored by a group of Episcopal churches in the Arlington, Virginia, area called Appalachian Crafts Fair where artists and craftspeople from the Appalachian region were invited to participate. This drawing was done from a photograph Willard saw in the home where he stayed during the fair. Thinking it "a really neat little photo," and with the permission of the child's parents, Willard did the drawing of little Melissa, who he says is probably grown up by now. "That was quite an experience, going up there and being with those folks and learning about Arlington and meeting the people." And he hopes the family has the print yet and enjoys it in their home.

Basketmakers
1991

This drawing depicts a well-known basketmaker and his son from around Springs, Pennsylvania, at a crafts show. The work was commissioned by the daughter of one of the weavers.

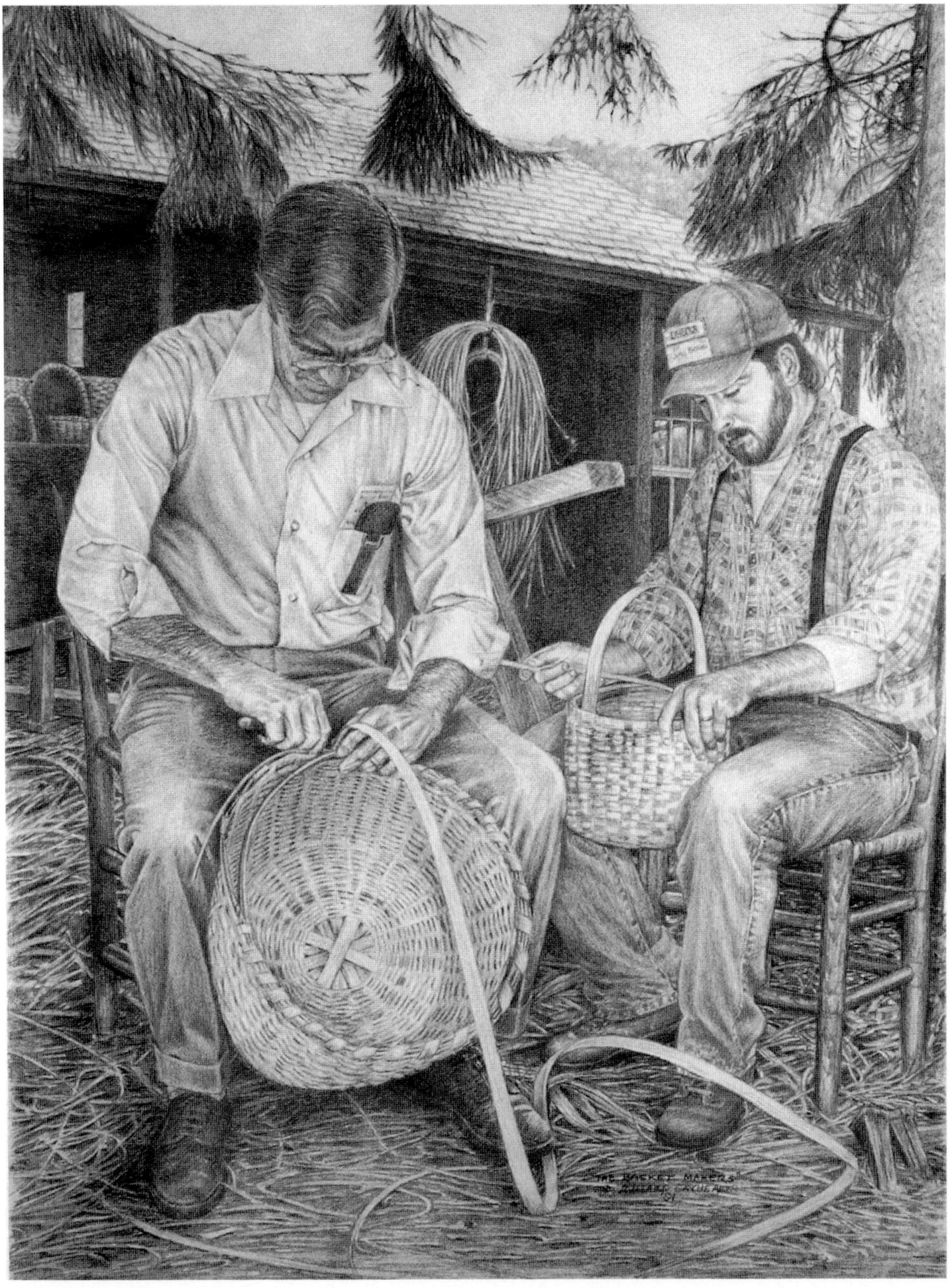
"THE BASKET MAKERS"

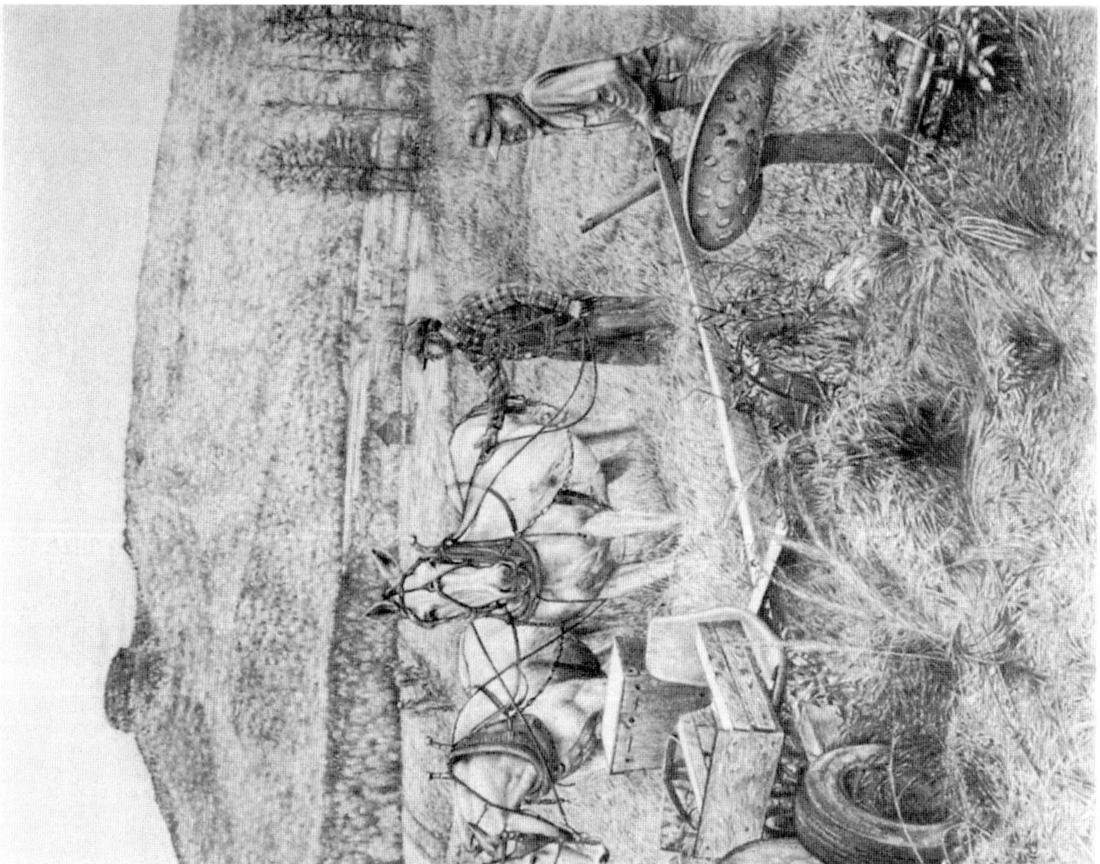

Return to Service
1991

This scene shows Pilot Mountain in the background, a unique cupcake-shaped mountain near Mount Airy, North Carolina, just across the border from Virginia. The main farming industry in the area was tobacco growing. Willard created a scene of getting ready to set tobacco in the spring with Willard, his son, and his son-in-law as models. He says he "just kindly put this one together in bits and pieces" from old photographs and some he took himself. The title comes from the old tobacco setter in the drawing. It has been sitting in weeds for a long while; the workers are pulling it from the weeds and getting ready to hook it to mules for setting out spring tobacco plants.

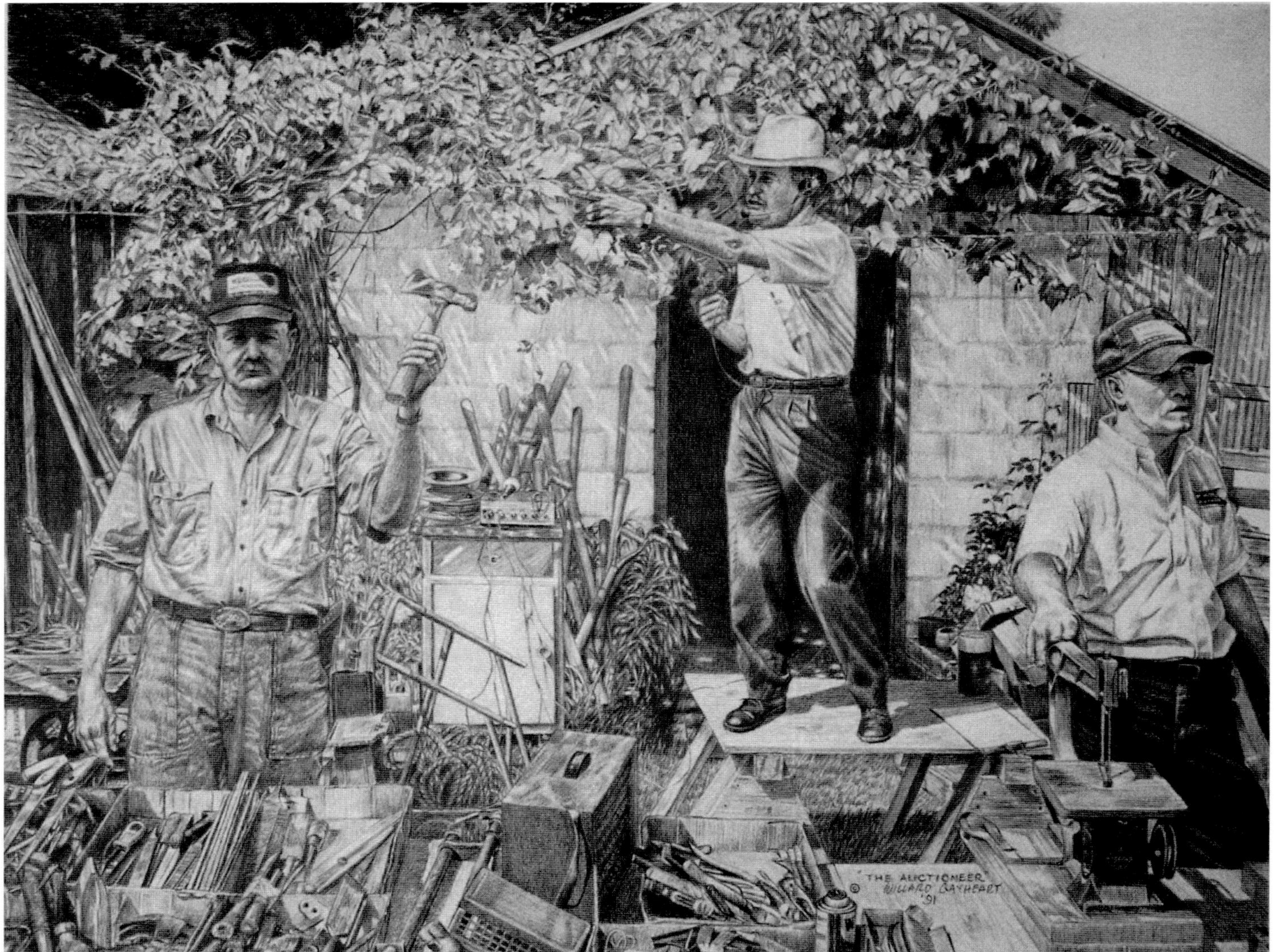
"THE AUCTIONEER"
© WILLARD GAYHEART
'91

The Auctioneer
1991

Most Saturdays in the summer one can find an auction conducted by the Dawn Auction Company going on in Hillsville, Virginia. This drawing resulted from several photographs and was commissioned by the auctioneer's wife as an anniversary gift. The auction took place somewhere in the Hillsville area as the "remains of a lifetime of collecting" were sold.

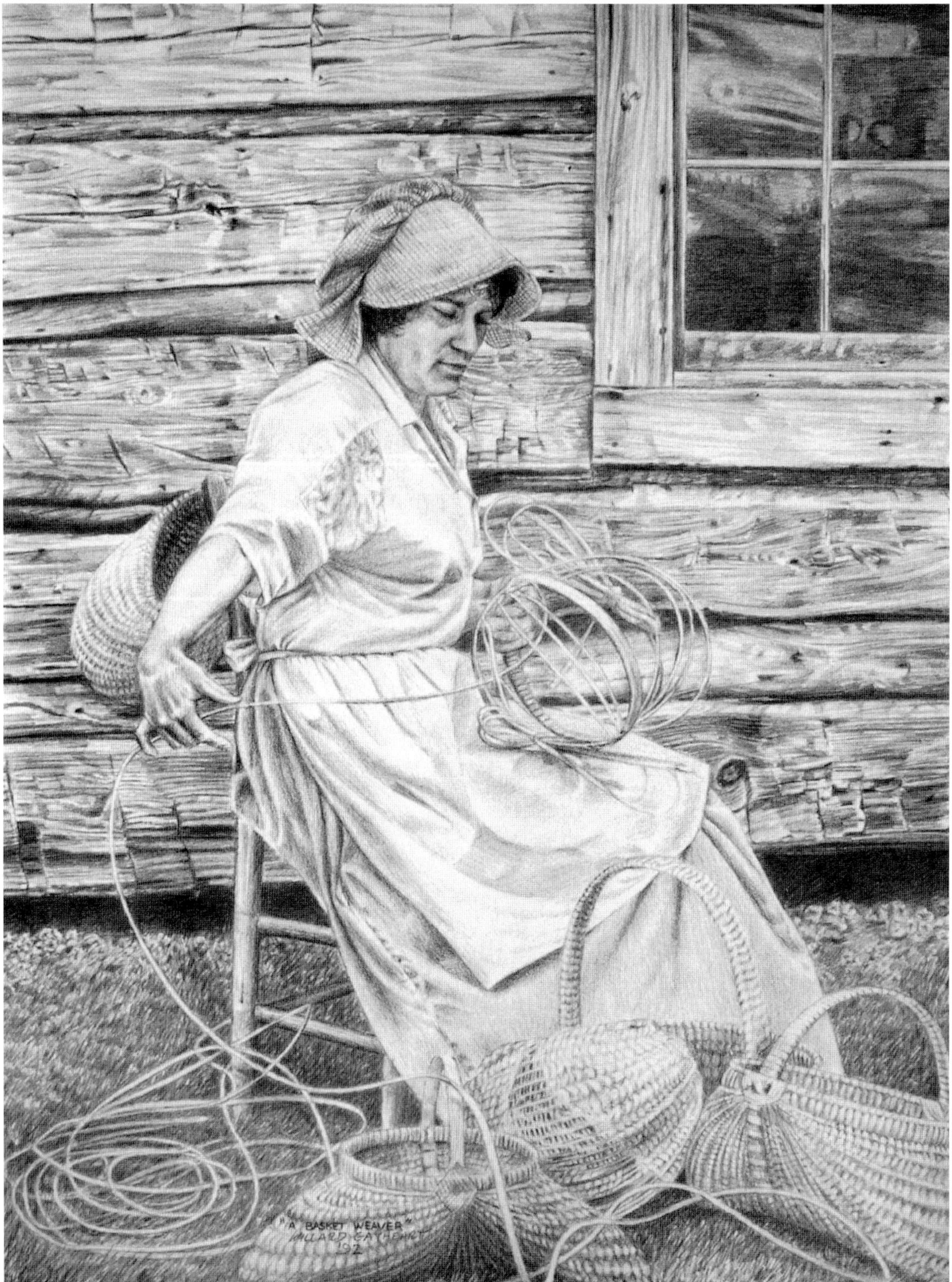
"A BASKET WEAVER"
'92

A Basket Weaver
1992

Frances Radford worked at scenic Mabry Mill, an area of the Blue Ridge Parkway in Floyd County, Virginia, which features a gristmill, blacksmith shop, and demonstrations of skills such as spinning, weaving, and basket making, as drawn here by Willard.

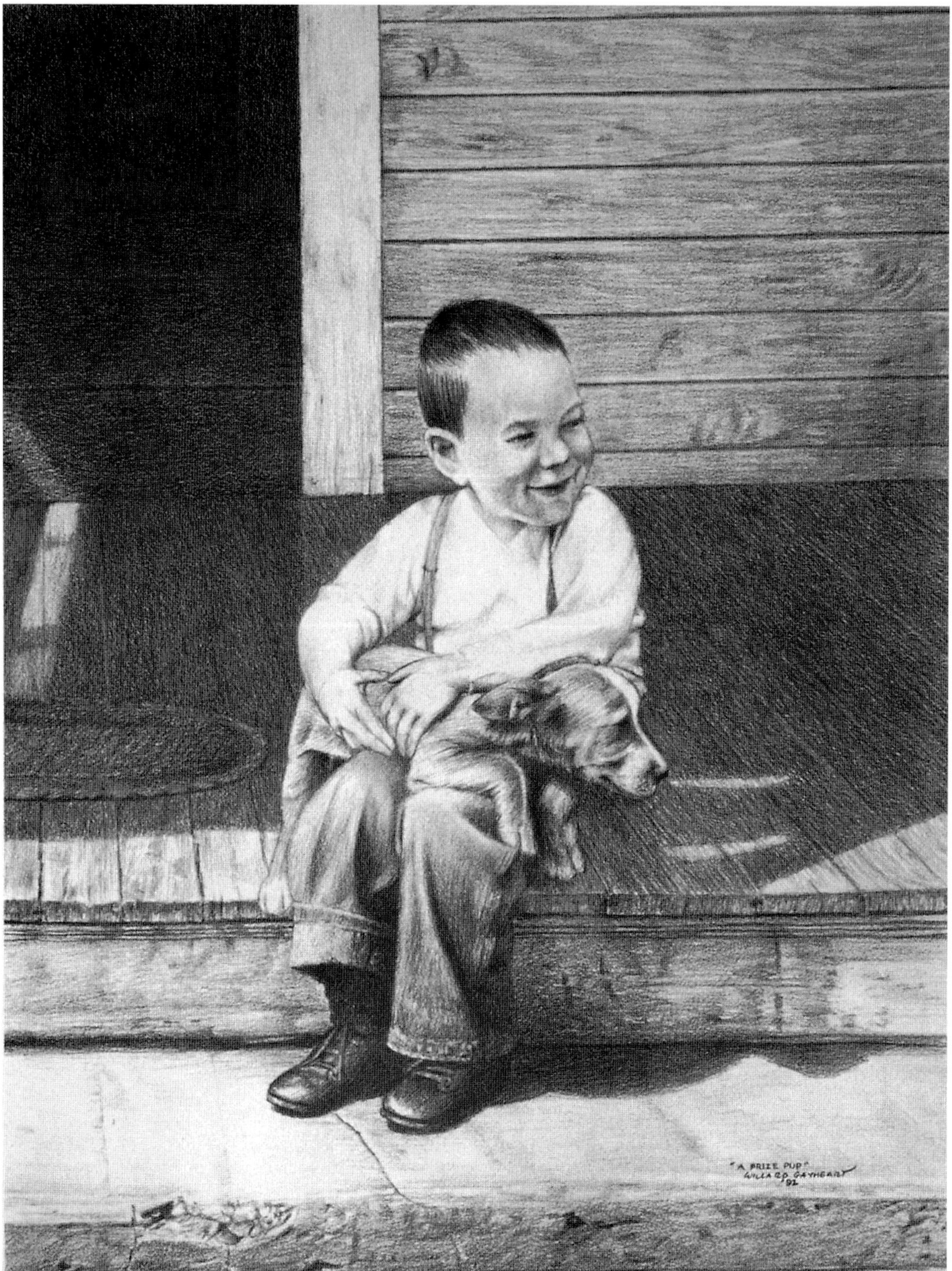
"A PRIZE PUP"
WILLARD GAYHEART
'92

A Prize Pup
1992

The Black Gold Festival is an annual four-day September event in Hazard, Kentucky, which brings in as many as 200,000 visitors to enjoy the arts, crafts, food, parades, dancing, music, and many other activities.

This drawing resulted from a photograph given to Willard during one of the years he participated, and he surprised the young lady when he returned the following year with the drawing completed. The boy featured was her father, and now the family owns the original and prints.

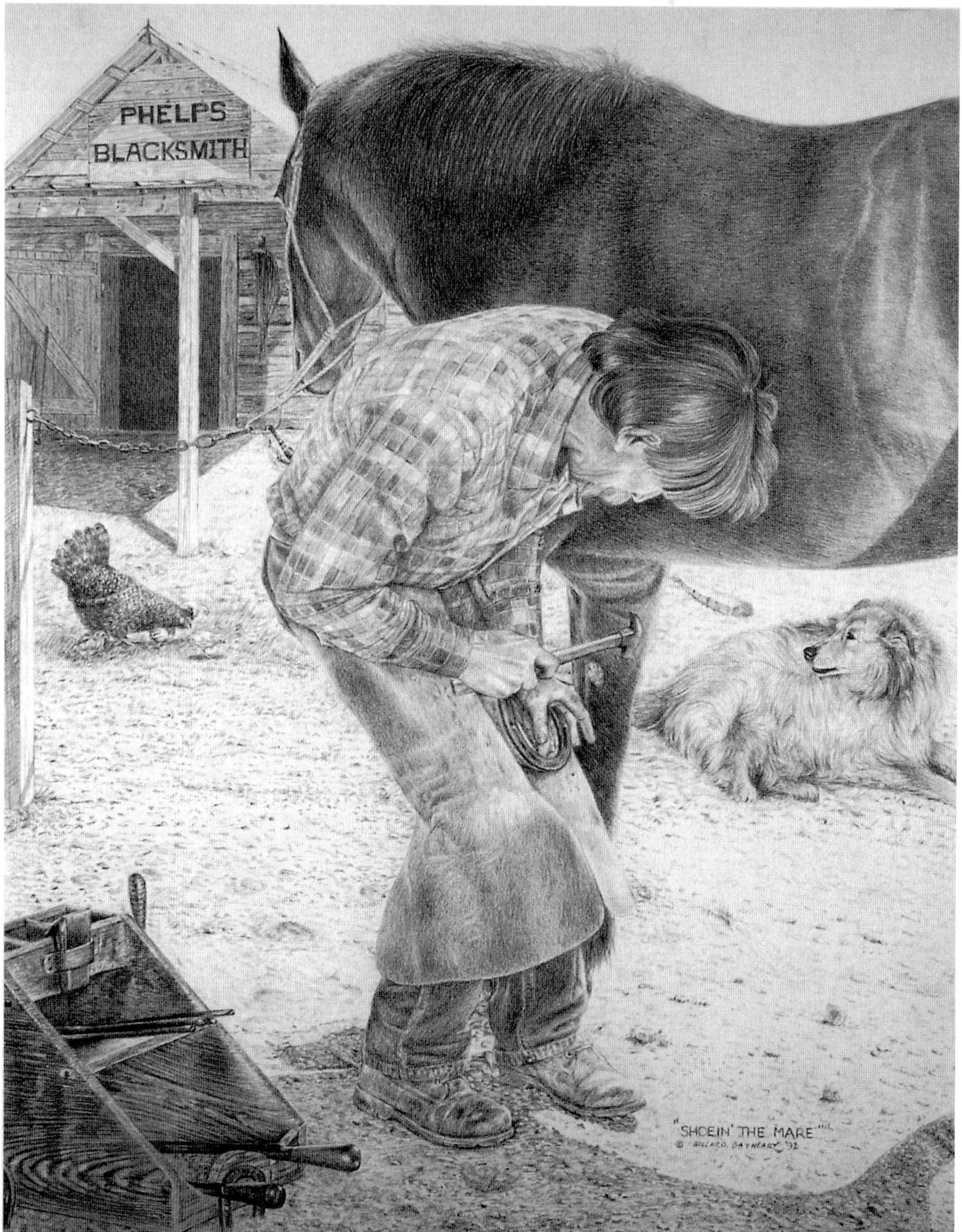
PHELPS
BLACKSMITH
"SHOEIN' THE MARE"

Shoein' the Mare
1992

Billy Phelps is a local blacksmith in the community of Laurel in Carroll County, Virginia, and he's a personal friend of mine. All through the years he's been associated with horses either through the rodeo circuit or as a farrier, and sometimes as blacksmith. In this drawing his blacksmith shop is in the background. Billy is one of these fellows that can do about anything and he really looks the part of a blacksmith or even a western cowboy with the way he dresses and the mustache. He made a good subject.

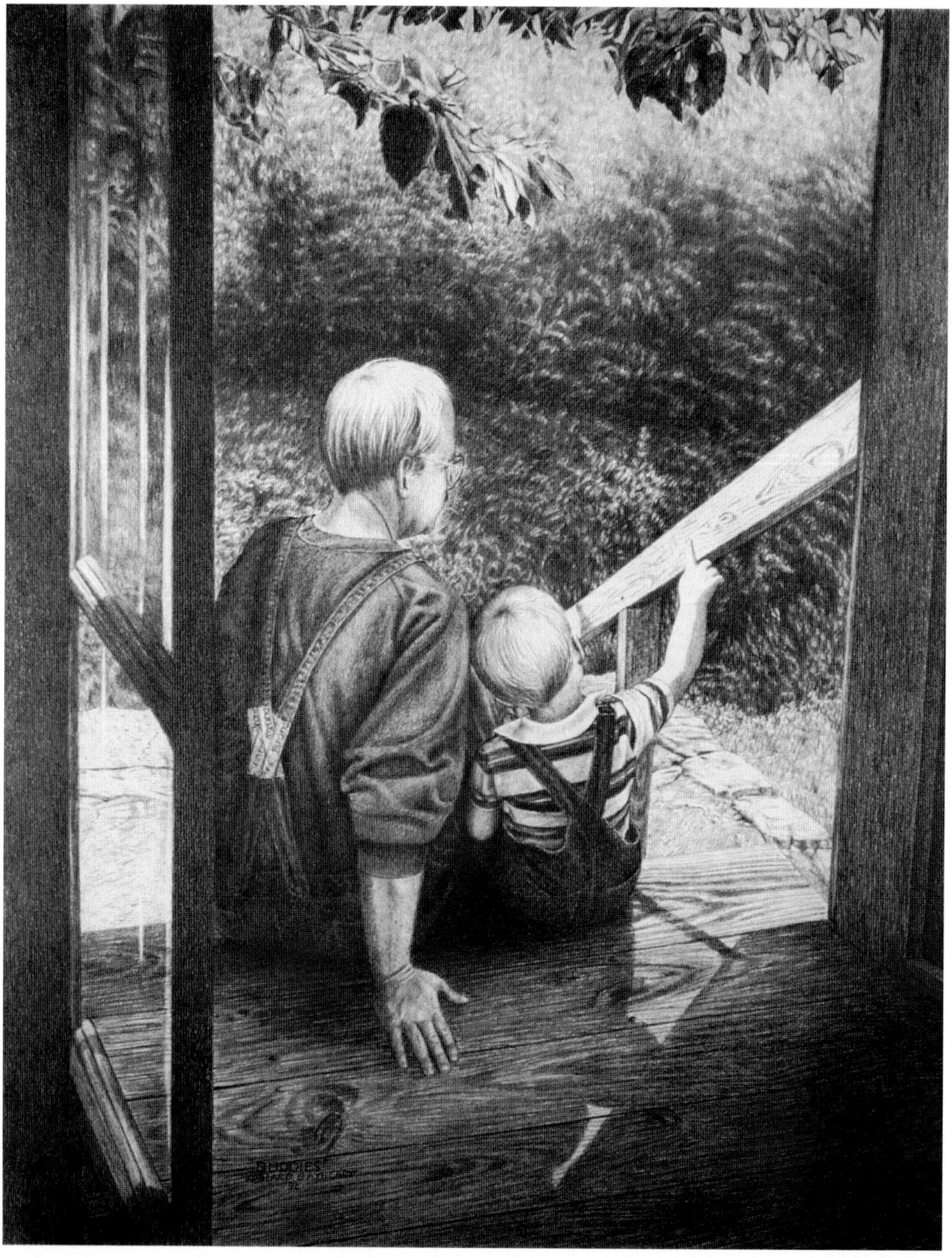
BUDDIES

Buddies
1992

Willard's daughter-in-law secretly took a photograph of her husband, Steven, and a young nephew they enjoyed during one of his visits. "They were good buddies," said Willard. He thought the photograph to be interesting and from an unusual angle, and sought to portray a relationship between a man and boy, whether it be father and son, a special friend or mentor. "From that angle it could be anybody," remarked Willard.

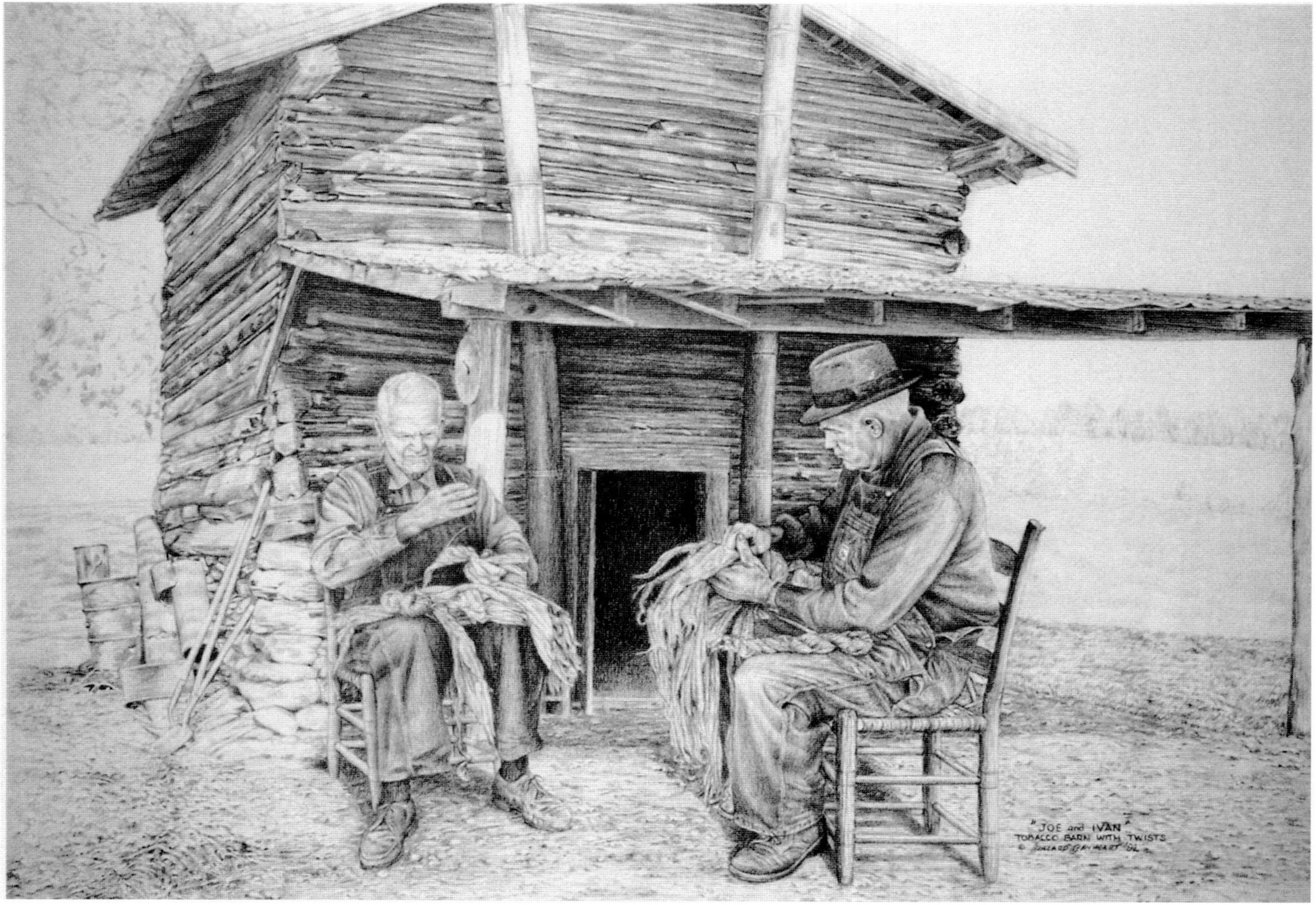
"JOE and IVAN"
TOBACCO BARN WITH TWISTS

Joe and Ivan
Tobacco Barn with Twists
1992

Years ago people would twist tobacco and hang it up and use it for pipe smoking or chewing through the winter. It's almost a lost art in tobacco. People just don't do it much anymore, although it was the way they used to preserve it for their own use.

Joe and Ivan, father and son, were tobacco farmers from Dobson, North Carolina, a community just off Interstate 77 between Elkin, North Carolina, and Hillsville, Virginia.

This drawing was commissioned by Ivan's daughter as a gift for Ivan, but there was some urgency for Willard to complete the drawing so that the father, Joe, could enjoy it. He was in his nineties at the time and in ill health. Willard completed the drawing and Joe did get to see and enjoy it, but died a short time later.

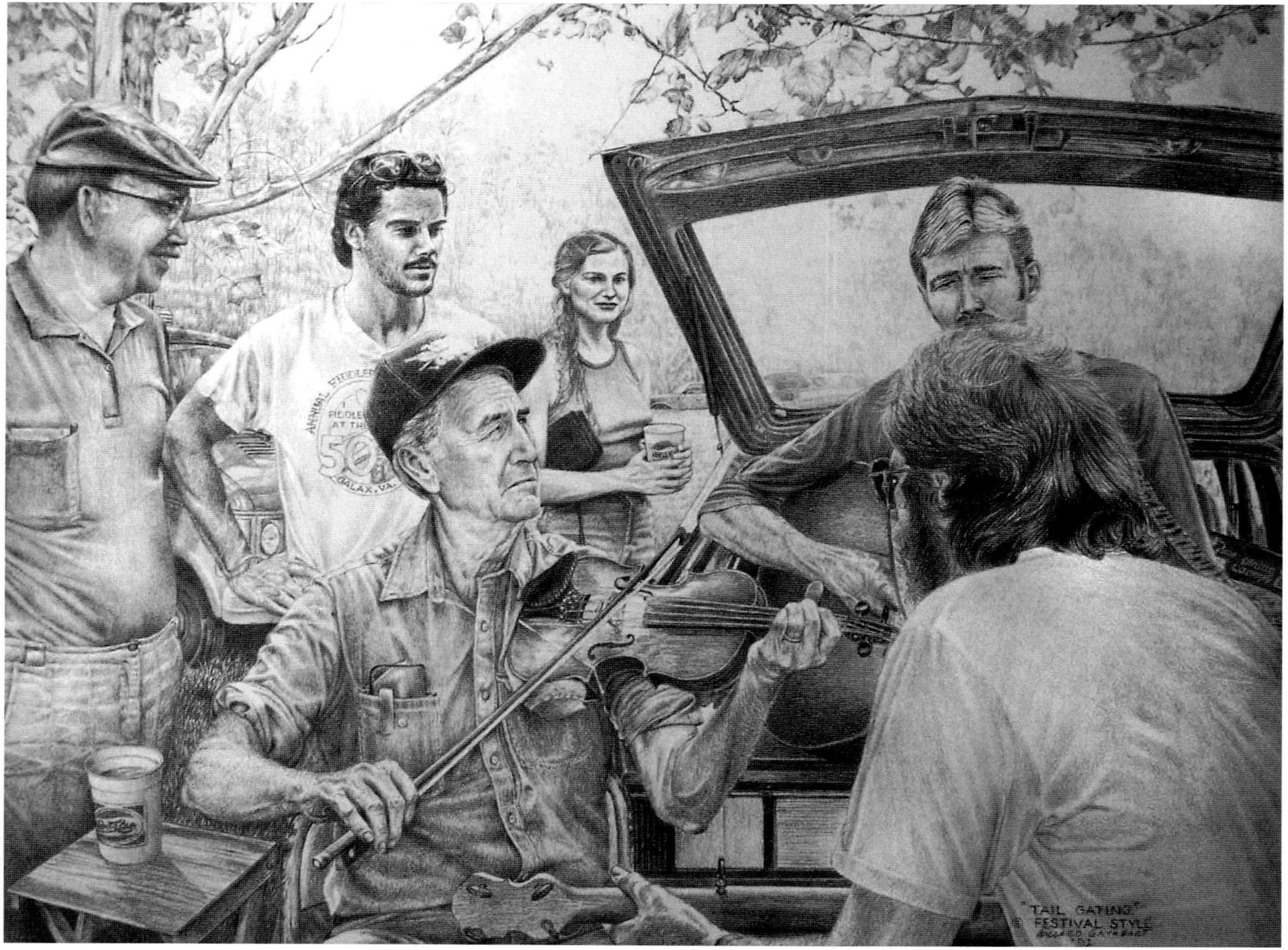
"TAIL GATING"
FESTIVAL STYLE

Tailgating Festival Style
1992

Ralph Blizzard, fiddler, and the New Southern Ramblers from Blountville, Tennessee, near Bristol, Tennessee, are drawn here as they played their music from a tailgate at the annual Old Fiddlers' Convention in Galax, Virginia, several years ago.

My idea is to show that bluegrass musicians tailgate, maybe not in the same way, but we tailgate the same as footballers do, except we play music where they're usually eating from their tailgates. It's typical at Galax every year.

Arthur Conner, Fiddle Maker
1993

First in a series called Blue Ridge Masters, this drawing shows Arthur Conner, a fiddle maker retired from Norfolk & Western Railroad Shops in Roanoke, Virginia.

> *If anyone qualifies to be a master, Arthur Conner does. He's a scholar of instrument making and really, really a truly great fiddle maker. He has made fiddles for Ricky Skaggs and George Strait, and also classical musicians in local symphonies have Arthur's fiddles. He really considers himself a violin maker and he's one of the best and an unusual, talented, one-of-a-kind guy.*

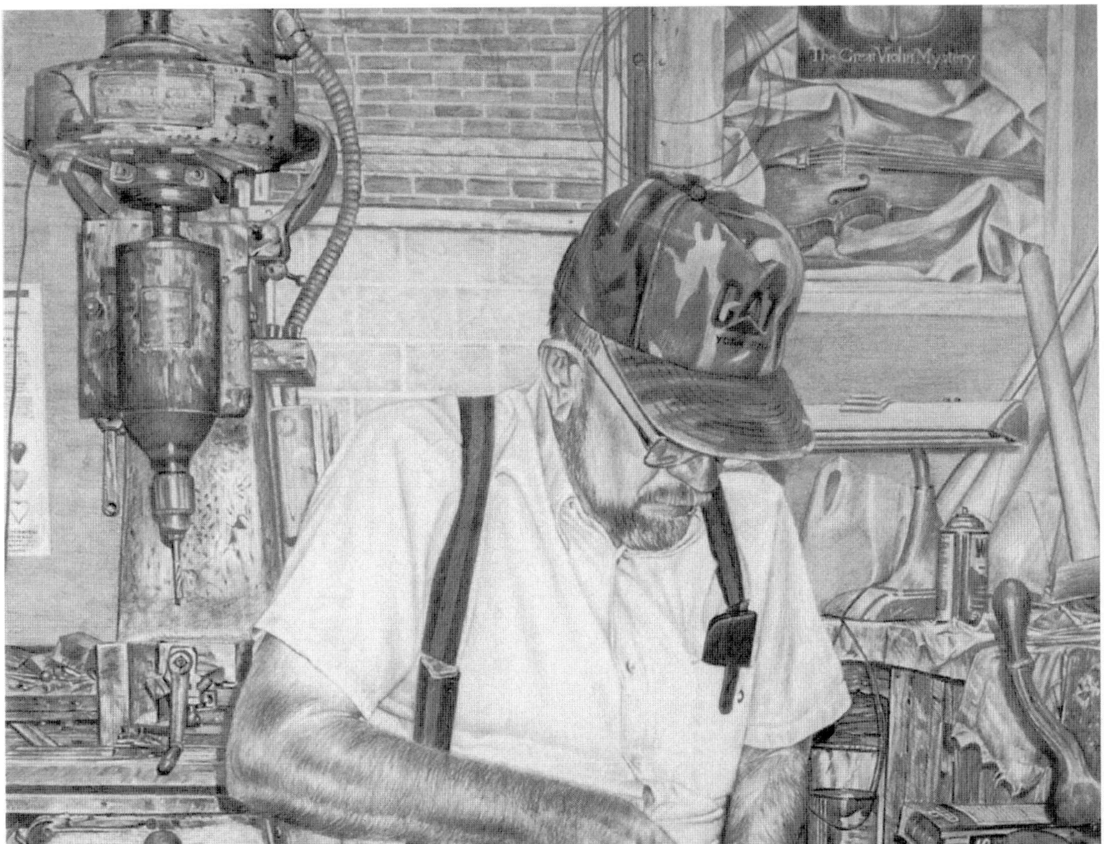
The Great Violin Mystery
Antonio
Stradivari
BLUERIDGE MASTERS
COLLECTORS SERIES
1
ARTHUR CONNER
FIDDLE MAKER
COPPER HILL
VA.
WILLARD GAYHEART '93

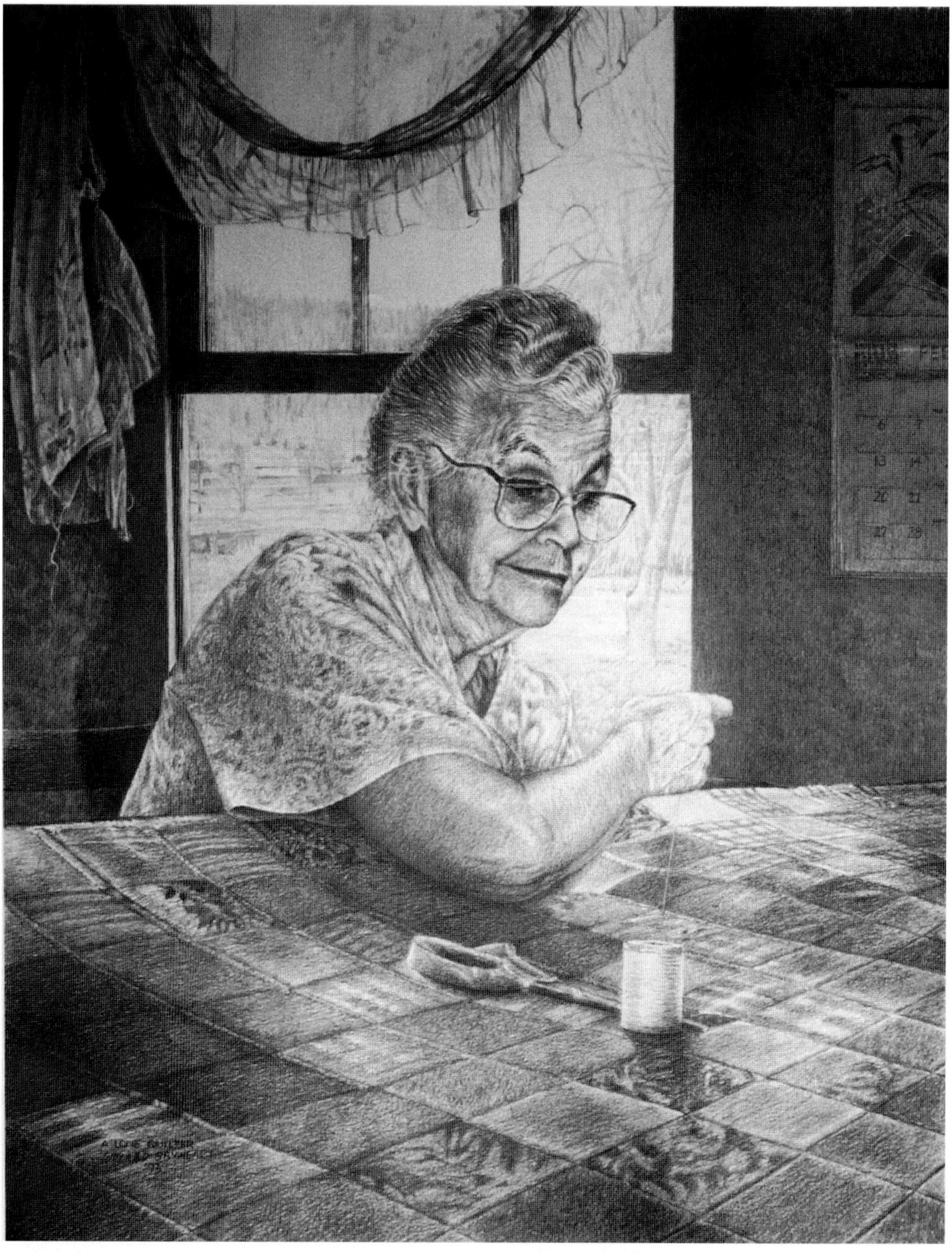

A Lone Quilter 1993

Mother still lives in the homeplace in Knott County, Kentucky. I think my mother always had the desire to play music and maybe even draw, but she never had the time because she had to raise a family, and conditions where I grew up were pretty hard and required a lot of attention and hard work. My mother is even to this day a very tough little woman. She's only about five feet tall, she's been very courageous all her life, very hard working, and has done a lot for her family.

After the death of his father, Willard wanted to do something for his mother, and so he did this drawing, which has been a very successful piece for him. The first 250 signed and numbered prints sold out and a smaller reprint is selling well. He's told his mother that she's in people's homes all over the United States.

Nina's Friend
1993

This is a commissioned piece for a lady from Florida who spent summers near Meadows of Dan, Virginia, off the Blue Ridge Parkway in Floyd County. The drawing is a scene from her Mississippi childhood. Sadly, she died before its completion. Family members have the completed drawing and prints.

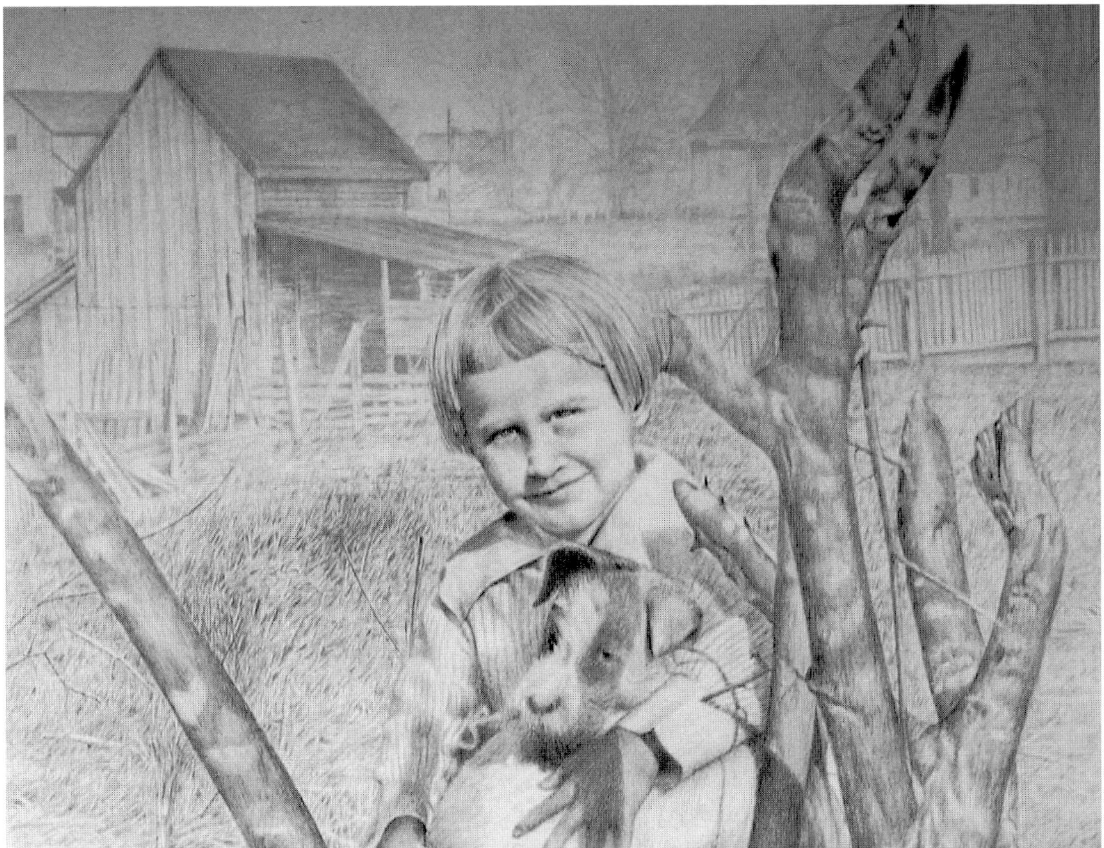

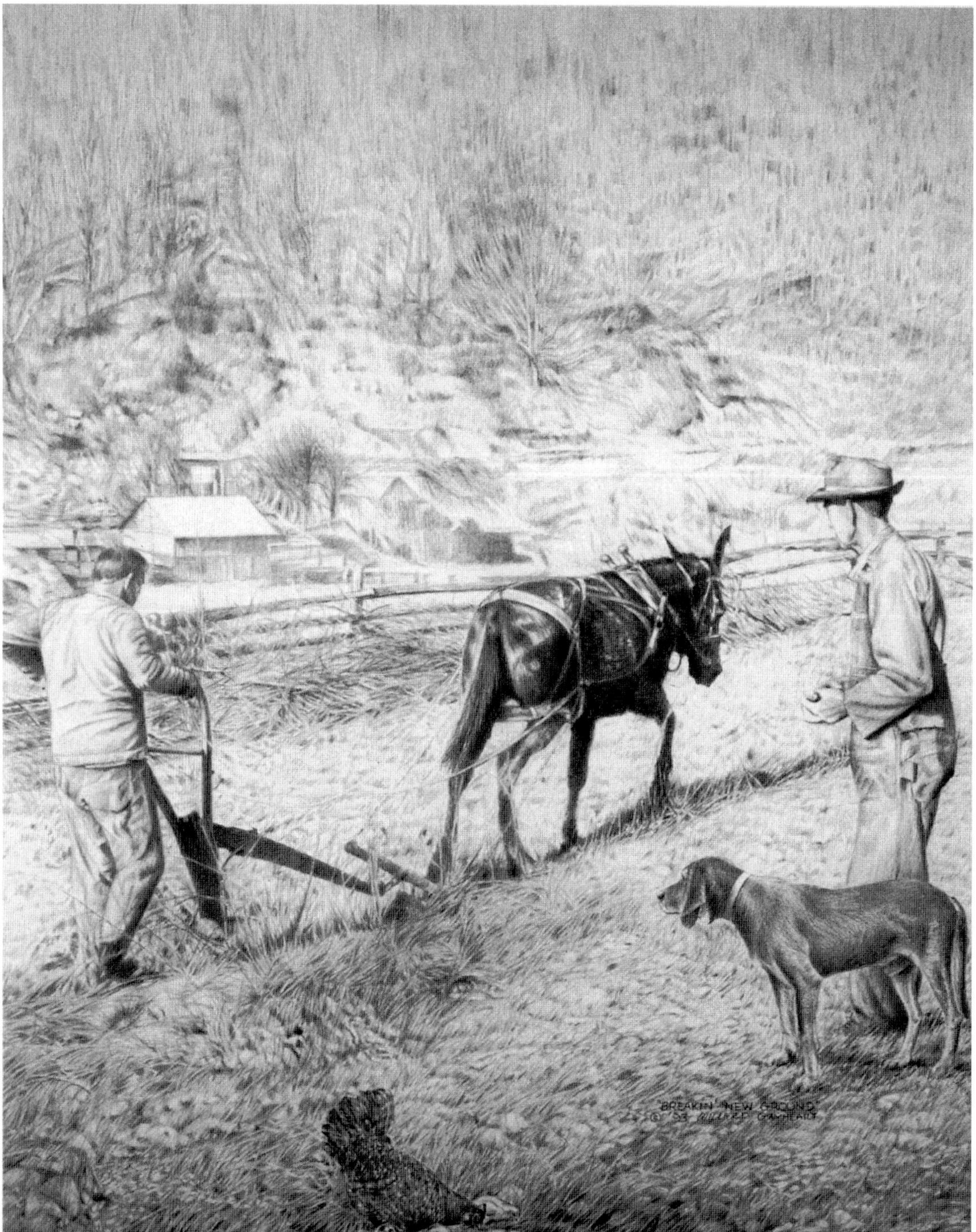
"BREAKIN' NEW GROUND"

Breakin' New Ground
1993

This is a drawing taken from a photograph given to me by a young man in Sullivan County [Tennessee] near Bristol, Virginia, of his grandfather and uncle working in fields in Eastern Kentucky in the forties. I added a dog and chickens and titled it. The men are named Cornett, a common name in Letcher, Perry, and Knott counties in Kentucky, which is also where my roots are. This is a typical scene from my youth.

Reunion in Wilkesboro
1993

Willard took this drawing to the annual MerleFest in Wilkesboro, North Carolina, with some hesitation because it features Doc Watson with his deceased son as kind of a spiritual figure in the background. It was Willard's way of showing Merle at the festival in spirit if not physically. The festival is in memory of Merle, who died in 1985 in a farm tractor accident. Bands and celebrities from the world of music convene at Wilkes Community College each April to remember Doc Watson's son.

Without consulting anyone and with some nervousness about how the drawing would be received, Willard went to the festival and set up his art space. One of the first people to see the drawing was Merle's daughter, who was very happy with it. Willard gave her a print, which she took to her grandmother, Merle's mother, and from there came the resulting three commissioned posters in 1995, 1996, and 1998. Also, Willard did a drawing commissioned by Wilkes Community College for Doc and Rosa Lee Watson's 50th wedding anniversary, a personal piece with no reproductions in print.

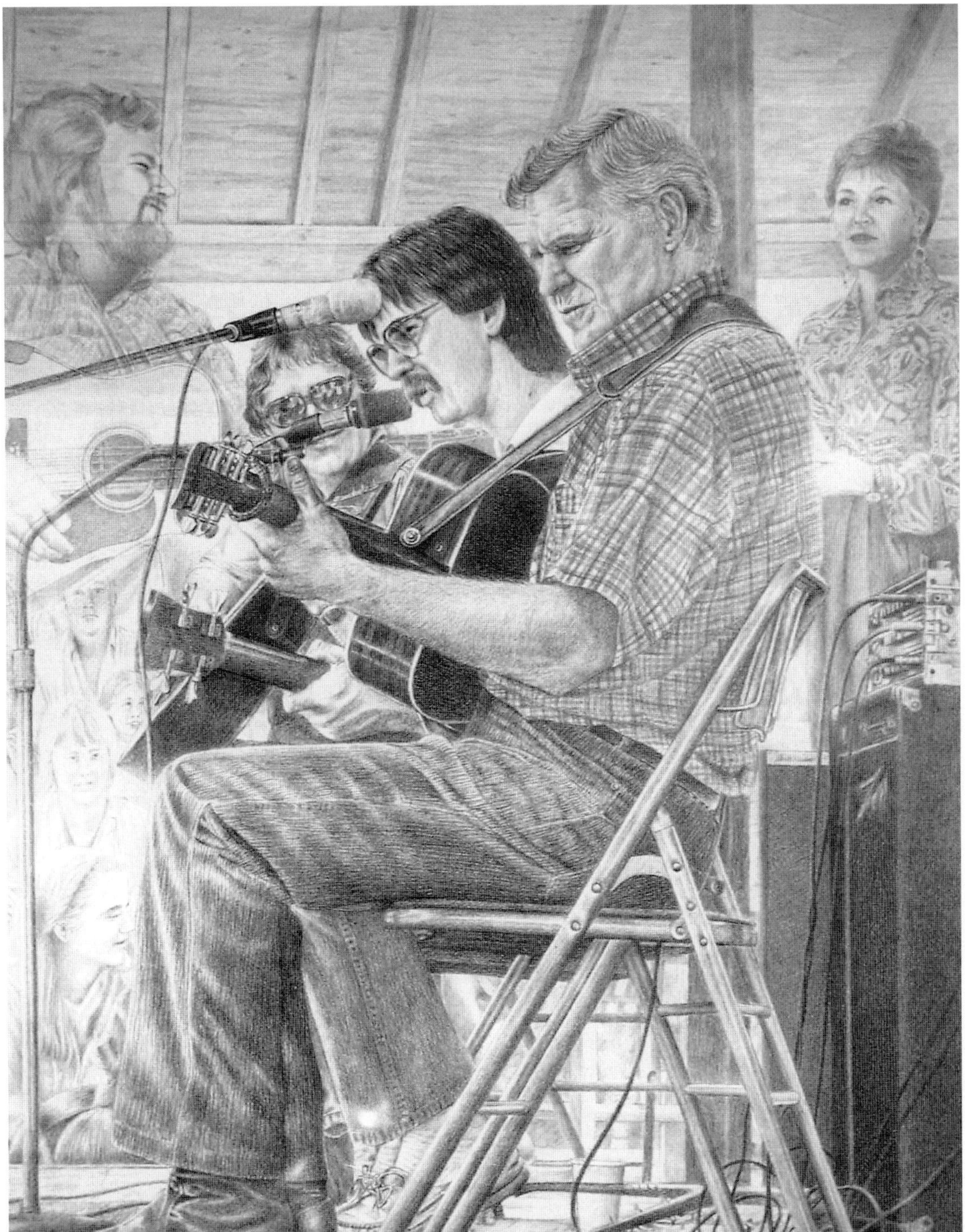
REUNION IN WILKESBORO

Mabry Mill Outdoor Quilting
1994

Frances Radford and a friend are demonstrating the art of quilting at Mabry Mill on the Blue Ridge Parkway, where old-time crafts are on display.

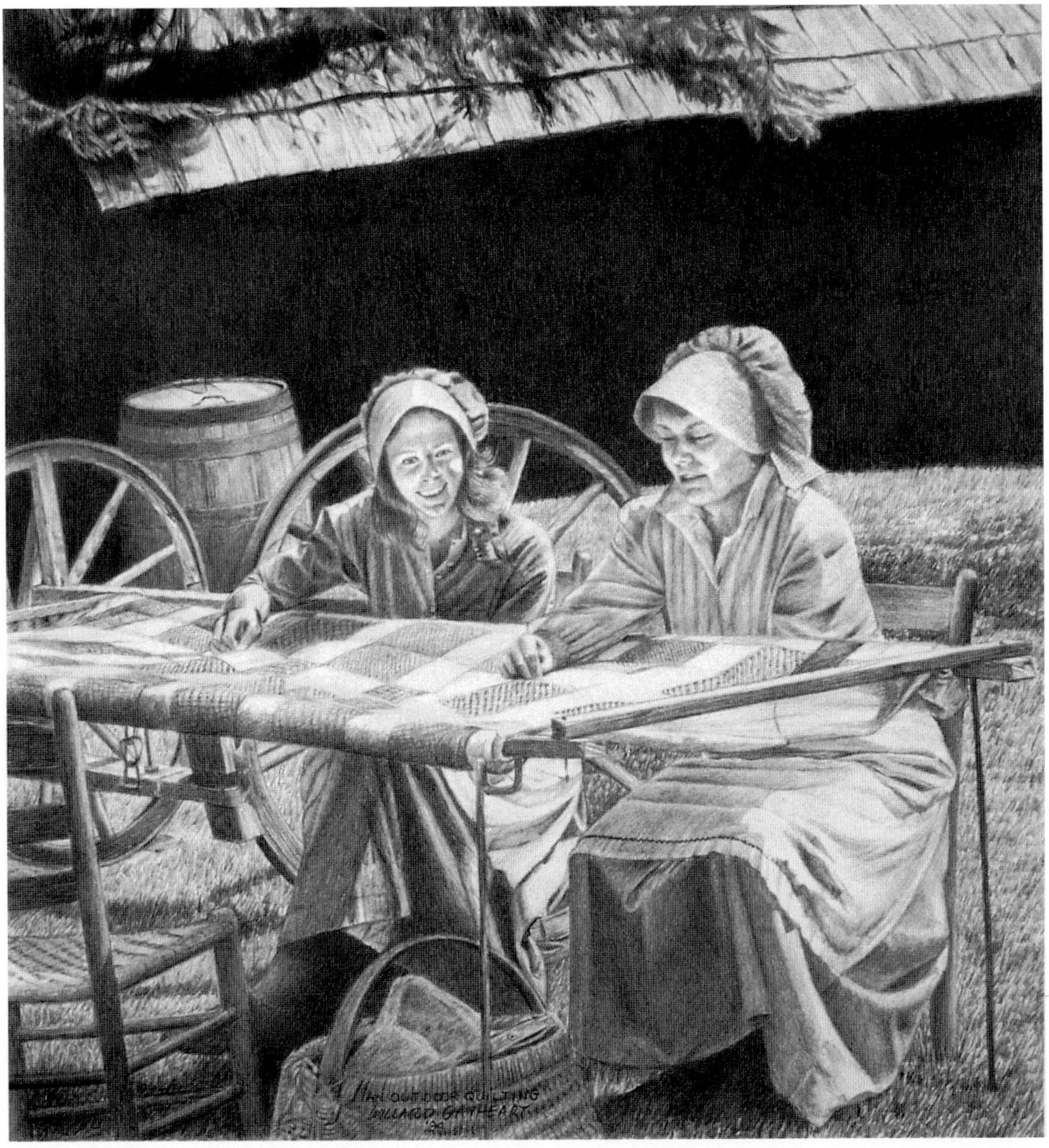
AN OUT DOOR QUILTING
WILLARD GAYHEART

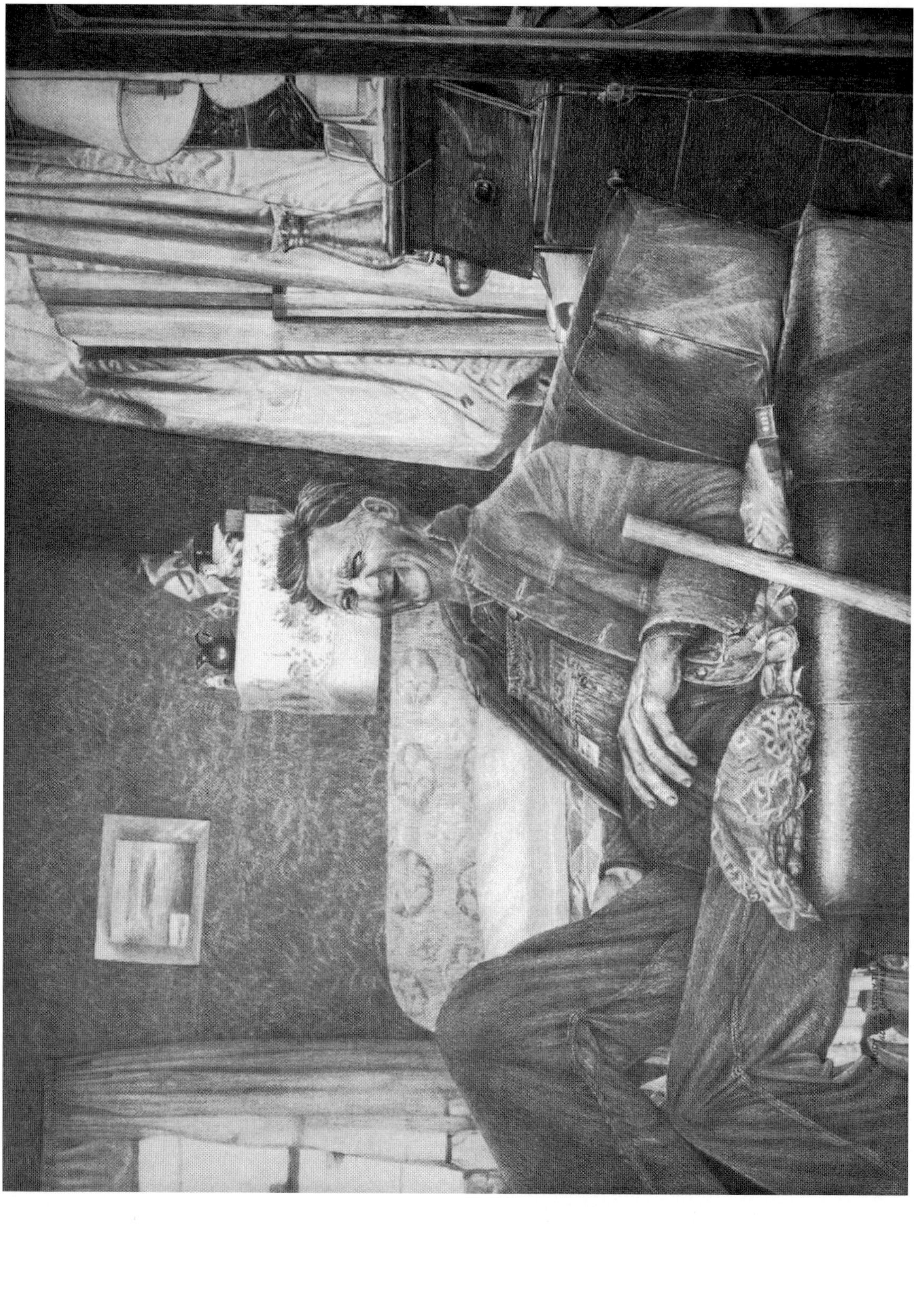

Study of a Storyteller
1994

A drawing of celebrated Appalachian storyteller Ray Hicks.

Ray Hicks lived with his wife, Rosa, on the back side of Beech Mountain, in western North Carolina, away from Beech Mountain Ski area and Banner Elk. He was born in the house he lived in all his life, a house with no indoor plumbing or other modern conveniences. Life was hard and simple, but full for Ray and Rosa.

A gifted storyteller, Ray was awarded the National Heritage Fellowship Award from the National Endowment for the Arts in 1983 and was listed as a National Treasure by the Smithsonian Institution. He was honored by the North Carolina Arts Council and featured in numerous articles, documentaries, videos, and books. Willard calls him "the grand patriarch" of the Jonesborough Storytelling Festival held in the fall of each year in Jonesborough, Tennessee.

Ray Hicks died April 20, 2003.

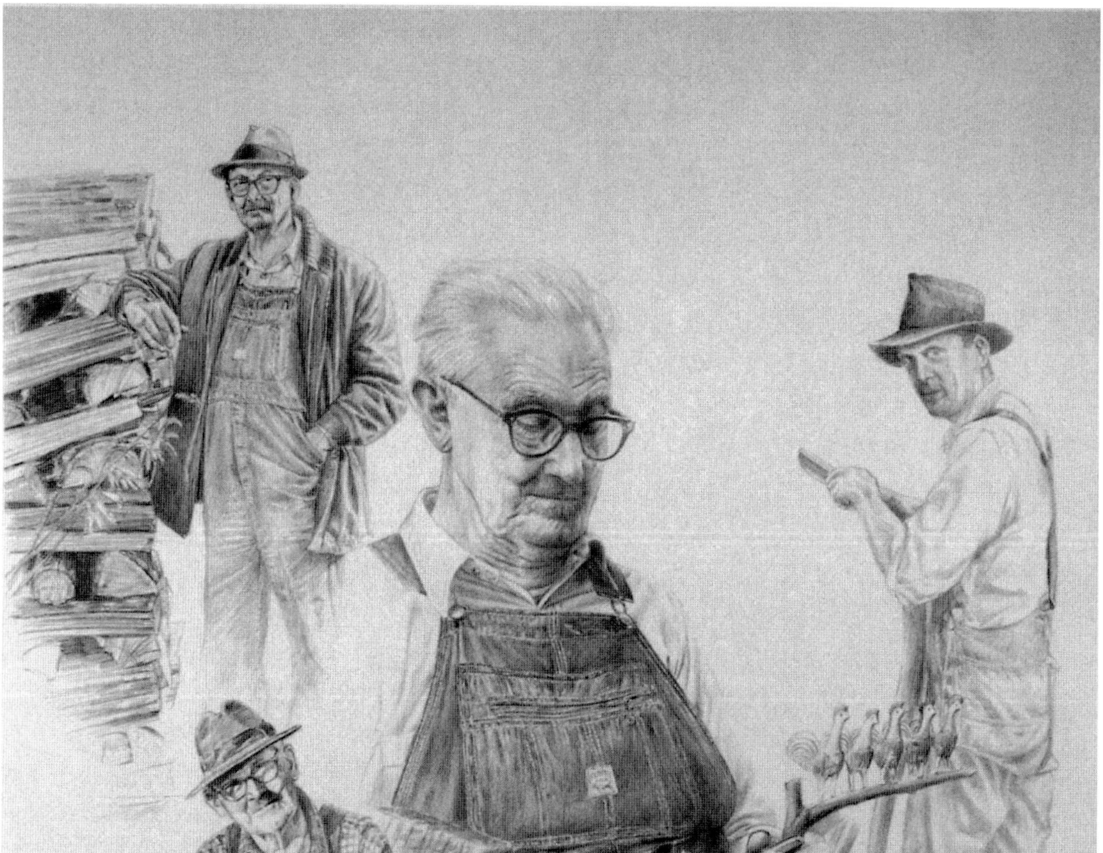
WALTER G. WILSON
"WHITTLING AWAY"
WILLARD GAYHEART
'94

Walter G. Wilson, Whittling Away 1994

Walter Wilson, retired, was a talented carpenter as well as a woodcarver and made many of Willard's frames from wood salvaged from old barns. He's shown here making little chickens on a stick, a craft he could produce quickly to sell in craft stores and at events.

> *He loved woodworking and was really a unique fellow who took a lot of pride in everything he created. He was very likeable, enjoyed gardening, but especially loved to whittle. He created many interesting things in his shop.*

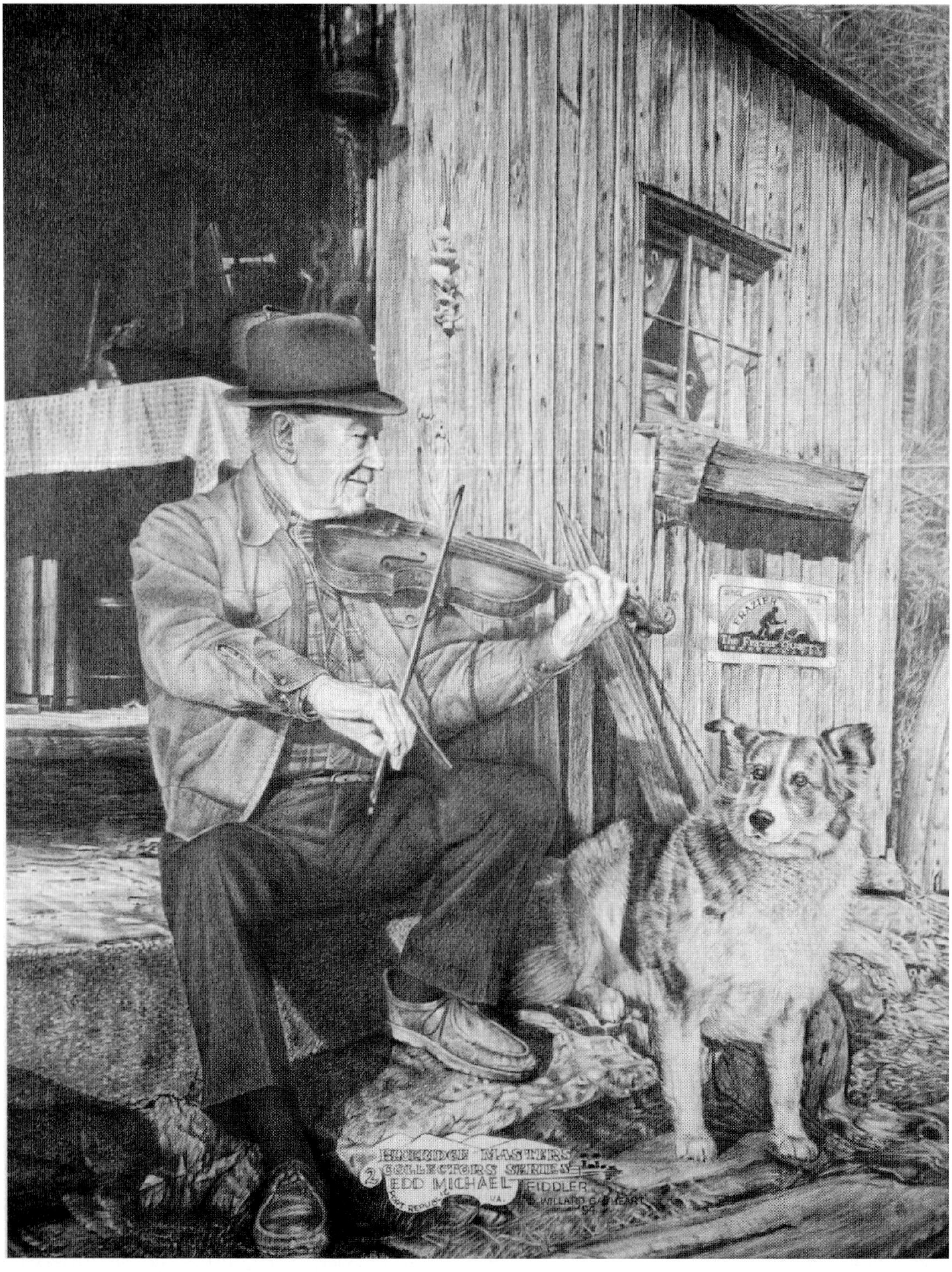
FRAZIER
MASTERS
2
COLLECTORS SERIES
EDD MICHAEL
FIDDLER
VA.

Edd Michael
1994

Edd Michael lives along the Shenandoah River on his ancestral farm in Port Republic near Harrisonburg in the Shenandoah Valley of Virginia. He is second in Willard's series called Blue Ridge Masters.

He truly is a master fiddler.

Willard says this drawing, created from photographs of Edd, took 80 to 100 hours to complete because of the significant amount of detail involved. The print has sold out.

Tips from the Master
1994

The Barr family from Galax, Virginia, own a music store there and are all musicians. This drawing resulted from a festival in North Carolina when the youngest member of the family, Stevie Barr, himself a bluegrass banjo picker, was fortunate enough to get a little personal time in his early years with legendary banjo player Earl Scruggs. The original of this drawing was bartered for a guitar.

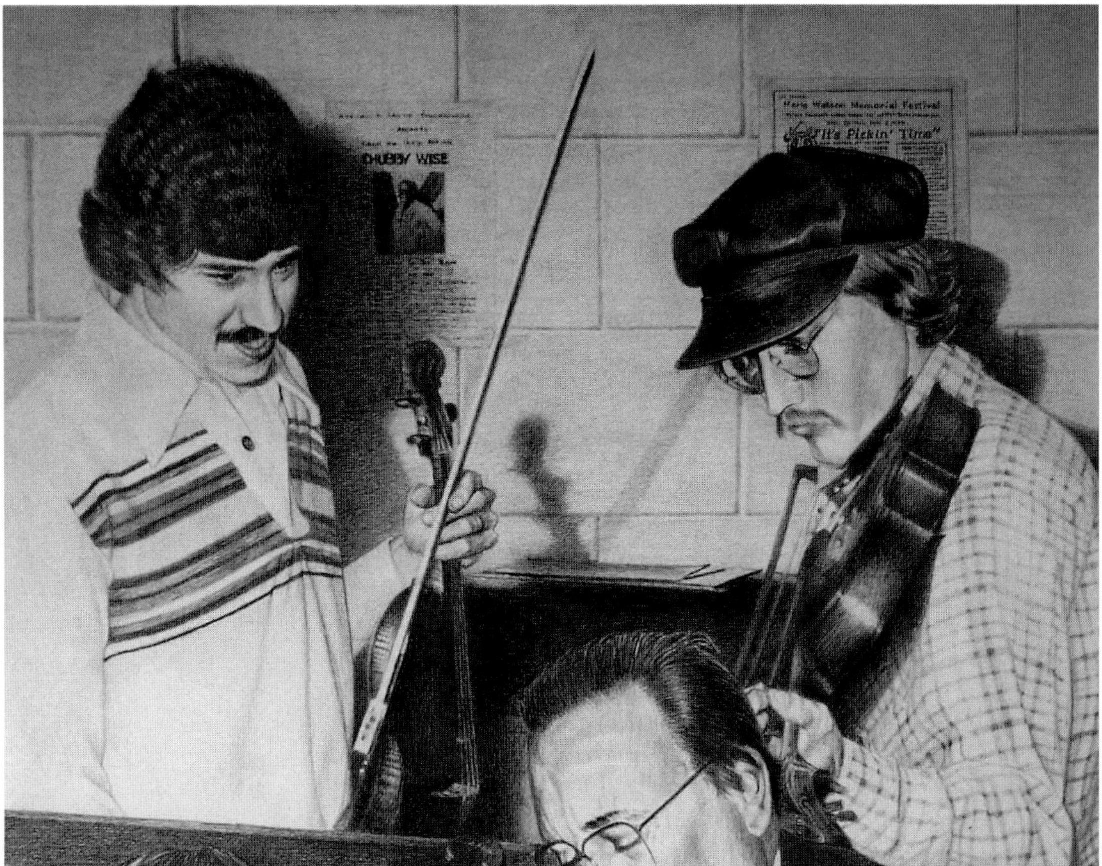
CHUBBY WISE
Merle Watson Memorial Festival
"It's Pickin' Time"
POTOMAC
TIPS FROM THE MASTER

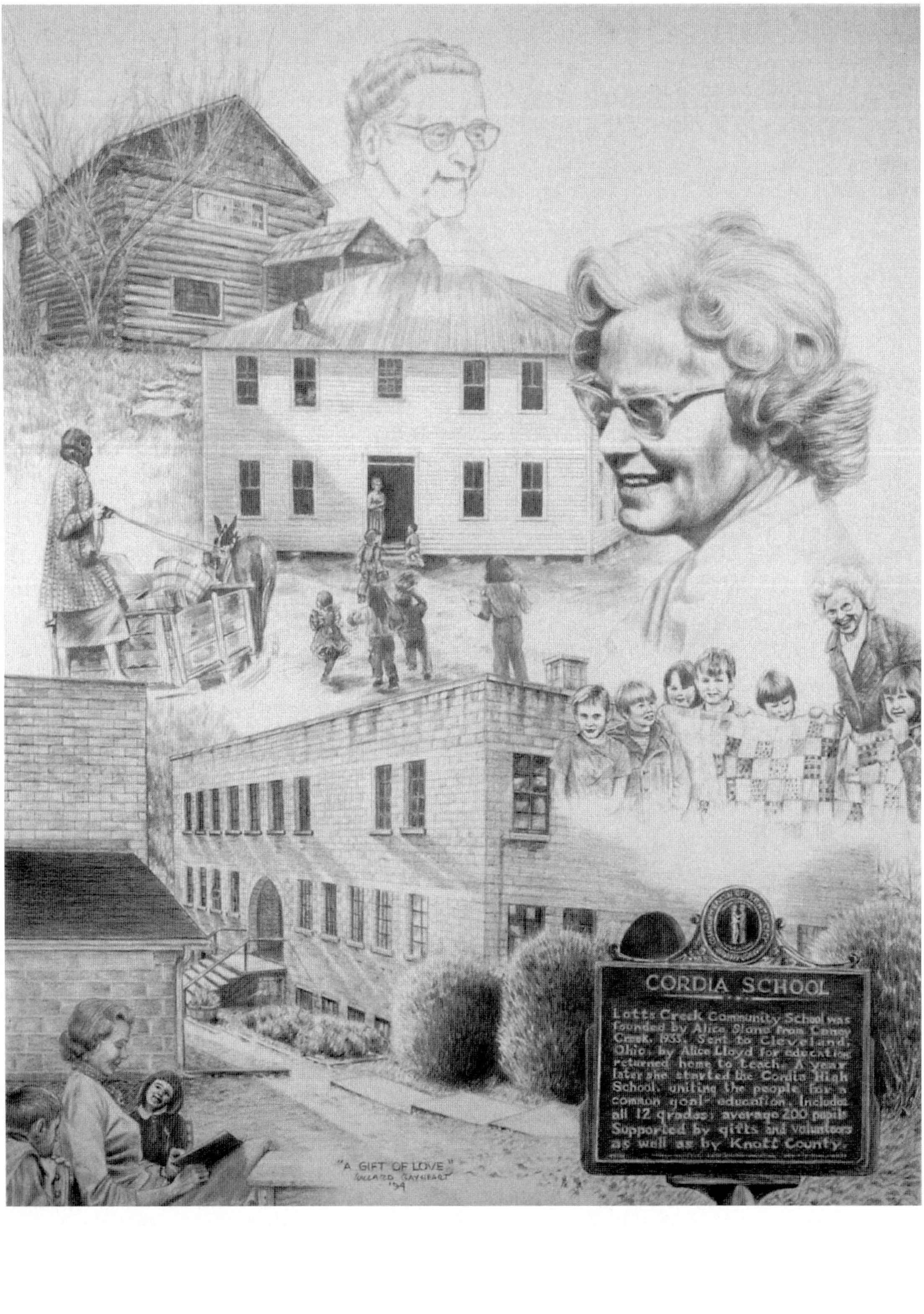
CORDIA SCHOOL
Lotts Creek Community School was founded by Alice Slone from Caney Creek, 1933. Sent to Cleveland, Ohio, by Alice Lloyd for education returned home to teach. A year later she started the Cordia High School, uniting the people for a common goal-education. Includes all 12 grades; average 200 pupils Supported by gifts and volunteers as well as by Knott County.
"A GIFT OF LOVE"
'94

A Gift of Love
1994

This is the best title I could come up with for this [drawing] because it's that and more. This is a drawing of Alice Sloan, who founded the little [Cordia] school where I went. She gave her life to that school, educating hundreds of kids that might not have had an opportunity to go to high school if she hadn't come when she was a young woman and started this school in our community. She was tutored by Alice Lloyd, founder of Alice Lloyd College, a private four-year college in Pippa Passes, Kentucky, offering tuition-guaranteed education to students from the Appalachian region. Then she went away to Cleveland, Ohio, to get her college degree and came back and founded our school. She gave us the opportunity to go on to a higher level of education.

[The school] had dorms for a while for the children who couldn't walk to school because of distance. They could stay during the week and go home on weekends, because there were no buses. The children did chores to pay for their keep. They chopped wood, brought in coal, and in summer worked the gardens.

[Alice Sloan] died about ten years ago at age ninety and is buried there on the little campus of Cordia School. There's a kind of memorial and little park there at her grave. It's a very special place, a place where she loved to go read. In the drawing I've actually portrayed the first building that she lived in, a log cabin built for her when she first came to the school. Later she moved into a larger log house. We went to school in the wooden structure in the middle of the drawing. We went to grade school on the bottom floor and high school on the second floor.

Miss Sloan started the school with nothing, and when she died she passed it to her niece, Alice Scoffield Whitaker. What started as a little log cabin is now about a four million dollar state-of-the-art school, second to none.

I think that's quite a legacy for Miss Sloan. Words or pictures can't express what this lady has meant to so many people.

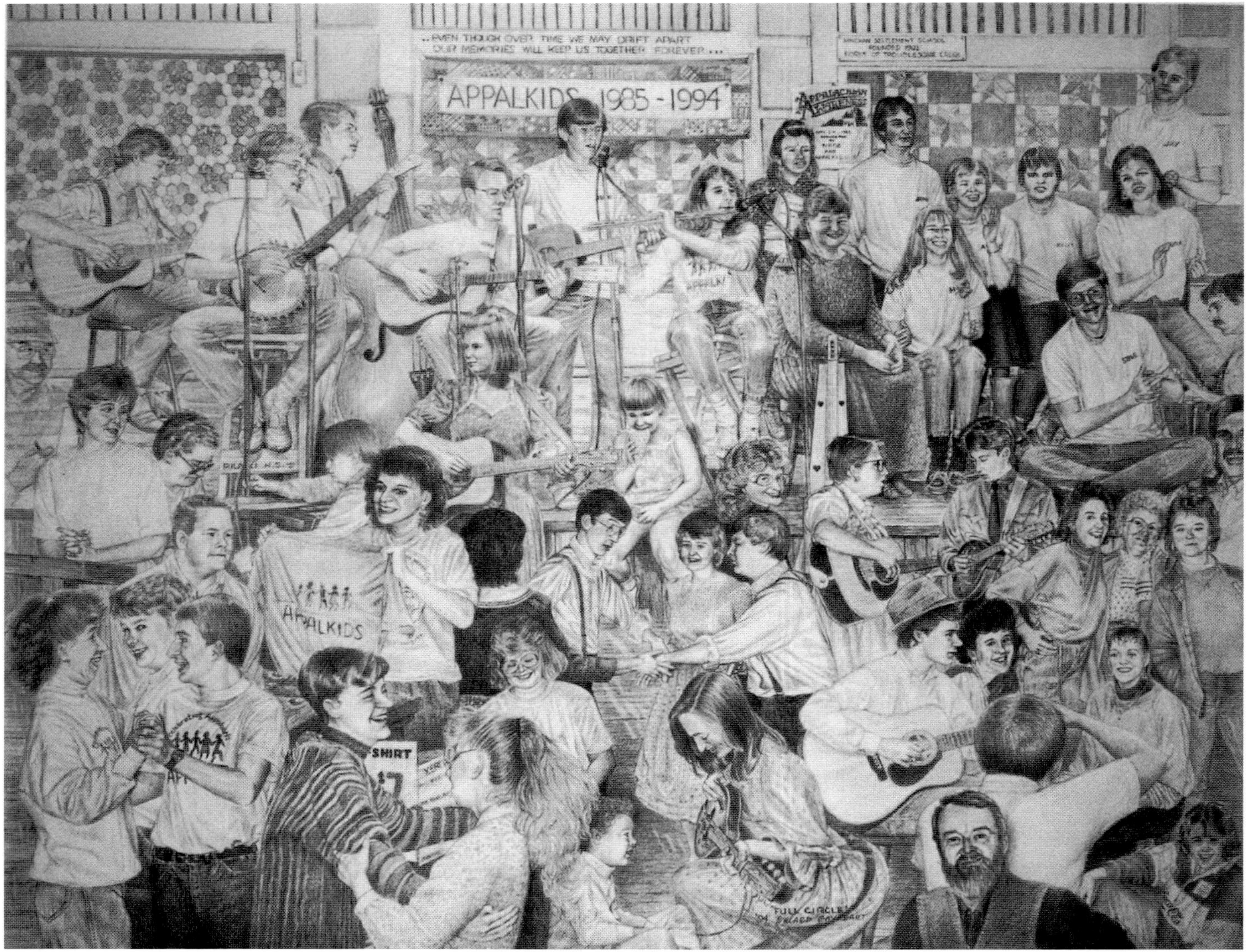
..EVEN THOUGH OVER TIME WE MAY DRIFT APART
OUR MEMORIES WILL KEEP US TOGETHER FOREVER...
APPALKIDS 1985 - 1994
APPALKIDS
SHIRT
FULL CIRCLE

Full Circle Appalkids 1994

The original of this drawing hangs at Pulaski County High School, home of the Appalkids in Dublin, Virginia, off Interstate 81 between the southwestern Virginia communities of Radford and Wytheville.

For a number of years I was involved with the Appalkids either at a festival at Pulaski High School they would host, or maybe I'd be invited to the school to help entertain. Just many instances I was around them and knew a lot of the kids. The kids did skits, played music, danced, all part of the Appalachian culture and a way of making them proud of being from the area. I'm not sure what you'd call them, but they were promoters of pride in our background as Appalachians. There must have been fifty or sixty of them over the years.

That's where I met Dr. Grace Edwards from Radford University. They weren't doing a program that day, but they were indirectly involved because the director invited me to come with my artwork and do some entertaining and invited Dr. Edwards. As a result I got to do things [festivals and other events] at Radford, but more than anything I received a lot of encouragement over the years from Becky Hancock, the director of the Appalkids and an English teacher at the school, and from Dr. Edwards. I must say I owe a lot to them for their encouragement in the early days.

When the group disbanded in 1994, I was asked to do a drawing. They wanted me to draw Hindman Settlement School where they used to go in Kentucky every summer. [Hindman Settlement School is located in Hindman and specializes in teaching children with special needs. Hindman also is active in carrying on the music, art, literature, and crafts of the Appalachian region through its many outreach programs.] So, that's the background and I tried to get all of the fifty some kids in the drawing dancing, playing music, talking, etc. That was quite an endeavor, but it was wonderful to be asked to do it.

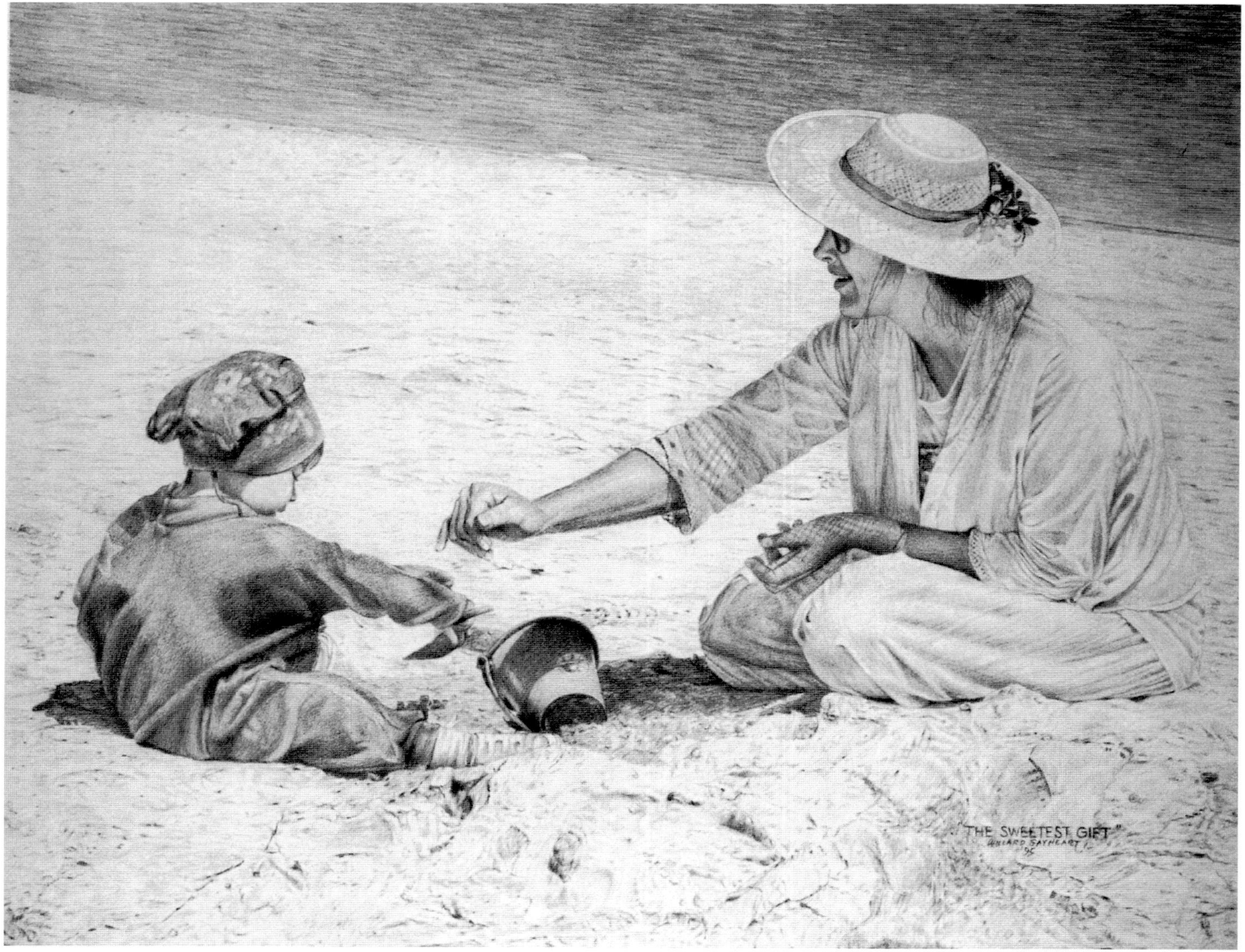
"THE SWEETEST GIFT"

The Sweetest Gift
1995

During a country music festival in Rocky Gap State Park near Cumberland, Maryland, where Willard's early band, Skeeter and the Skidmarks, were performing, he also had his artwork set up along a lake there at the park. Set up alongside him was a couple, Kathleen and Carl Gotzmer, and their daughter Sarah. Kathleen and Carl were friends with Willard and they had done shows together before this event. Carl is an "excellent dulcimer maker," says Willard, "and Kathleen sings and plays really well."

During one of the days there Willard noticed Kathleen and Sarah playing in the sand near the water, and the way they were dressed looked "kind of old-timey and unusual" to Willard. He photographed them there.

The title of the drawing, "Sweetest Gift," actually came from a line from an old song called "The Sweetest Gift (A Mother's Smile)." Willard didn't know until later that this meant even more to Kathleen. The couple bought the original and explained to Willard that the title of the drawing meant so much to them because they'd waited so long to find Sarah, their adopted child, a child so special to them, and indeed "the sweetest gift."

Kathleen had such a pretty smile and was always smiling, especially when she was with Sarah.

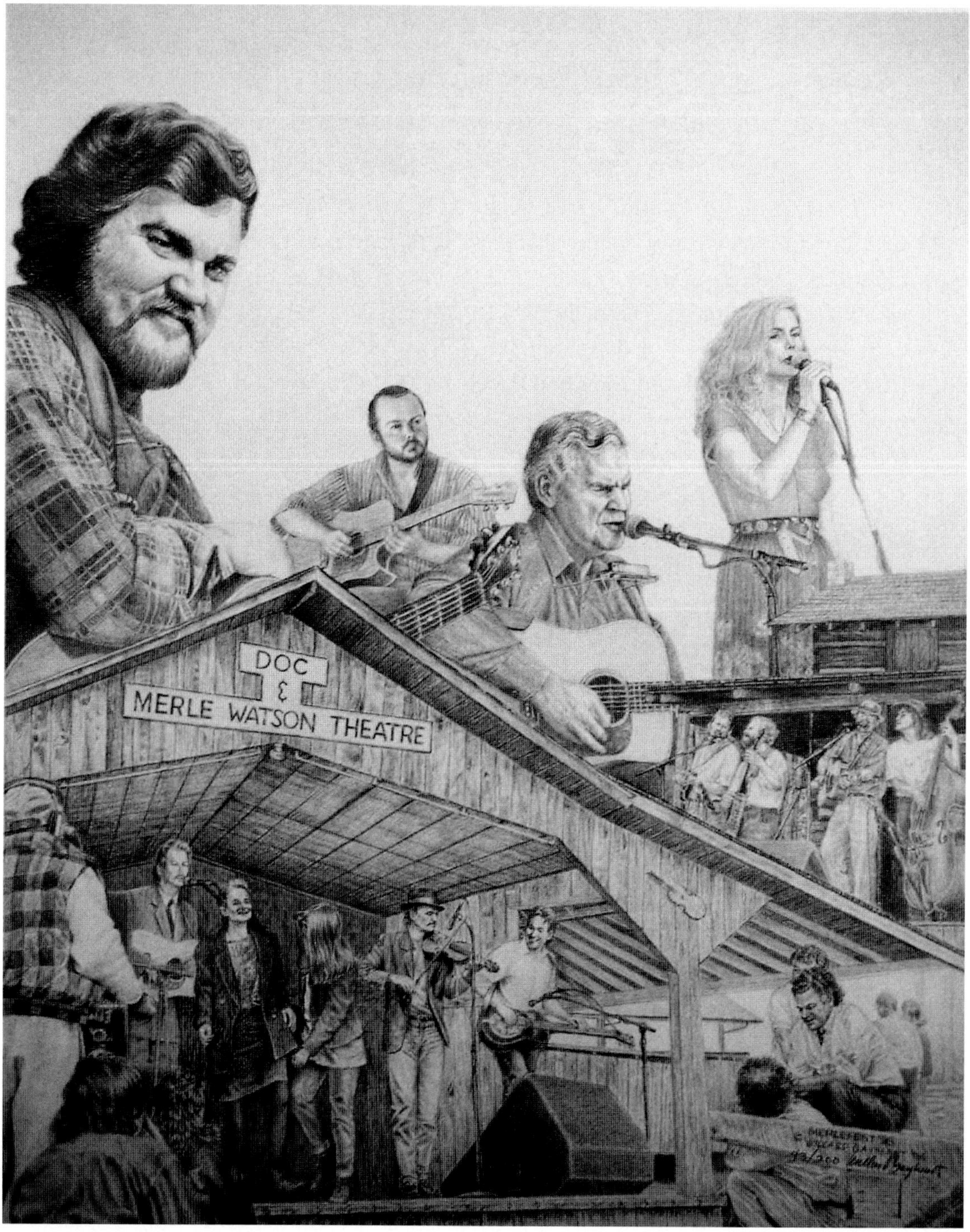
DOC
&
MERLE WATSON THEATRE

Merlefest 1995

This second drawing of a poster for the annual MerleFest "includes lots of people," explains Willard.

> *Emmy Lou Harris is in there and Doc and Merle, and Merle's son Richard, Jerry Douglas, probably the best Dobro player in the world, and Mark O'Conner, not only a bluegrass fiddler, but a classical violinist. He was there and Tony Rice, who probably has the reputation of being the greatest bluegrass guitar picker there is. They raffled the original, had stationery made from it, little badges, and various things they sold at the festival to raise money. In one of those coincidences the fellow that won the original was someone I've known for years from Galax, and out of all those thousands of people who registered, it was coincidental that he won it.*

The Gardeners
1995

Willard's strong sense of family is obvious in many of his drawings where faces of his children, grandchildren, and other family members appear.

In this drawing Willard recalled a November day when "the time was just right to set out tulip bulbs" his wife had brought him. Dori was around three years old and lived in sight of her grandfather. She spied Willard working in the flower bed and came to help set the bulbs.

He remembers thinking as Dori "got hold of a little hand tool and got to digging in the dirt to help me" that this would make a good drawing. It has been one of his more popular drawings and is a favorite of his "since it's a drawing of my little buddy and me doing things together."

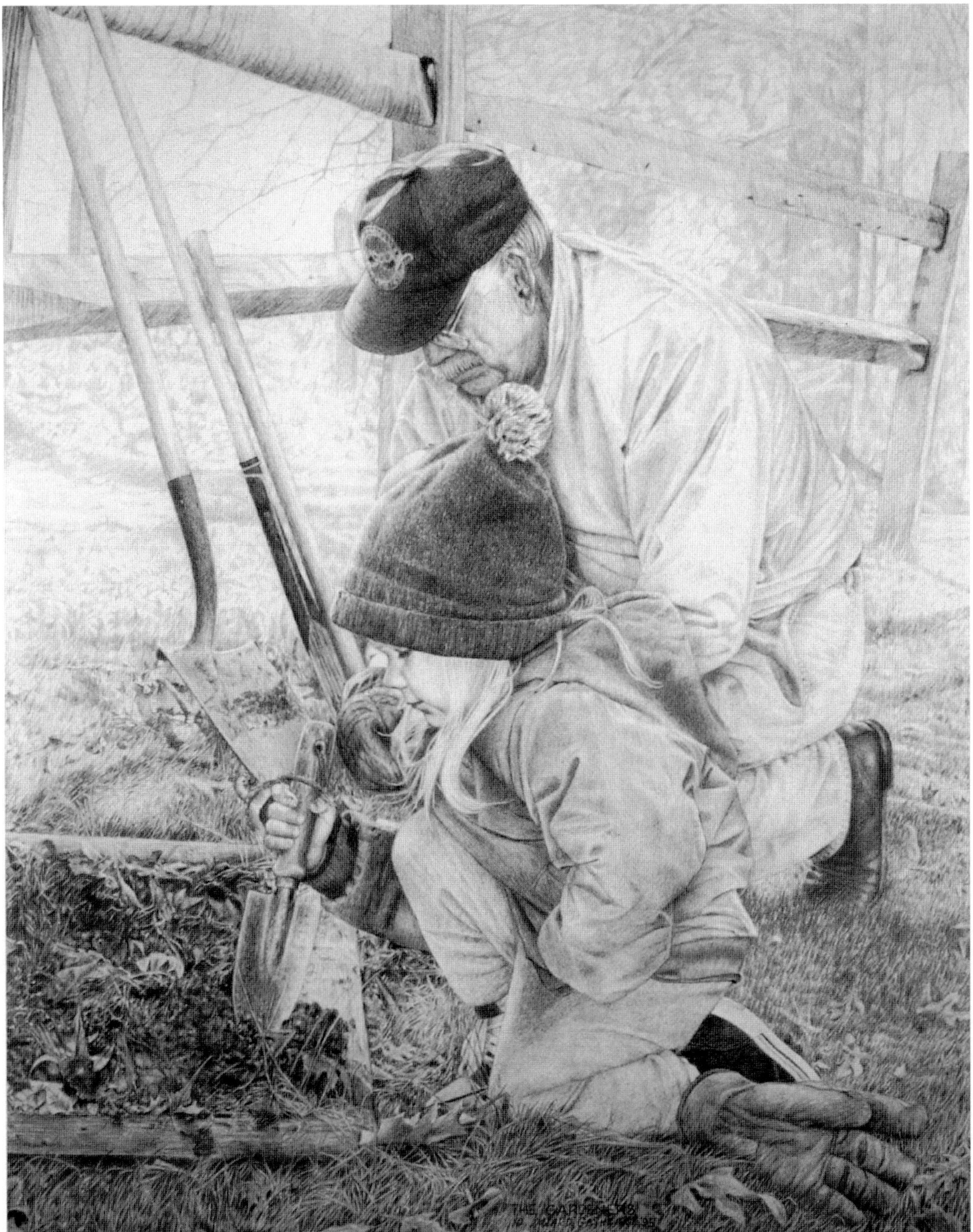

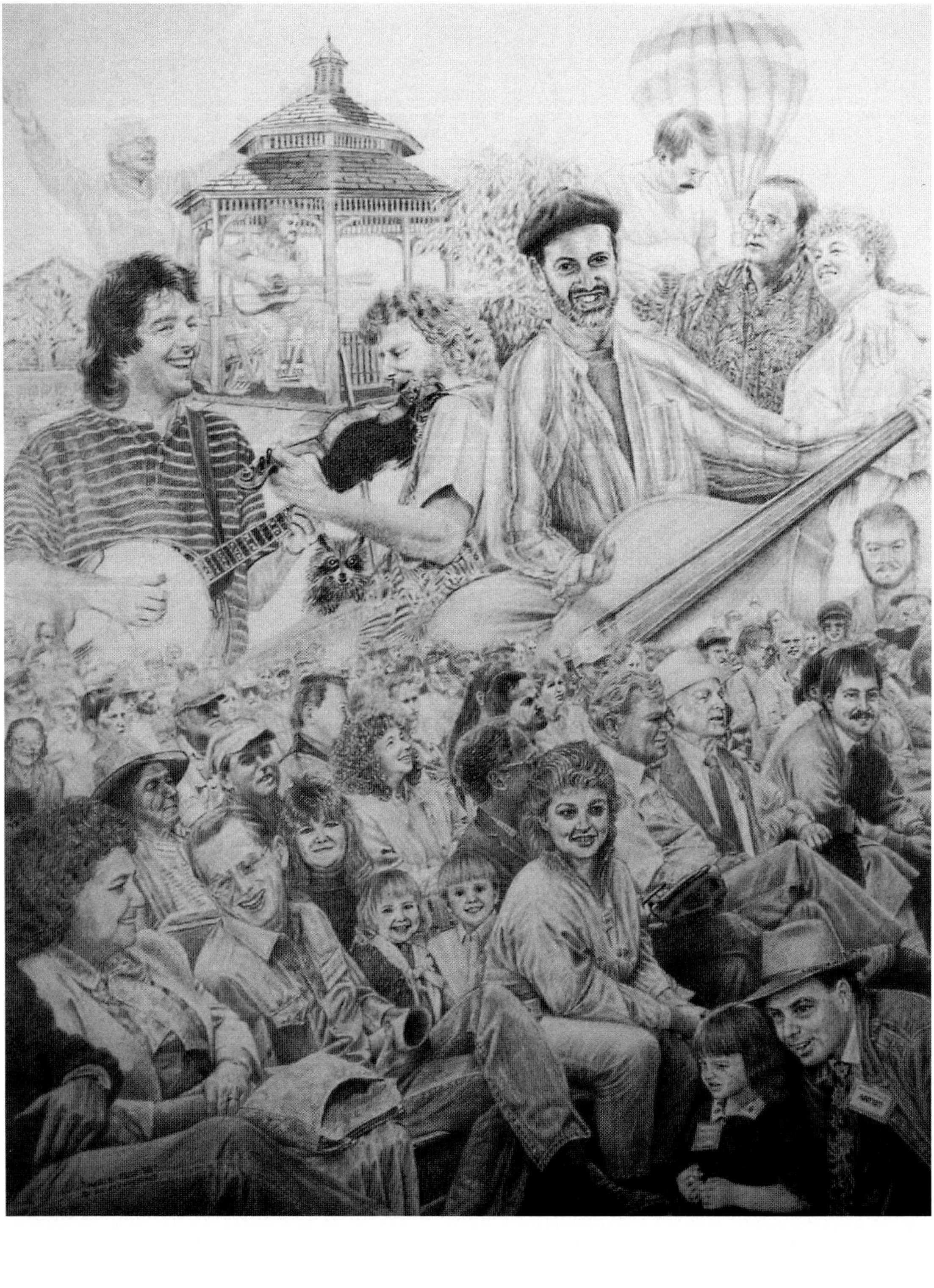

Merlefest
1996

This drawing portrays the MerleFest as it might be with the gazebo in the background. Several musicians are performing while others are drawn sitting in the audience, such as Doc Watson and Bill Monroe with some of the Nashville Bluegrass Band and members of Doc's family. The original was raffled at the event.

Homer Young
Master Quilter
1996

Through the medium of barter, this drawing became a prized possession of quilter Homer Young, and Willard and his wife have the pleasure of owning one of Homer's hand-stitched, king sized, double wedding ring patterned quilts.

> *It's very unusual to see a man quilting, but this man is a friend of mine who is disabled, a big stout man who looks like he could do anything, but he's not able to work, the last fellow you'd expect to be quilting. It's something he did as a little boy with his grandmother, and later when he became disabled, he and his wife started quilting. His wife would piece the quilt and Homer would do the intricate stitching designs. He's really good and has won lots of prizes. I see him at the annual Black Gold Festival in Hazard, Kentucky.*

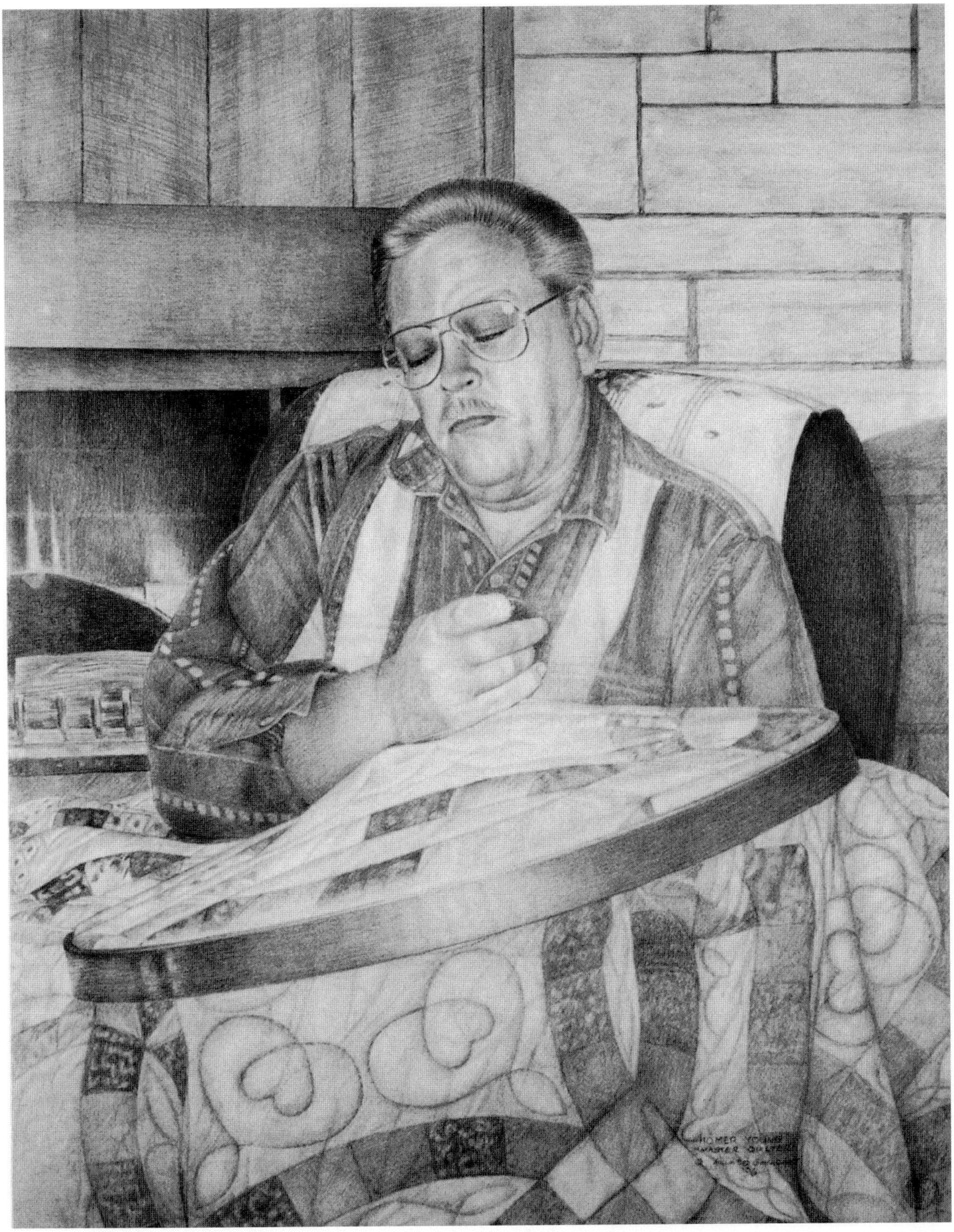
HOMER YOUNG
MASTER QUILTER

Grandma with Sweet Corn
1996

After the artist completed the original commissioned work for a family reunion, he received permission to reproduce prints. The print then completely sold out because the woman reminds so many people of their own grandmother in a similar scene of preparing sweet corn for canning, freezing, or just good eating.

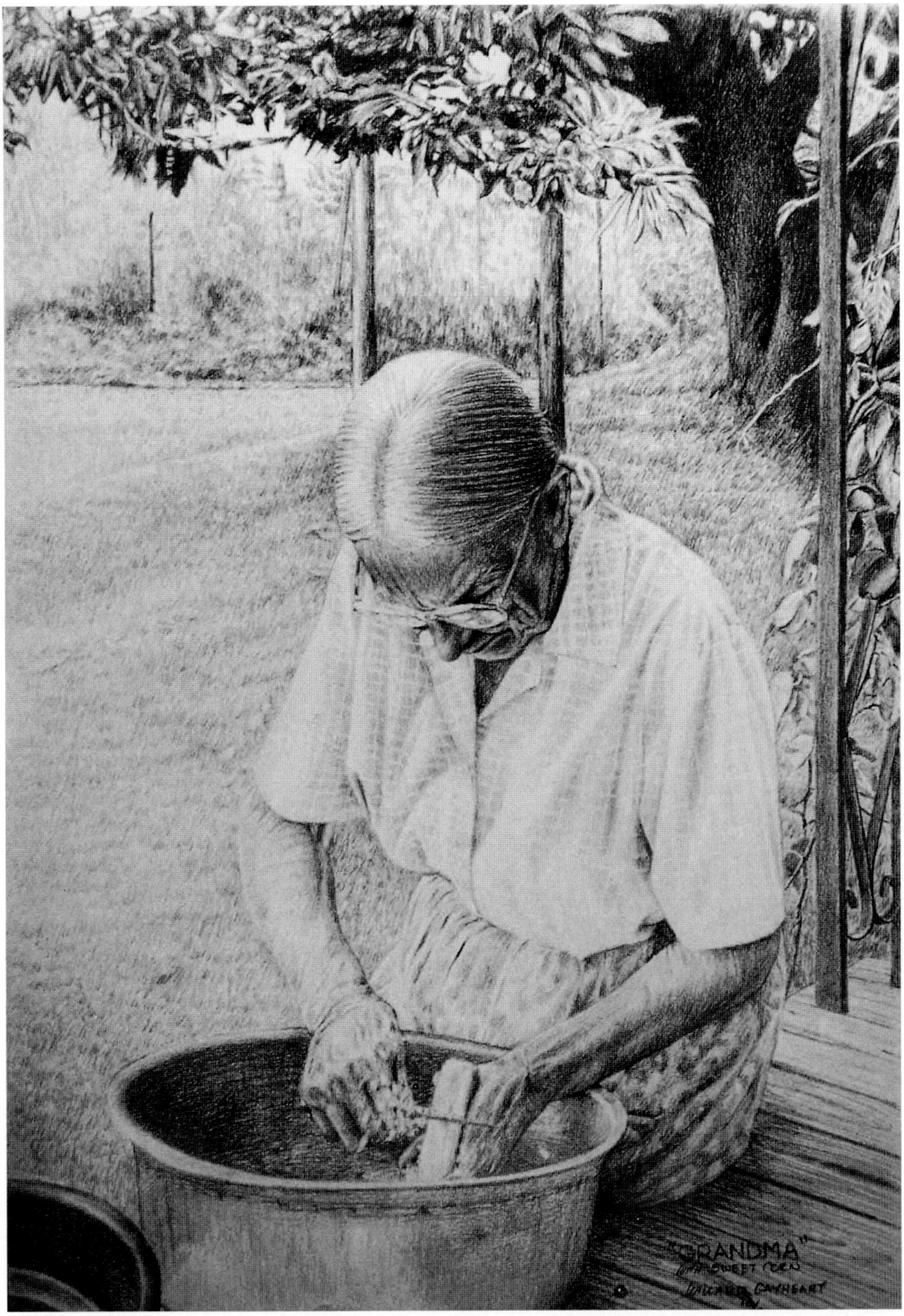
"GRANDMA"

Study of a Chairmaker
1996

Sherman Wooten is 91 years old and still making and selling chairs. From Wendover, Kentucky, where he lives in a cabin he built for himself and continues to work, this master crafter gets between $800 and $1,000 for his handcrafted rocking chairs.

Willard describes him as a "stately looking old timer with a long white beard and a heavy head of hair." His strong hands have been featured crafting his chairs in shows throughout the country, he's been written about many times, and Willard says he has "probably been the subject of a lot more art than I'll ever do."

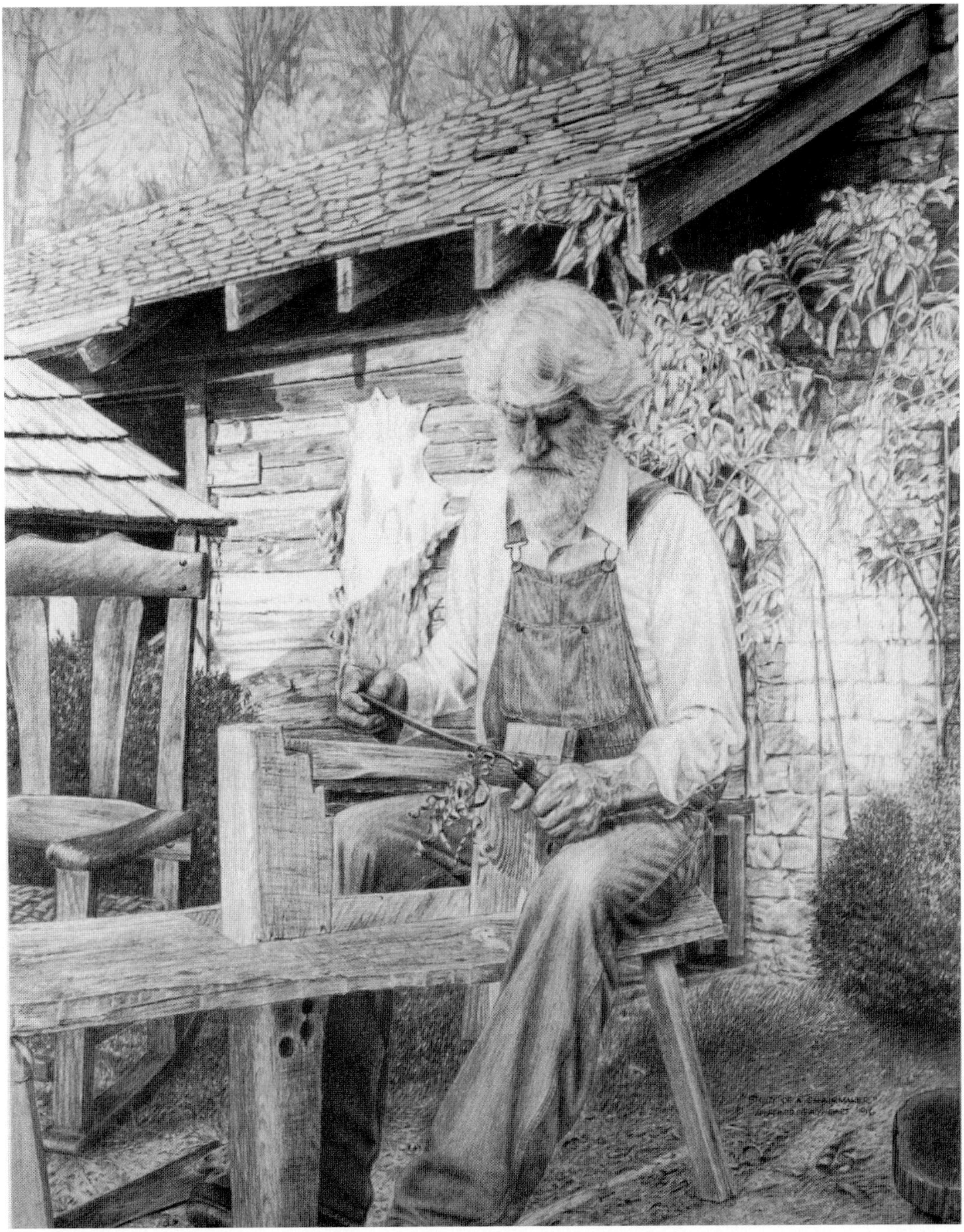

Country Music in the Beginning 1997

It is believed that the first commercial country music recordings were done in Bristol, Virginia, in 1927 by a representative from Victor Recording Company, later known as RCA Victor.

This is the beginning of what we know today as country music. The Victor label company rented a space in the old Taylor Christian Hat building in Bristol and invited people from all around to come and record. The Carter Family from over at Maces Springs near Hiltons, Virginia, heard about it or maybe read about it in the newspaper and decided to come and see if they could record. Jimmie Rodgers was working with a group down around Asheville, North Carolina, at the time and they came; and as it turns out, Jimmie's band fell out with him somehow and abandoned him and he wound up recording by himself, which is the best thing that ever happened because from those sessions Rodgers became famous and is today considered the father of country music. The Carter Family also became famous and it was from those sessions we get all the classics we listen to and have been kind of the standard for music down through the years. The Carter Family songs and Jimmie Rodgers songs are still being sung today. Jimmie Rodgers is probably the most popular country music star that ever lived.

The Birthplace of Country Music Alliance has established a Country Music Museum, and in 1997 Willard was commissioned to do a drawing in celebration of the 70th anniversary of the recordings.

Featured in the upper left of the drawing is the Stoneman family from Galax, Virginia; down to the right and dressed in a suit is Ralph Peer, the Victor representative; the Carter Family are at right in front of Peer; and Jimmie Rodgers is in the cap.

He was known as the Blue Yodeler and died at age 32 or so of TB in New York during a recording session. He was so well known that people gathered all along the train route used to take his body for burial in Meridian, Mississippi.

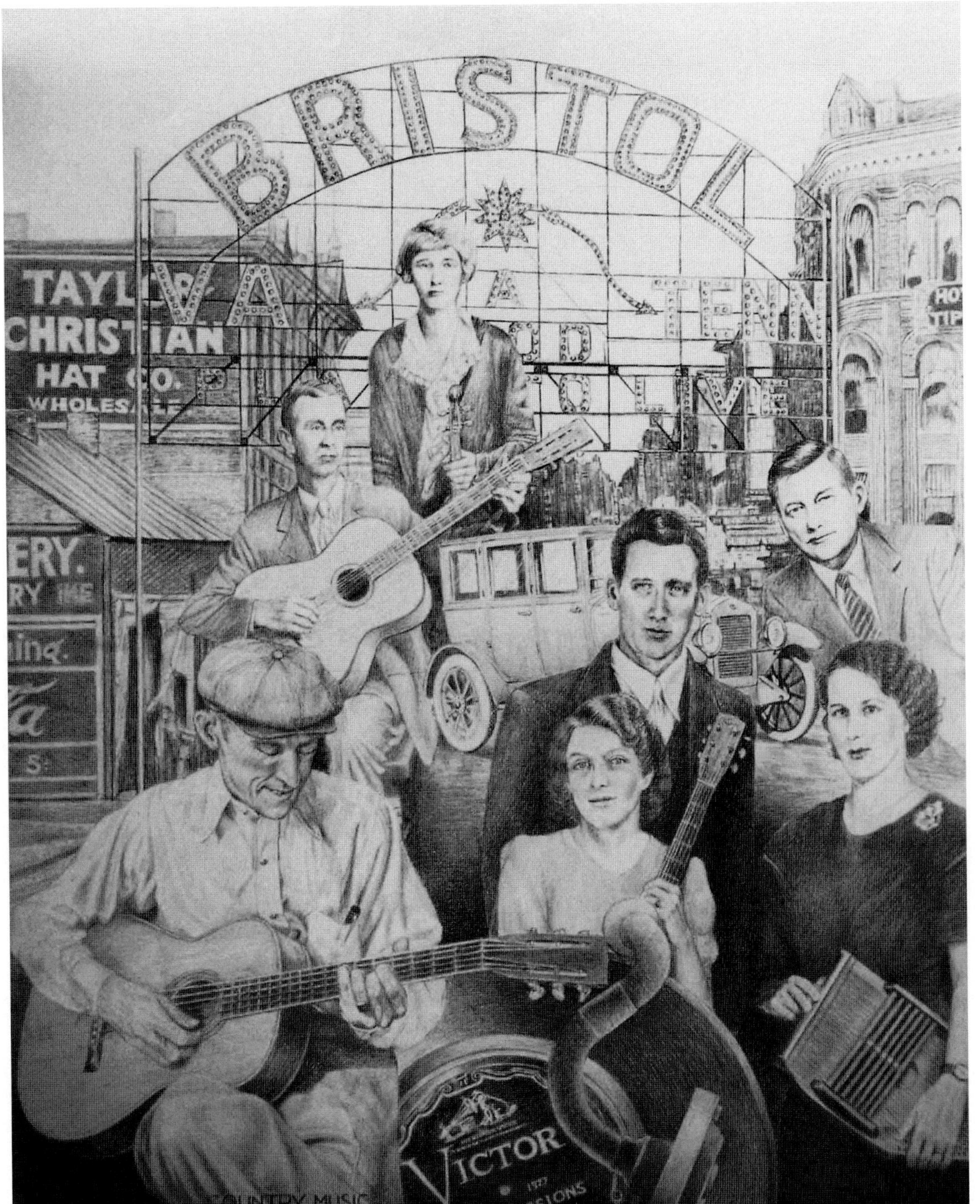
BRISTOL
VA
TENN
CHRISTIAN
HAT CO.
VICTOR
BRISTOL SESSIONS
COUNTRY MUSIC
in the beginning

Dori **1997**

Dori is Willard's granddaughter, and she was five years old at the time of this drawing with her cat, Minnie. A friend had visited members of the Gayheart family and snapped a picture of Dori standing in the family carport with her cat. She later mailed the picture to Willard and he set about with his thoughts of children and their pets to create this drawing with a very different background than the carport, one he felt better represented the region.

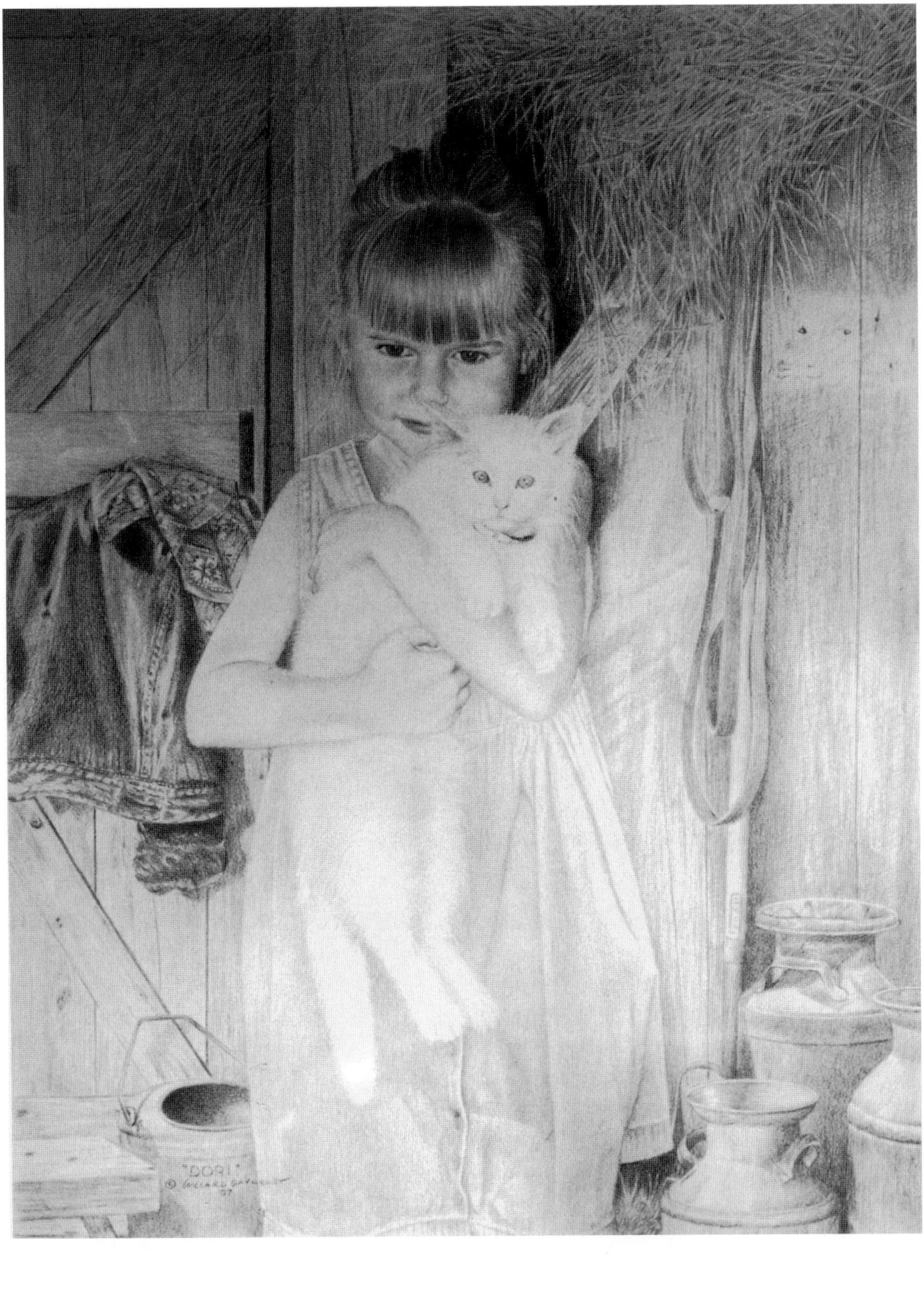
"DORI"

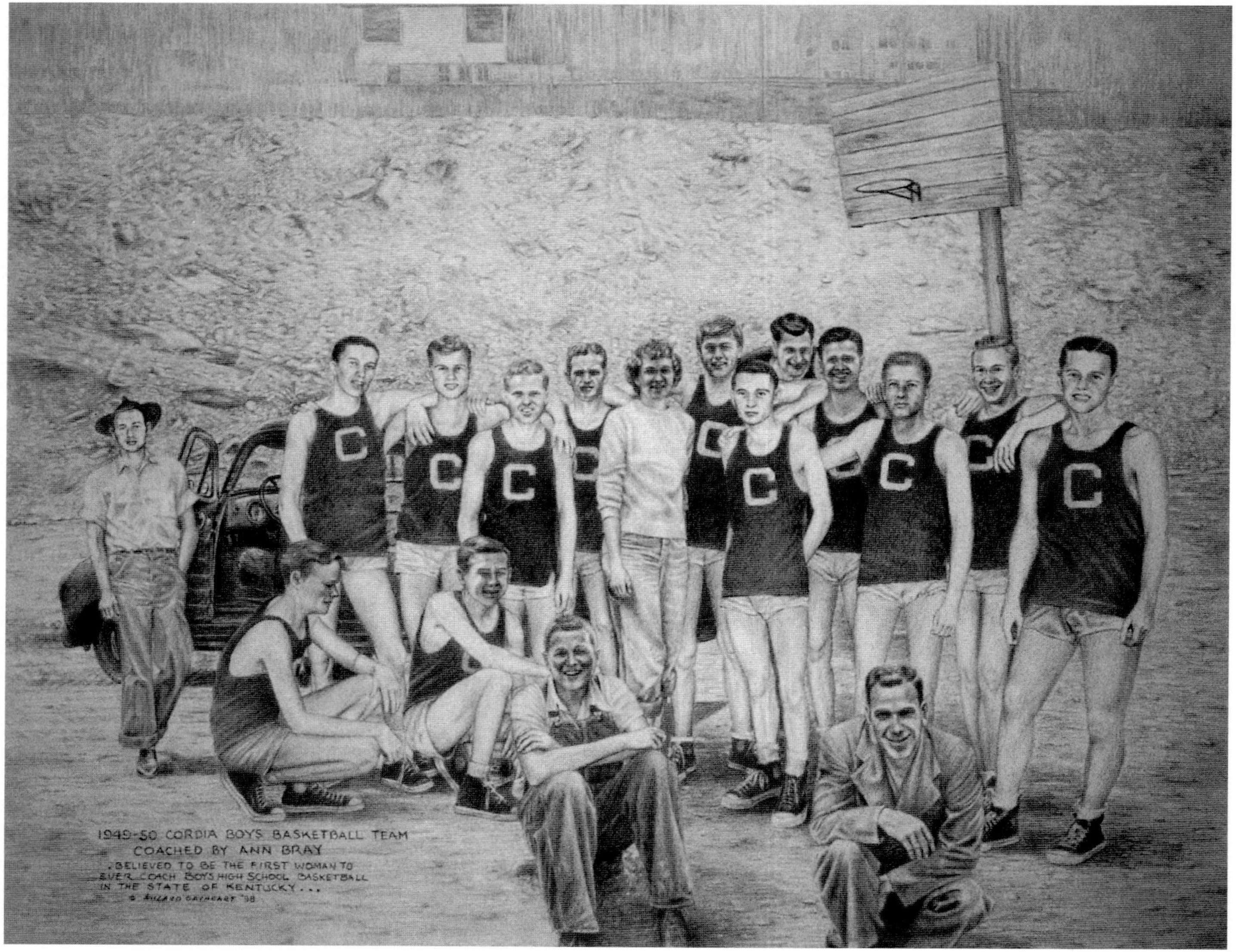
1949-50 CORDIA BOYS BASKETBALL TEAM
COACHED BY ANN BRAY
.BELIEVED TO BE THE FIRST WOMAN TO
EVER COACH BOYS HIGH SCHOOL BASKETBALL
IN THE STATE OF KENTUCKY...

1949-50 Cordia Boys' Basketball Team 1998

In 1998 the 1950 graduates of Cordia School, where Willard graduated in 1949, asked Willard to reconstruct what might have been if a team photograph had been made. The boys' basketball team of 1950 did not have a coach, and Miss Ann Bray volunteered to coach them her first year out of college and first year of teaching at the school.

> *That year the boys played their normal schedule and did fairly well and enjoyed playing, but especially enjoyed their young woman coach, which was highly unusual. They didn't have a photograph taken that year of their team and a few years ago thought it would sure be nice if they had some depiction of what their team would have been like if they'd had a photograph made, and so they commissioned me to do a drawing. We found all kinds of photographs that were scattered of each of the men on the team and Miss Bray and, as best we could, recreated what might have been if they'd had a camera and taken a photo out on the old dirt court with the basketball goal in the background.*

The resulting original was given to Miss Bray, and she in turn donated it to the school. Miss Bray married Bill Webb of Pulaski County, Virginia, and is now retired.

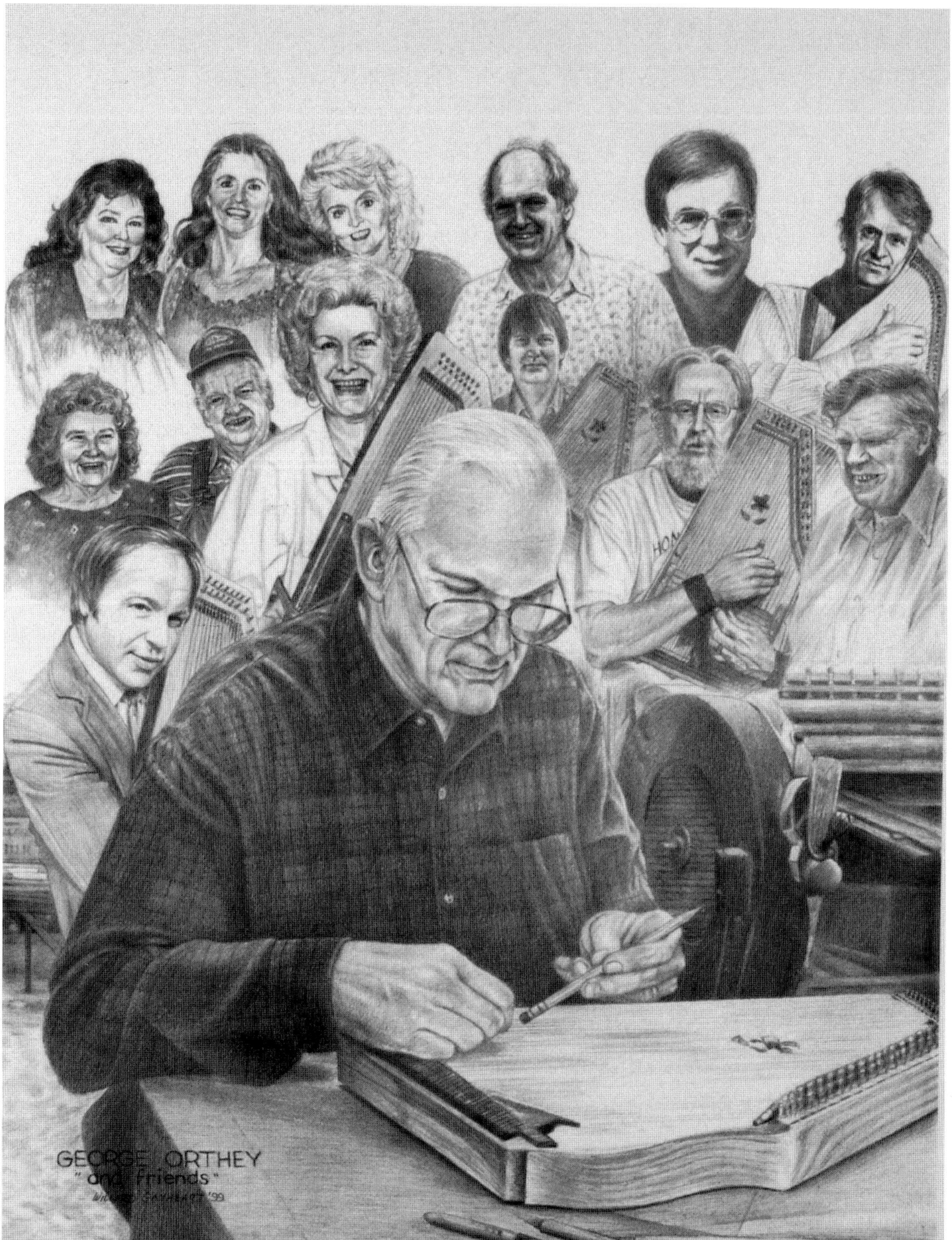
GEORGE ORTHEY
"and Friends"

George Orthey and Friends 1999

After seeing the drawing Willard did for the Birthplace of Country Music Alliance in Bristol, Mary Lou Orthey requested that he complete a drawing of her husband with some of his musician friends in the background.

George Orthey is a well-known autoharp maker from Pennsylvania, and when his wife asked the price of an original drawing, Willard says, "a little bartering went on." Consequently, George Orthey received the portrait of himself surrounded by his wife holding an autoharp, Anita, June, and Helen Carter, Bill Clifton, John Sebastian, and Mike Seeger along with Janette and Joe Carter, Patsy Stoneman, Bryan Bowers, Doc Watson, and Little Roy Lewis. Willard received "a beautiful Orthey autoharp."

Her First Castle
1999

A drawing of Willard's granddaughter, Sarah, at age two playing in her sandbox, but recreated to look like a visit to the beach. Willard had lots of pictures of Sarah in her sandbox and decided to pursue his vision of portraying her as if she might be on her first visit to the ocean.

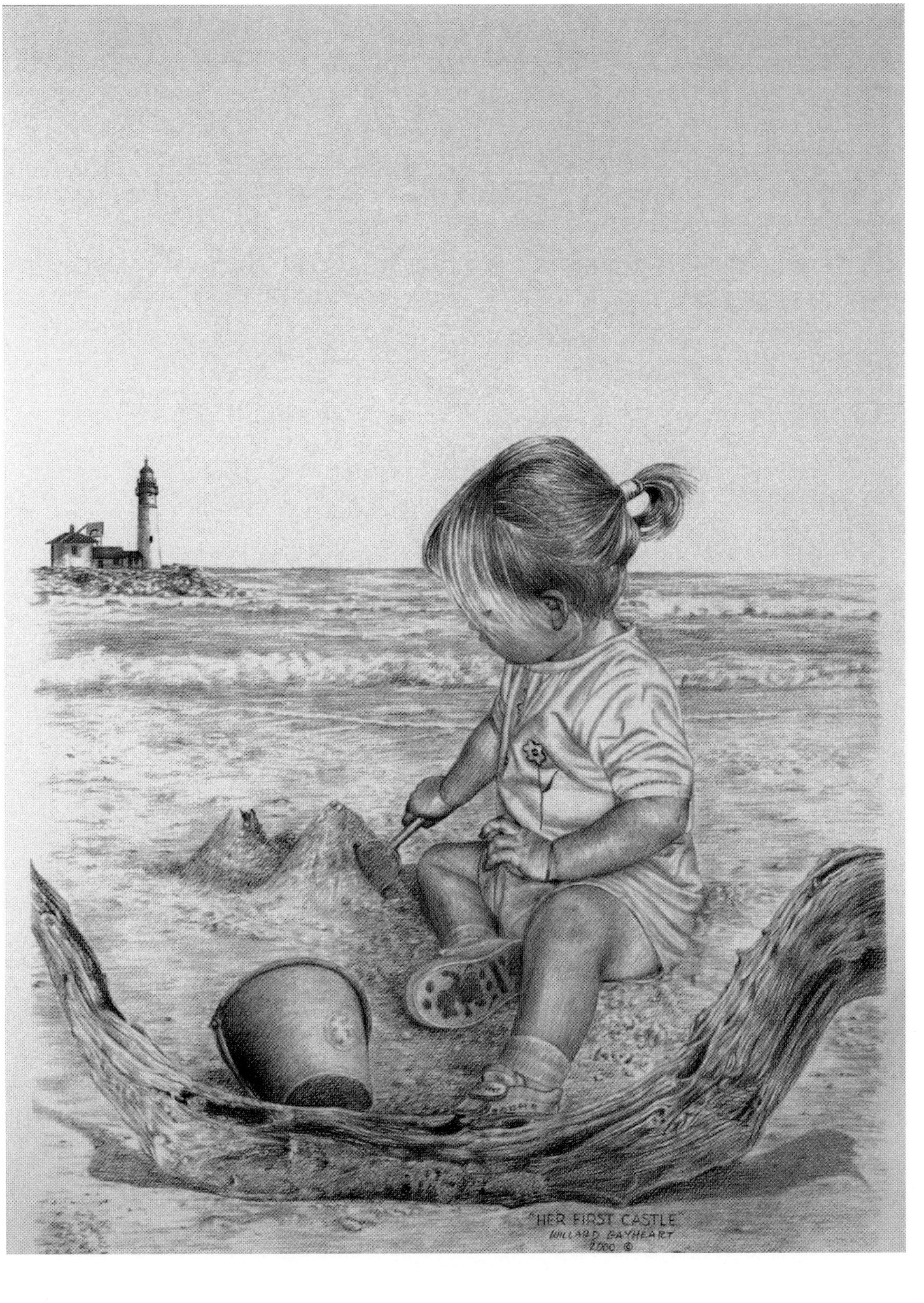
"HER FIRST CASTLE"
WILLARD GAYHEART
2000 ©

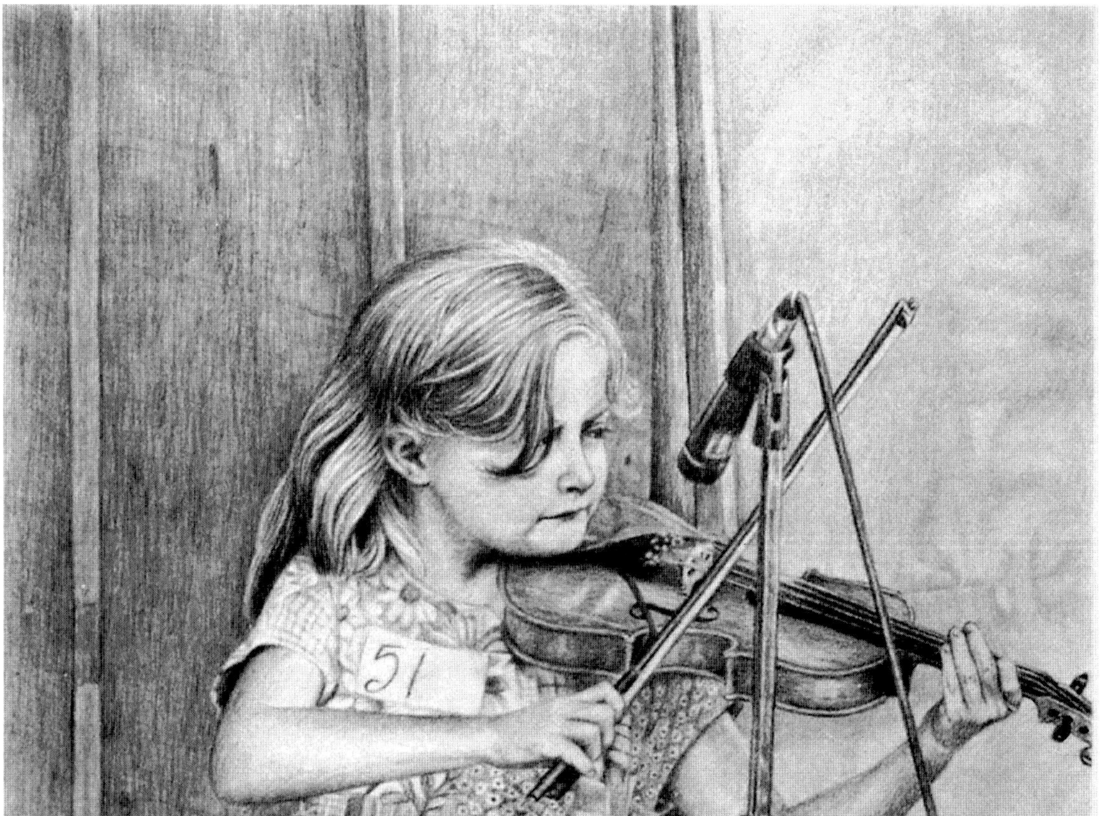
51
Both share a name and beauty
Told through Song & Sight
The leaf that carpets mountain folds
As Fiddles Echo August nights
Scott Freeman '98
CONTESTANT NO. 51
© WILLARD GAYHEART
'98

Contestant #51
1999

Following the 1998 Old Fiddlers' Convention in Galax, Virginia, visitors Willard had met from Vancouver Island, Canada, sent him copies of photographs from the convention.

The child in this drawing participated in the 1998 fiddle playing competition with her father, and Willard did the drawing of her for the Chamber of Commerce fundraising raffle at the 1999 convention. Attempts to find the young family were unsuccessful and they did not return to the event in 1999. However, in 2000, Willard was pleased that they did attend and sought him out after hearing about the drawing of the girl. Much to his surprise, the subject of his drawing appeared at his art booth with an identical twin sister. Though from a musical family, the twin sister did not play the fiddle.

All in the Family I
1999

Jack Tottle, director of the Bluegrass and Country Music Program at East Tennessee State University in Johnson City, Tennessee, asked Willard to complete a drawing for him showing the relationships among various styles of tradition-based American music. After a great deal of research time, Willard did the drawing depicting many of the country's famous musicians.

The drawing includes: the A.P. Carter Family, influenced by Leslie Riddle, a guitar player from Kingsport, Tennessee; Jimmie Rodgers, influenced by Louis Armstrong, who actually performed with Rodgers on some of his recordings; Bob Wills, influenced by Bessie Smith, a jazz singer; Bill Monroe, influenced by Arnold Schultz, a blues guitarist who lived near Monroe's home place in Rosine, Kentucky; Dobro player Bashful Brother Oswald, who played with Roy Acuff on the Grand Ole Opry and was influenced by Joseph Kekuku's Hawaiian guitar, an instrument much like the Dobro in how it's played and its sound; Earl Scruggs, influenced by an African American banjo player also named Scruggs from near Shelby, North Carolina; Elvis Presley, influenced by a guitar player, Arthur "Big Boy" Crudup, from around Memphis; and Hank Williams, influenced by Rufus "Tee Tot" Payne, a street guitar player from Alabama. With the exception of Joseph Kekuku, each of the influences listed here was an African American musician.

An enlarged mural of Willard's drawing, entitled *All in the Family II*, was completed by North Carolinian muralist Marianne DiNapoli Mylet and now hangs as the focal point in the lobby of Sherrod Library at East Tennessee State, where Willard was honored in February 2002 for his work.

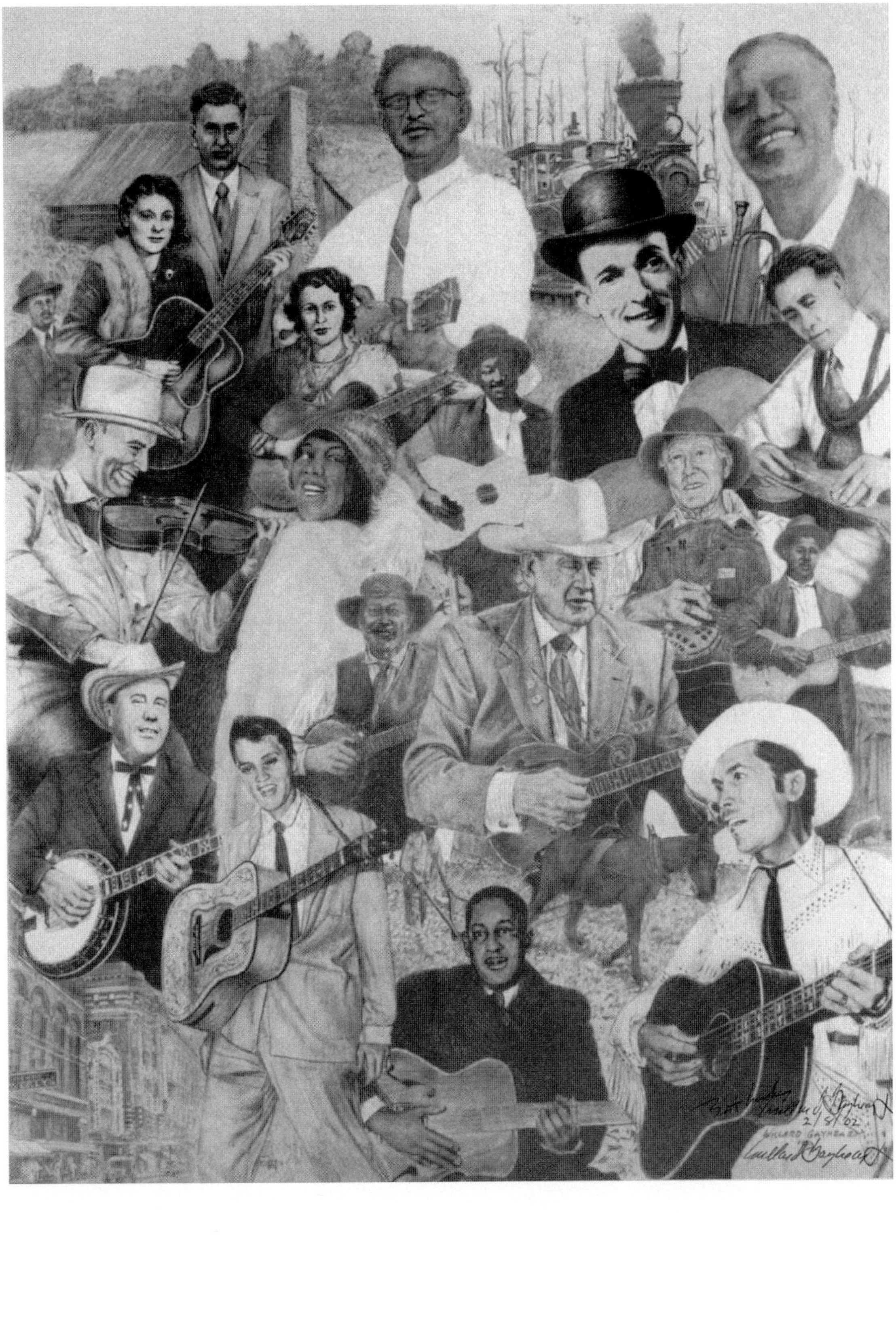
2/8/02
WILLARD GAYHEART

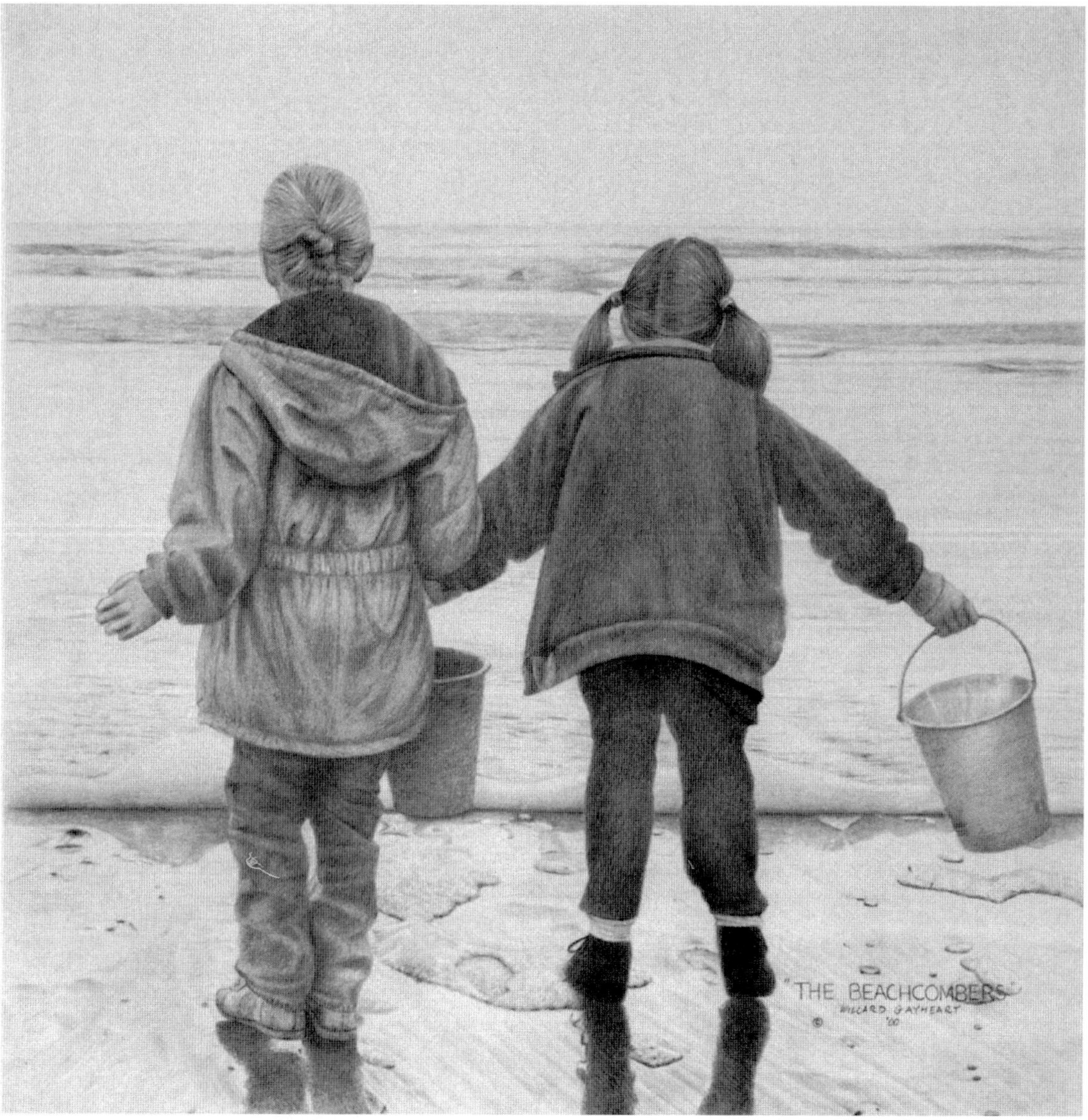
"THE BEACHCOMBERS"
WILLARD GAYHEART
© '00

The Beachcombers
2000

Willard's granddaughter, Dori (left), at the beach in winter with her friend Nikki.

With no faces showing, these children represent many children.

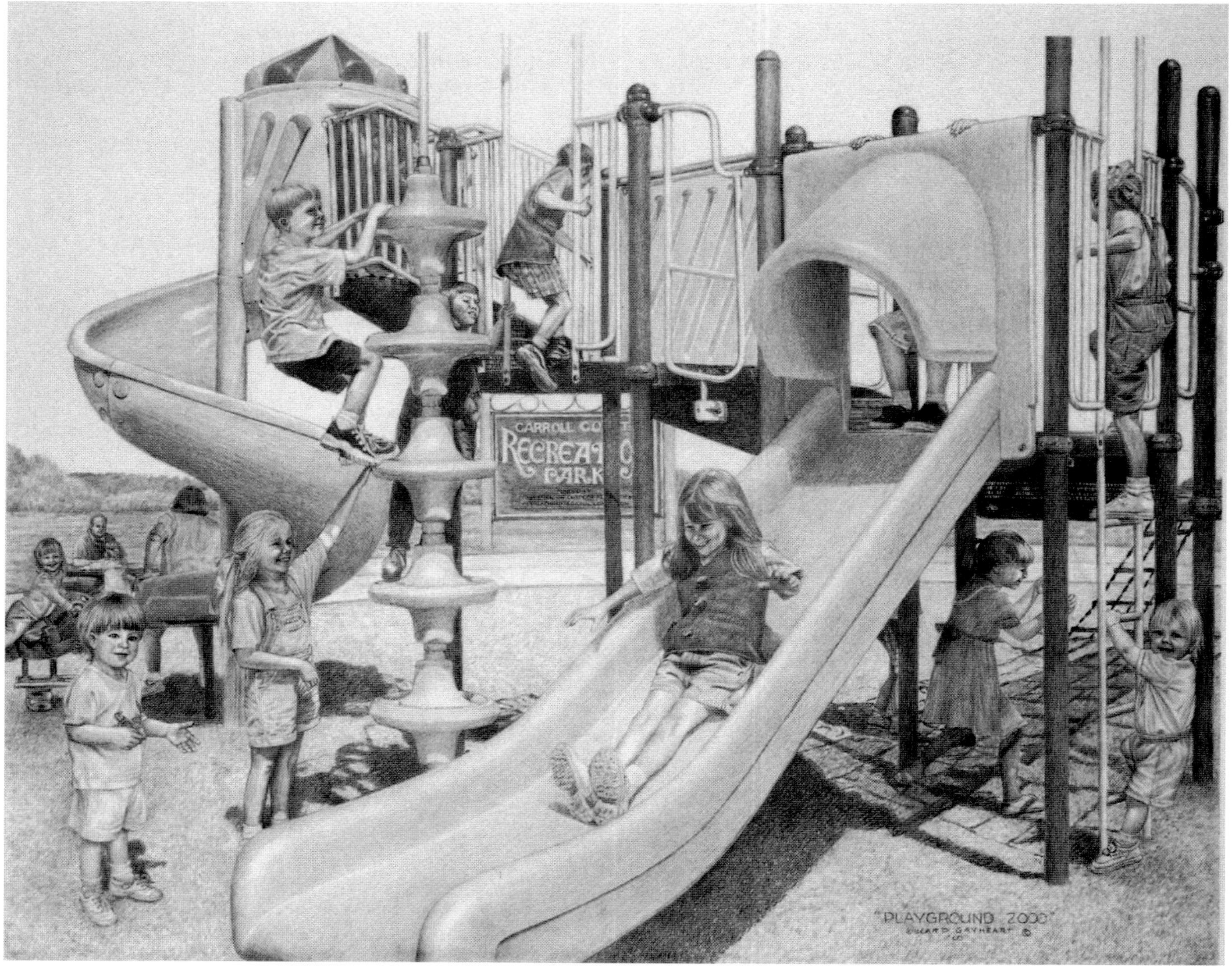
CARROLL CO
RECREA
PARK
"PLAYGROUND 2000"
GAYHEART ©

Playground 2000
2000

I donated this drawing as a fundraiser for a community playground at the intersection of Interstate 77 and Route 58 near Hillsville, Virginia. Brian Spencer, manager of the Shoney's Restaurant, headed up a drive to build this playground close to Shoney's on county property. He got the idea to build a state-of-the-art playground that would cost about $100,000 and he spent a couple of years soliciting donations and raising money, and I did the drawing as a fundraiser and Brian sold the prints and made several thousand dollars.

Mary Faith
2000

Bumper stickers and tee shirts display Mary Faith's patented motto, "Music really does make the world a better place." A former professional musician during the folk boom of the seventies, she currently is the owner of the John Pearse Company in Pennsylvania, a company which sells strings for musical instruments.

Willard says, "She's such a neat person." He met her nearly ten years ago after he did the first drawing of Doc Watson. On Doc's guitar and other instruments he drew a little arm rest, which protects the edge of the guitar, with the Pearse label drawn on the piece and met Mary Faith after she saw the drawings and was so pleased at the advertising resulting from sales of his prints. Like Willard, she is a regular at the Old Fiddlers' Convention, and this drawing was raffled at the event in 2000 to raise money for the Galax Chamber of Commerce.

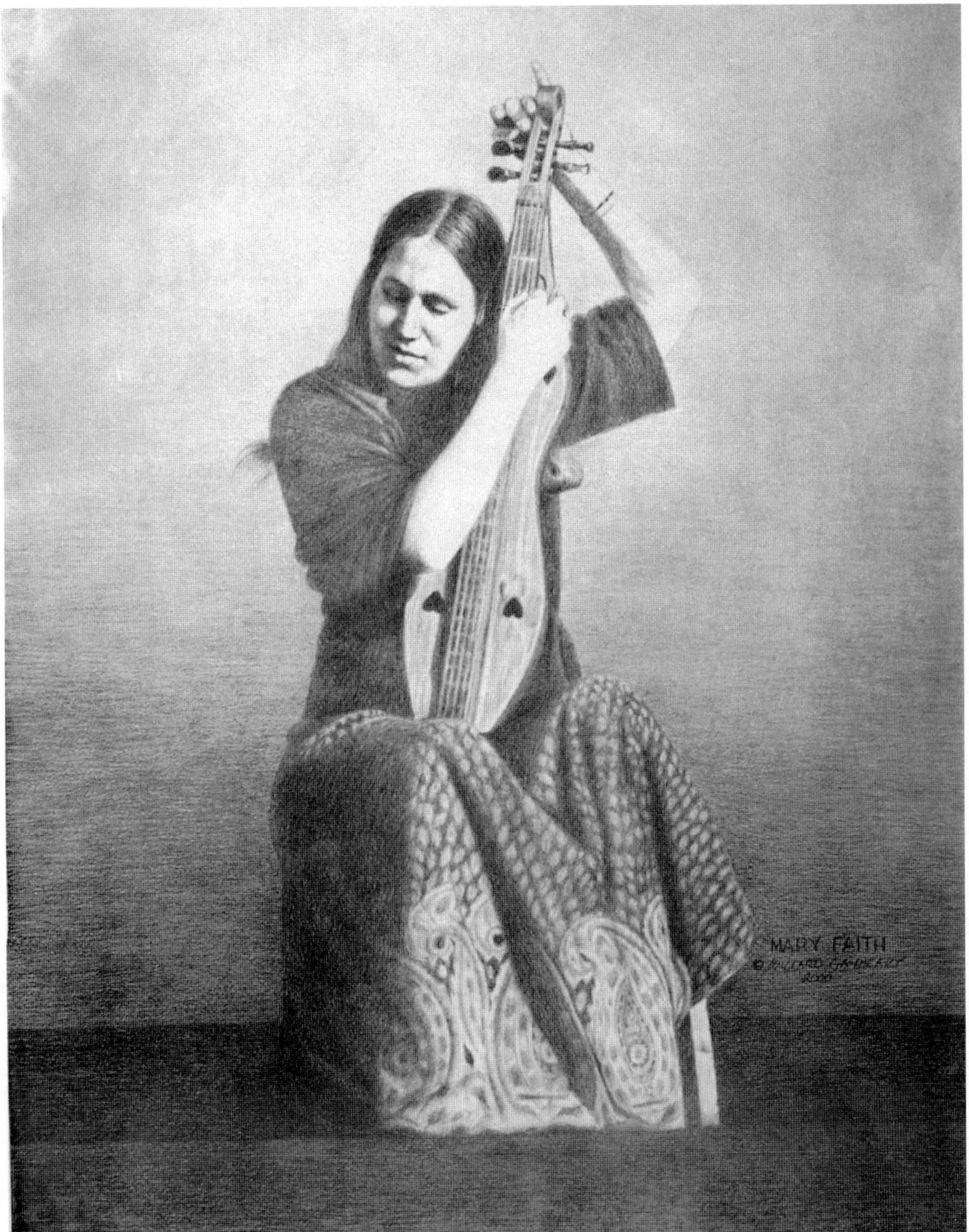
MARY FAITH

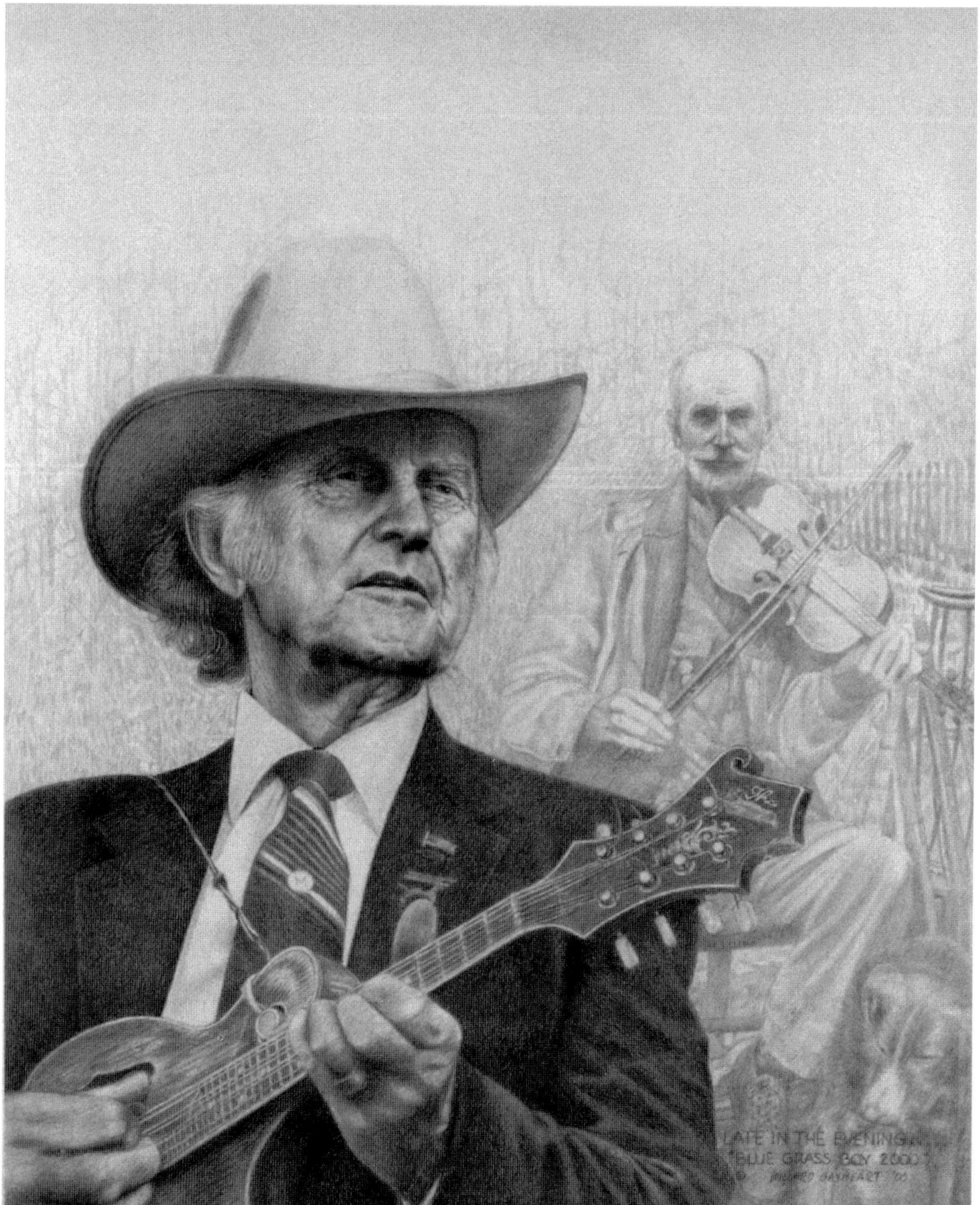
LATE IN THE EVENING
"BLUE GRASS BOY 2000"

Late in the Evening 2000

This is just a dream of mine, to do these drawings each year and know where they're going, and hopefully the originals will someday be displayed in the museum at the homeplace of Bill Monroe. I hope it happens.

Willard is sincere as he talks about the commissioned works he's already completed and those yet to be done.

Late in the Evening, lifted from the famous Monroe song "Uncle Pen," was a tribute to an uncle with whom the bluegrass legend spent a great deal of time in his lifetime. Uncle Pen was a musician and had a great influence on Monroe. This is the first in a series of eleven drawings commissioned by the Bill Monroe Festival held annually in Rosine, Kentucky. The commissioned works are to continue until the year 2011, the 100th birthday of Bill Monroe. Over the fifty or so years that Monroe played, there were over two hundred Bluegrass Boys who performed with him, and each year different performers are presented with one of Gayheart's prints.

This is quite a thing for me, being a bluegrass musician, to be able to do these drawings.

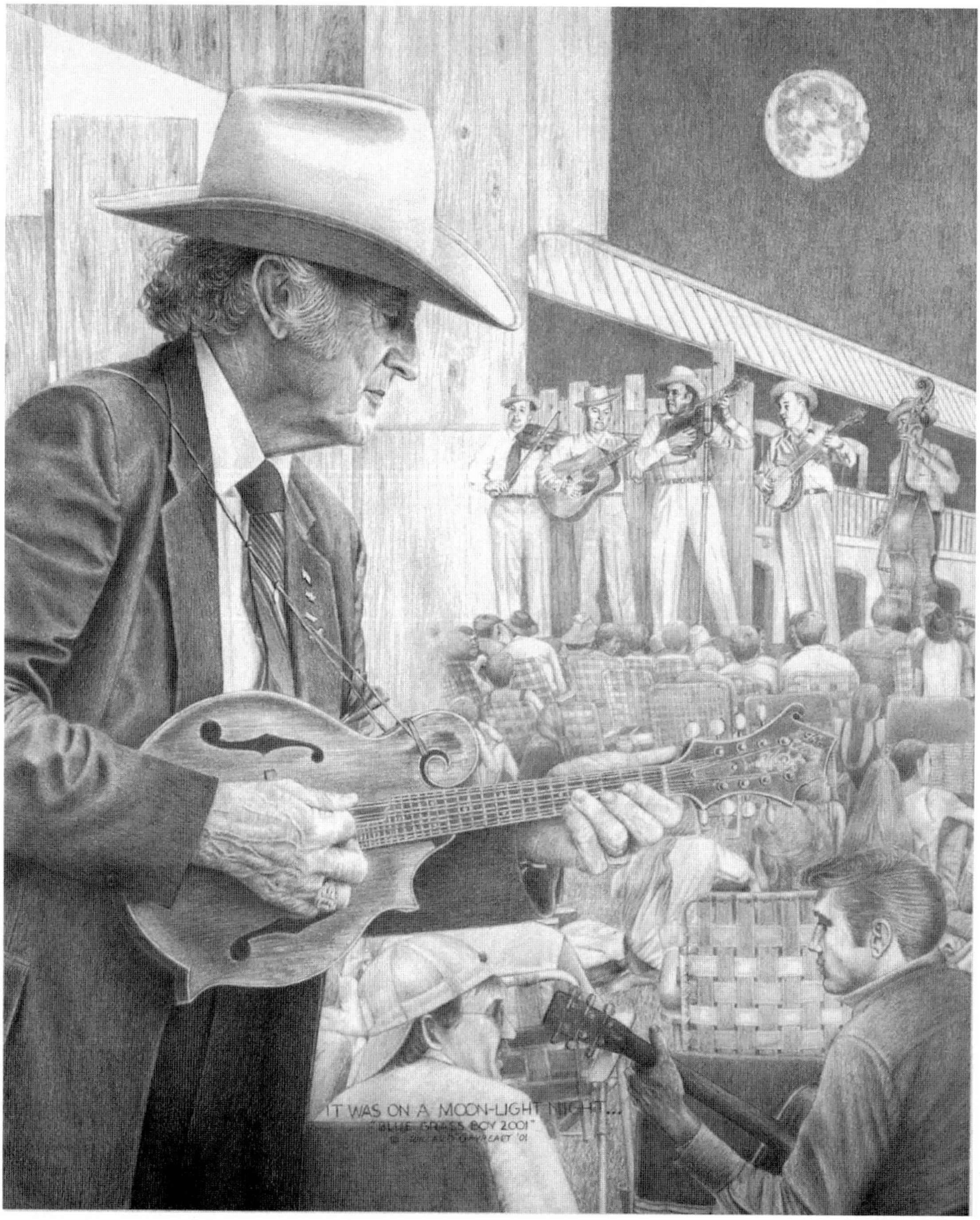
IT WAS ON A MOON-LIGHT NIGHT...
"BLUE GRASS BOY 2001"

It Was on a Moonlight Night
2001

Each title in the series of Bill Monroe drawings is taken from a line from one of Monroe's songs. This is the second in the series of eleven, and the title is taken from the first line of "Blue Moon of Kentucky." Featured in the drawing are Lester Flatt and Earl Scruggs, members of Monroe's band around 1946. Elvis Presley is drawn in the front because one of his first recordings was a rendition of "Blue Moon of Kentucky," which flattered Bill Monroe. Willard's group of musicians, the Highlanders, opened a few shows for Bill Monroe and his Blue Grass Boys.

Doug Hutchins, a schoolteacher from Stokes County, North Carolina, who once played with the Blue Grass Boys, works with Willard in suggesting the titles for the drawings. He also acquires the original and sees that each of the former Blue Grass Boys, numbering around 200, gets a copy of the print at their annual reunion held each Memorial Day weekend at Monroe's home in Rosine, Kentucky. Then, about 1,500 of the prints are available for public purchase.

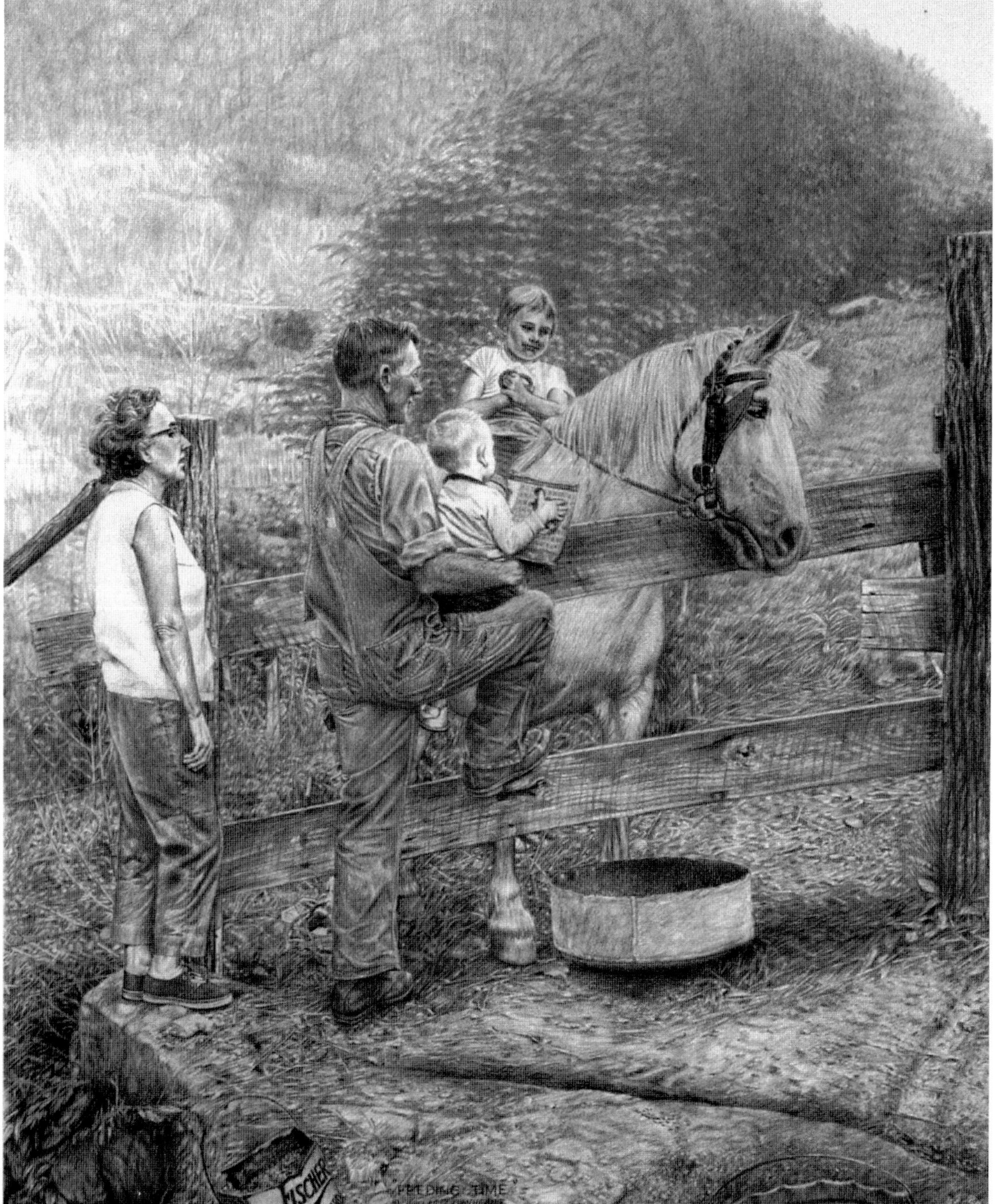
FISCHER
PURE LARD
FEEDING TIME

Feeding Time
2001

A commissioned work, this is a scene along Lotts Creek in Knott County, Kentucky, where Willard grew up. David and Mabel Russell are holding a grandson. A daughter, one of eight children they raised and college educated, is on the horse at their farm.

A Bird in the Hand
2001

Several years ago Willard was given a photograph by a man at a festival in Kentucky with a request that a drawing be done for the man's family. The man's daughter had photographed him holding the hummingbird and surrounded by the grandchildren. Without the family's knowledge, he wanted this drawing done as a surprise. Interestingly, Willard did not see the man for a while and when he finally completed the drawing and returned to the Kentucky festival with the original and prints, he tried to locate the man with no success. Finally, he found someone who recognized the family and learned the man had died. Willard eventually located the remaining family members who were "shocked and happy" to see the drawing. They now have the original and each family member has a print.

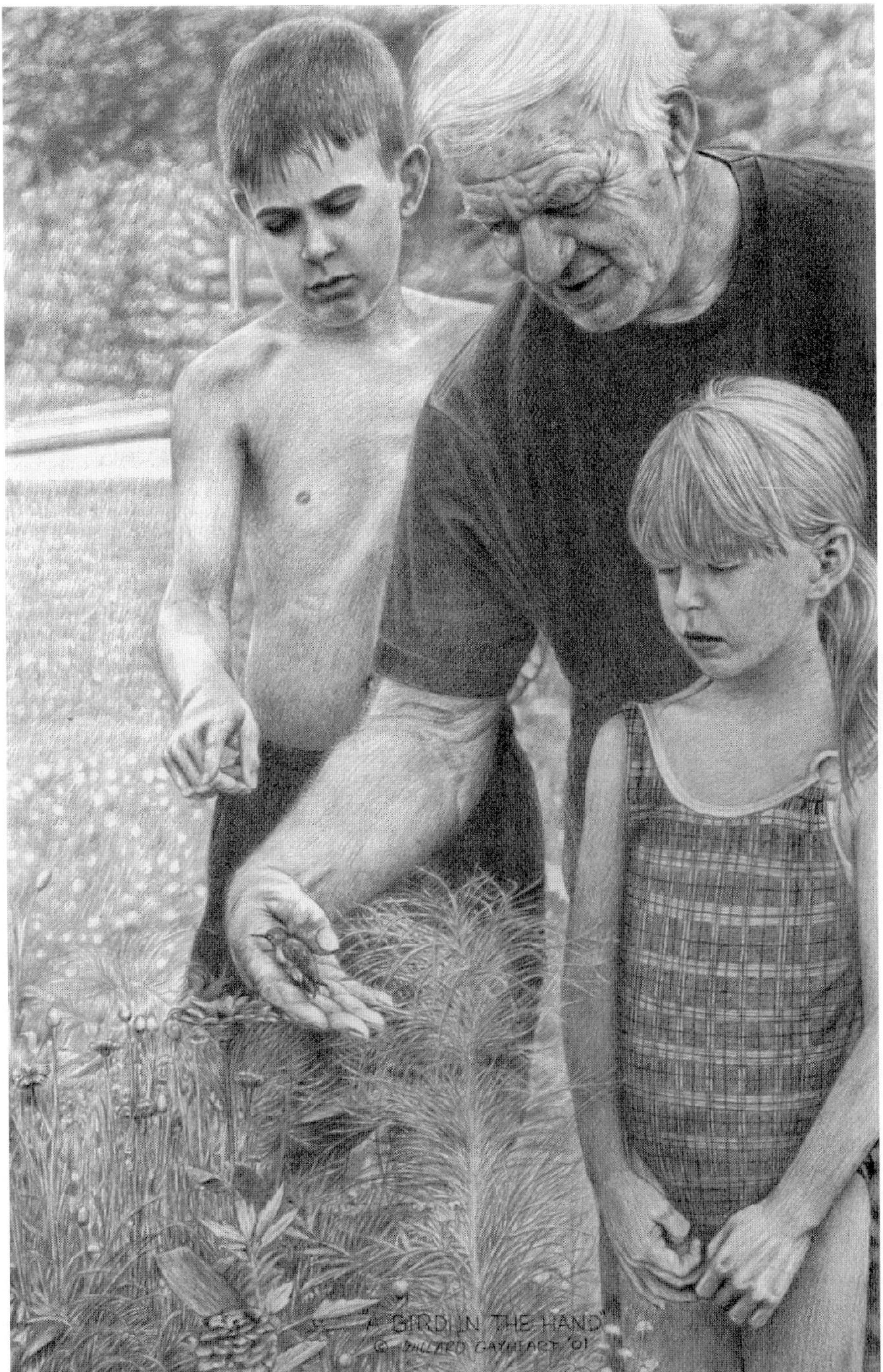
"A BIRD IN THE HAND"
© DILLARD GAYHEART '01

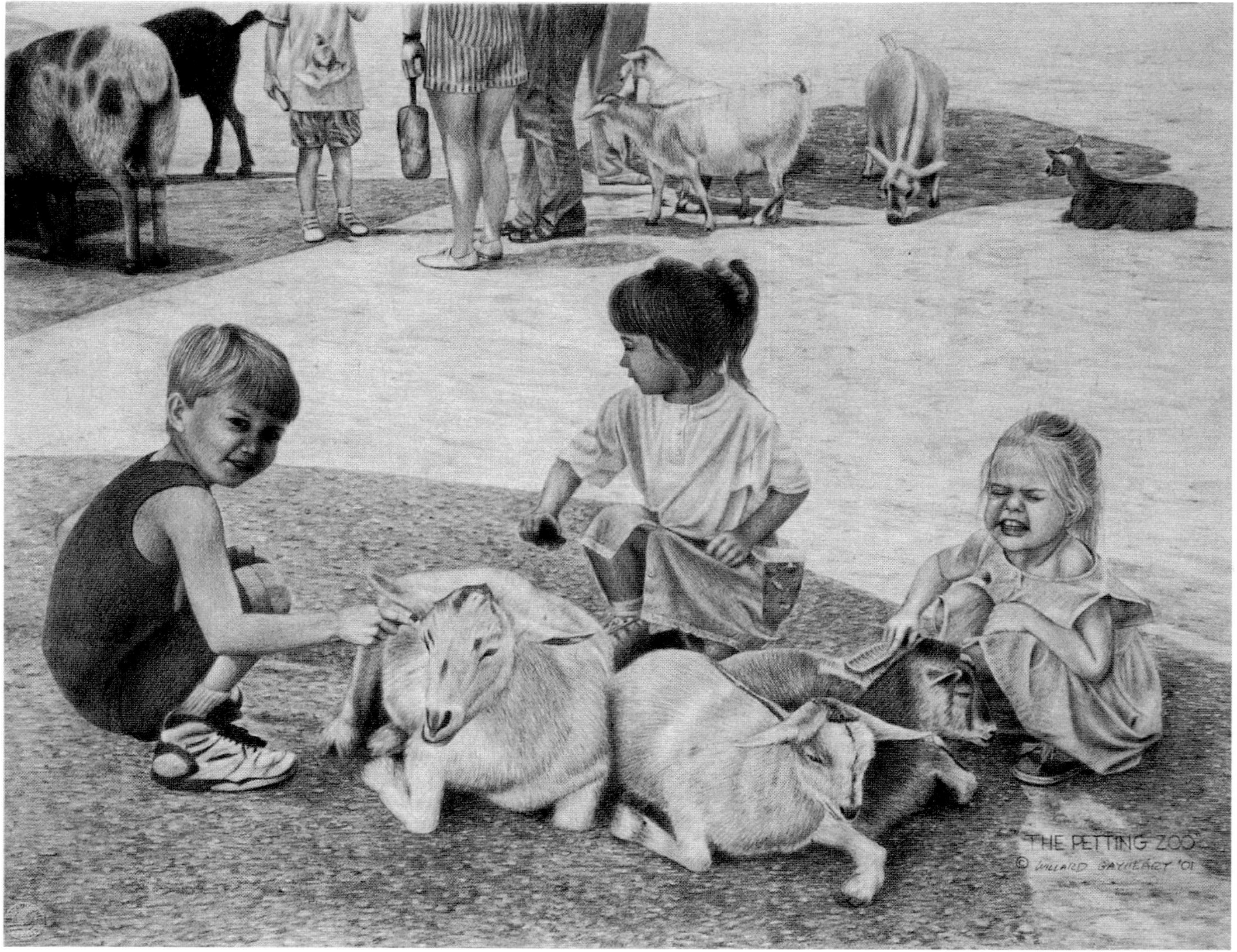
"THE PETTING ZOO"

The Petting Zoo 2001

A drawing featuring the grimacing granddaughter, Dori, and her friends Nikki and C.C. Conner at a petting zoo.

The Dreamer
2001

Representing anyone who aspires to be like the legendary Doc Watson, this drawing was completed in 2001 and presented to the Galax Chamber of Commerce to raffle as their 2002 fundraiser at the annual Old Fiddlers' Convention.

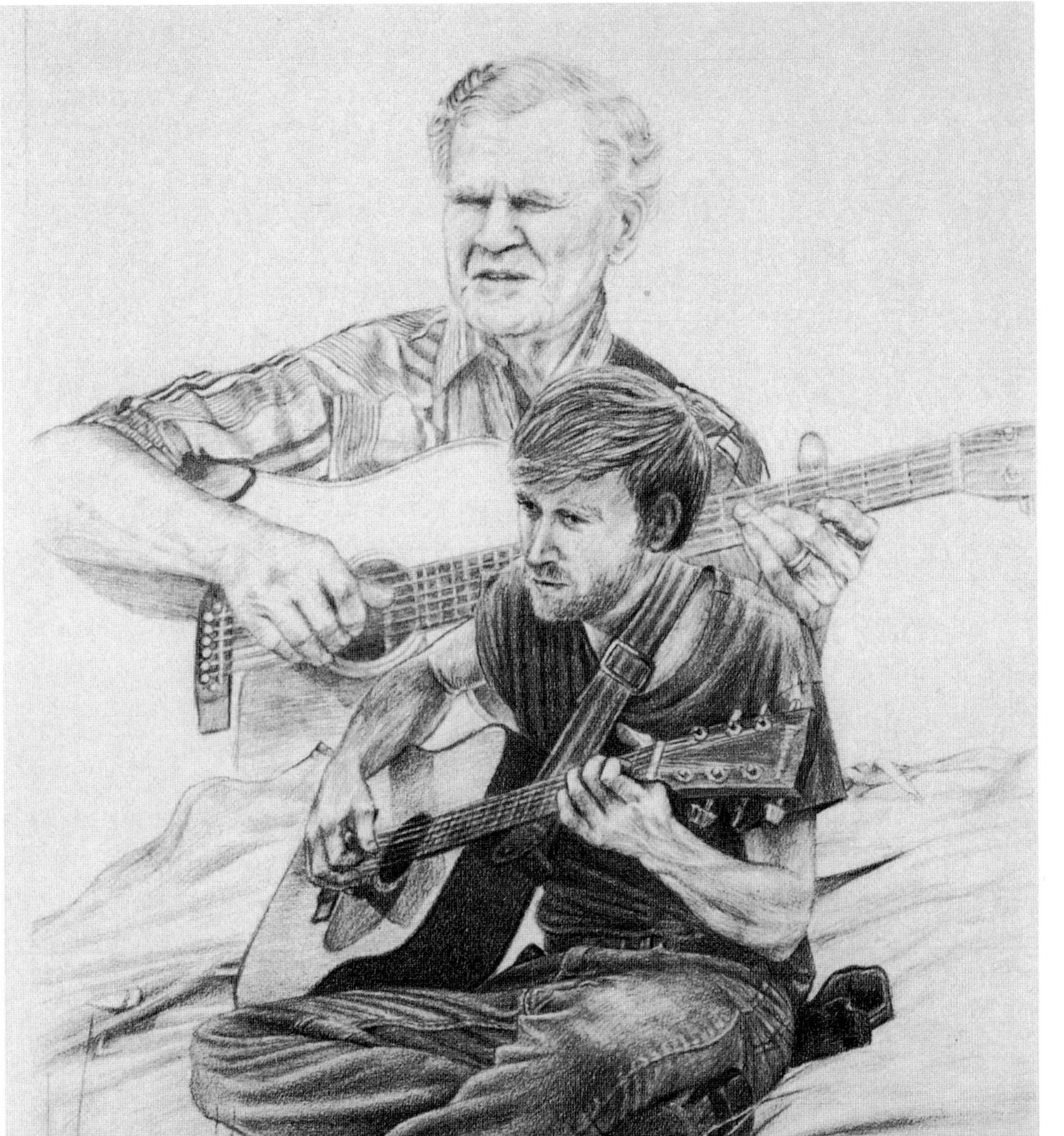
"THE DREAMER"
© Willard Gayheart
'02
John Pearse
Strings
THE WORLD A BETTER PLACE

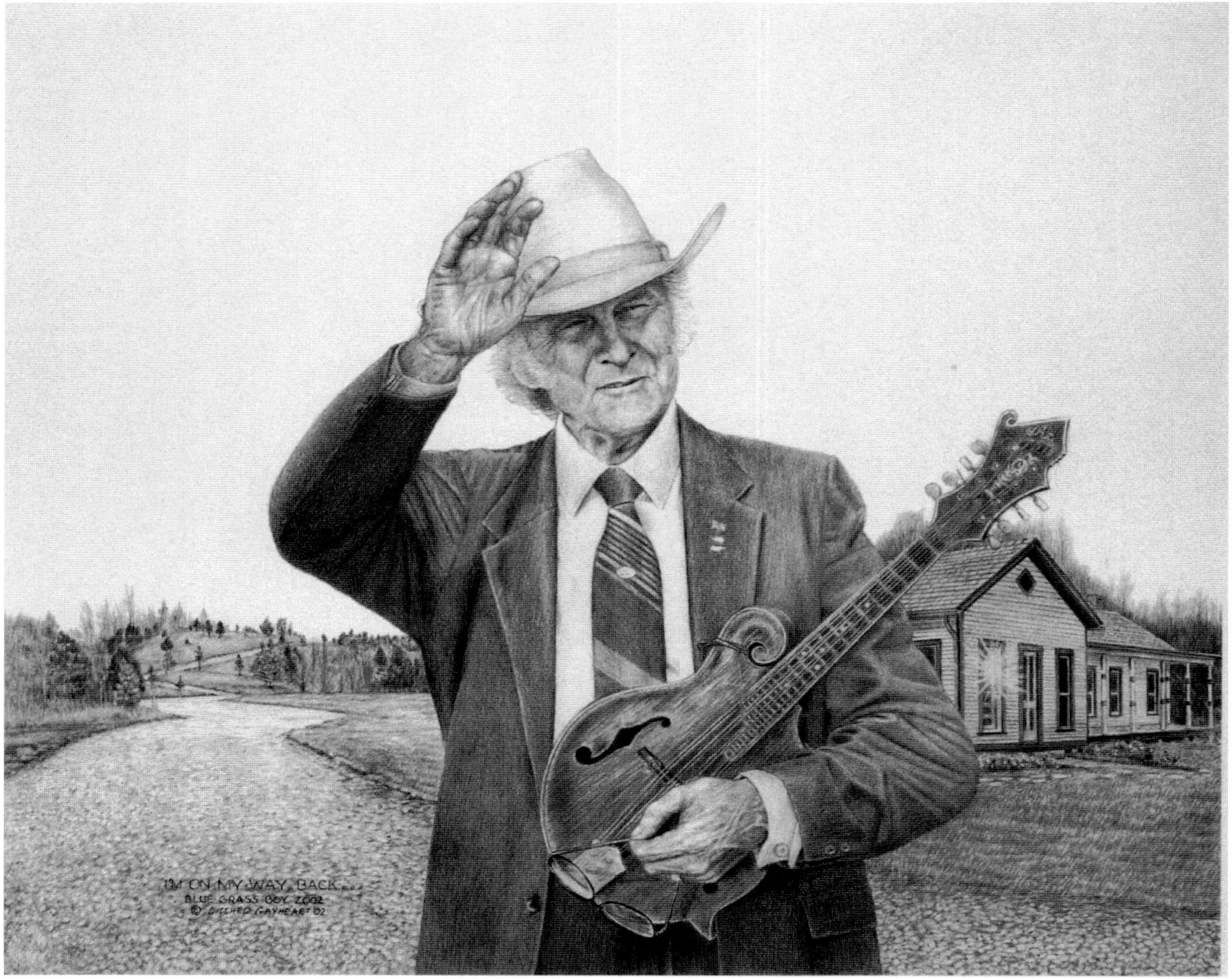
I'M ON MY WAY BACK...
BLUE GRASS BOY 2002

I'm on My Way Back
2002

Taken from the Monroe song "I'm on My Way Back to the Old Home," this is the third drawing in the series of eleven to be done for the Bill Monroe Festival. The road featured in the drawing is the road leading to Monroe's childhood home.

BIBLIOGRAPHY

Arnow, Harriett. *The Dollmaker*. New York: Macmillan Publishing, 1954.

Bolgiano, Chris. *The Appalachian Forest*. Mechanicsburg, Pennsylvania: Stackpole Books, 1998.

Constanz, George. *Hollows, Peepers & Highlanders*. Missoula, Montana: Mountain Press Publishing, 1994.

Dunn, Durwood. *Cades Cove: The Life and Death of a Southern Appalachian Community*. Knoxville: University of Tennessee Press, 1988.

Dykeman, Wilma. *The Tall Woman*. Newport, Tennessee: Wakestone Books, 1962.

Eller, Ronald D. *Miners, Millhands and Mountaineers*. Knoxville: University of Tennessee Press, 1982.

Higgs, Robert J., and Ambrose N. Manning. *Appalachia Inside Out, Vols. 1 & 2*. Knoxville: University of Tennessee Press, 1995.

Jones, Loyal. *Appalachian Values*. Ashland, Kentucky: The Jesse Stuart Foundation, 1994.

Mashburn, William H. *Mountain Summer*. Blacksburg, Virginia: Pocahontas Press, 1990.

McNeil, Nellie, and Joyce Squibb. *A Southern Appalachian Reader*. Boone, North Carolina: Appalachian Consortium Press, 1989.

Miller, Jim Wayne. *The Brier Poems*. Lexington, Kentucky: Gnomon Press, 1988.

Olson, Ted. *Blue Ridge Folklife*. Jackson: University Press of Mississippi, 1998.

Paludan, Phillip Shaw. *Victims: A True Story of the Civil War*. Knoxville: University of Tennessee Press, 1981.

Smith, Lee. *Fair and Tender Ladies*. New York: Ballantine Books, 1998.

Still, James. *Pattern of a Man*. Lexington, Kentucky: Gnomon Press, 1998.

_____. *River of Earth*. Lexington: University Press of Kentucky, 1978.

Suter, Scott Hamilton. *Shenandoah Valley Folklife*. Jackson: University Press of Mississippi, 1999.

INDEX

Boldface numbers indicate drawings